ENERGY and SPACE

Liebe Swamishi
von Dr. Rosi
May 2009

ENERGY and SPACE
Within/Outside and Beyond

Swami Maheshananda
Dr Stuart Rose

The Dual Publishers

First published in the United Kingdom in 2009 by The Dual Publishers
Cover design by Dany Paal

The authors may be contacted at
sr.kaivalya@yahoo.co.uk

ISBN 978-0-9562112-0-0

Contents

Introduction	i
Prologue	1
The Text	19
Epilogue	265

Introduction

To start the dialogue

ENERGY and SPACE: Within/Outside and Beyond is written to answer, or lead the reader to explore, the fundamental questions which can be asked about life and existence. It gives a factual and experience-related picture of oneself providing answers, and hopefully clarity, to our deepest thoughts without being dogmatic, religious, psychological, scientific, or philosophical, yet it can also be read from these perspectives or any other.

ENERGY and SPACE is a book and it is not a book! What is said appears to be like a book as it is necessary to present this wisdom in an understandable and communicable form. It is written in an English and it's not an English standard style. It is an art to convert the full stop into a comma, and it is a mistake to convert the comma into a full stop! So a question arises: who is the editor, who can be the editor when the Lord is writing the sentences of life? For instance, suicide is considered as a full stop of the life sentence which is written by ONE and edited by the other one; it can be a foolish stop, also.

Instead of enjoying the meaning of the sentence that is the life written by the Lord, the reader becomes the editor and edits the sentence, and finds out there is a mistake and decides to cut short the sentence with a full stop. And that full stop becomes the foolish stop, because how can a reader become an editor. Instead of enjoying the meaning of the sentence that is the life, who is it that gives him the task and the mistaken sentence?

About the dialogue

The writing throws light on life and its components: Space and Energy, within, outside and beyond – from the simplest cell to the far reaches of deep space – identifying and searching for the cause of the existence of one's own beingness. That's why the questions arise from within: Who am I? How am I? Where am I? This is why the primary concentration is focussed on Energy and Space within, outside and beyond the individual, and the universe as an individual, thereby pointing to the inner work that is necessary to be done to overcome the ego, consequently changing from 'I-am-ness' to 'am-ness'. The work becomes successful when unlimited happiness is found – not happiness particular to the individual, but a universal happiness, a happiness which knows no bounds.

Readers may be scientists, astronomers for example, and 'travel' from the depths of outer space to inner space and beyond; or readers may be more interested in their inner depths, their 'gastronomic' depths, so to speak, and 'travel' in different directions from inner space to outer space and beyond. This means that all of this text can be read and explored from any single standpoint or many standpoints together – the final outcome is likely to be the same.

ENERGY and SPACE starts with a Prologue to the whole of the thinking.

The main text identifies five levels of reality and their combinations, and various titles may be given to each level. The subject of energy and space – their interplay and characteristics – is introduced and continues to be discussed until the writing ends. 'I-am-ness' is energy and 'am-ness' is space: energy is disturbance itself; space cannot be disturbed. All life, all material, all and every 'thing' is energy – the human being him or herself is described as countless energies and nothing else – in and through space. Space is a place for energy to play.

The interplay of energy and space takes place in the human psyche: greed, anger, pleasure, relationships, parentage, ignorance and illusion, ego, beauty, creation, the sun, moon and planet Earth, cultural and social change, connections, money, are all met with and, together with these themes, death (including dying, decomposition, and being prepared for its occurrence) is also a major subject – but what is it that dies?

Until the end, this thinking gives all who care to know a map to read and follow in order to reach the 'destination'. This 'map' can be torn up or it can be used to move forward to fully realize the truth about existence, thereby satisfactorily resolving the questions, Who You are, How You are, Where You are, Where do you want to be and What do you want to be or become.

India and United Kingdom
March 2009

Prologue

The writings on Space and Energy, Within, Outside and Beyond are possible to present because inspiration and motivation were given to write through using common terminology accepted by different communities of the various societies.

The terms are 'Space and Energy'. Today we have many different terms and all are collected in dictionaries and thesauruses which are the storehouses of those terms known as phonemes because their sounds are different.

Sound becomes the creator and creates different phonemes (letters of the alphabet), which are the creation of the sounds whereby the literary world came into existence with its own literature. The sound is the cause and it is the creation; the creation is the literary world because it has its own dynamic. On the other side of the sound the creator is there who creates and produces the sound, so sound is a creation also. Sound is produced by, created by, a CREATOR, a PRODUCER, that ONE who is not the sound itself.

As a tree produces an apple and is also different from the form of the apple, we cannot say that the apple is the tree itself, but the seed within the apple, having the plant within of that apple, that is the potential and the potential power to produce/create the tree again and again and again, which can give many fruits – here comes the re-cycling and multiplicity. Roasting of the seed means that the potential power to sprout is seized, nullified, zero. To avoid the fruit, how many seeds need to be nullified? How many trees to cut and uproot? Outside many, inside one! Instead of 'uproot' better to have 'root up' in connection with THAT ONE.

Existence of the seed is one form, while on the other hand the fruit is in another form. The distance between the two points is considered as Space, and the journey between the two points is achieved by Energy. Crossing that Space, and during the journey, transformation takes place in that

Space, and the journey continues and continues because Space is always available between two points, from point to point, and Energy is always happy to travel in that Space. And that journey, how can it be stopped? That is the question even today. How can a constant moving principle – Energy – stop? It is relatively possible. So, we can say it is a stop and it is not a stop; then, what is it? What is continuously moving with a pause which appears as a stop?

We have an active and a passive voice. This means, for example, to do and to get it done, and it is done by the doer. Doer is doing, or is getting it done by the doer. Then, who is that one who has got it done through the doer?

Energy appears as a direct doer, while Space is the doer indirectly and gets it done by everybody, so Space is the doer and is not the doer. In the same way as Space, Energy also cunningly tries to manifest as "I am the doer" and "I am not the doer"; at the same time, through 'making it happen', energy tries to establish itself on an equal level or in an equal position with Space. It has developed oneness and becomes one with Space, and has another term – Ether, which today is considered equal to Space.

Space and Energy have two different forms and that's why transformation and reformation is possible in two different ways. The formless form is ONE, while the other one is made by the combination or help of many other forms which are measurable and miserable also.

Now comes the mixture and we can straight away say a mixture exists or the existence of the mixture is possible to prove with evidence. So, we can say that the mixture is prepared not by the mixture itself, or is it by the mixture itself? Both are possible because mixture is a creation and mixture can be a creator also, the same as sound. The two are different as a creator and creation, and the two are similar because both are a creation, but in these two, one appears as a creator. So, we can say that one is a creator and not a CREATOR also.

Our existence is the creation, the 'being-ness', which we experience in the form of life. We can say, "I am alive and not dead", but I can be a dad or mum (not a mummy – again dead). Life is a mixture, and the one who 'lives the life' is inside that mixture; although the mixture is the mixture which is the life, it is separate from other mixtures that are the life of others. In that way, each mixture, each life lived by each one, is different in a different way – so we can say: one is born, one is child, adult, old, sick and ill, and dead – all are different phases and transformations on the one. They are separate also, because it is seen by the seer altogether in one spectrum of time; that is, Energy and the seer principle is different from that, while the witnessing principle has witnessed the different phases and transformation of that life, lived by each different one. The time spectrum has a continuous flow of energy in it, and that flow of time/energy is seen by the seer (seer principle), witnessed by the witness (witness principle), so the question arises: Who are we?

In this way, we can have two different standpoints: on one side where the scene, the happening, is taking place within the time spectrum and, on the other side of that, the seer principle and the witness principle are there, the observer is there. The principle is one and the functions are many. According to the functions, the principle is known by many different terms such as seer, witness, observer, doer, listener etc., etc., – 're' and 'er' are applied to this principle and then the principle gets different titles as above, to 'play' a role in the lifetime spectrum. How long can they remain in that particular role without changing or transforming into another role?

The unchangeable is ONE, and the other one has the possibility to change according to own wish and will, as a chameleon. That's why the questions: Who am I? and Who are You? Is it unchangeable or changeable? As and when the role is changed, how it can be unchangeable? And how many roles do we frequently play, and how many dresses do we frequently change? When there is disharmony between the dress or uniform and the role, it brings down the established values related to them. A living body is also considered as a dress for that one who is living inside. That one is different from the dress or uniform and the role. So, on one side, there is one who is different and, on the other side, the two are together. Who is behind whom and supporting whom as a ground? On which ground does change take place, is it unchangeable or changeable?

The flame is constantly changing while burning – a constant energy flow in the form of fuel, and the ground becomes the cotton wicks; again, that ground is going to change and turn to ash, and the flame goes out. So, a question: to whom does the flame belong, to the fuel or to the cotton wick, or to the pot which keeps the fuel and wick inside it?

The pot is a place where the flame is, and that pot as a space has a fireball in it which is the sun. Can you go out of that pot which is the space? The pot: either to be or to become the pot which is a space – that is one option; on the other side of that – to be inside the pot which is the space, to have a life that is the flame on the basis of the cotton wicks and fuel, which are different from each other and help the flame to burn steadily without wavering, by protecting from the wind.

The fickleness, the wavering condition, becomes the cause inside the pot of the changes. Shelter and protection bring security, which helps to develop steadiness, and the flame – the life – burns steadily, giving light and warmth until the end that is death, separation. The flame has gone, the wick has turned to ash, the fuel spent, the pot remains – that is space. It is a death because there is no life (no flame) and it is not a death because it is a separation of the flame from the wick and fuel, but not from the pot which is space.

The use of specific terminology, for example 'flame', 'fire', 'heat', etc., and their synonyms has created confusion, conflict and confrontation on one side and, on the other side, the terms are being used to remove the confusion, conflict and confrontation. Finally, the terms themselves can be friendly or not depending on how they are used. The user becomes the owner or authority and insists on using a specific term, but not the synonyms of it which were coined by the other, who is opposing. This is as good as denying or not accepting the synonyms coined by the opposition, thus denying their authority, freedom and right to coin a term, so a clash occurs between the two to prove who has the authority, freedom and right. The clash – mild, moderate, and intense – then becomes fight and war begins; this means denial, refusal and non-acceptance turns into clash, then clash transforms into fight and war. To transcend this there has to be no clash; instead there has to be acceptance, peace, harmony, and happiness.

For example: The old, popular and commonly accepted term 'father' becomes a biased term because of its masculine nature. This becomes the specific term on one side and, on the other side, it is considered as a commonly related term to both the son and daughter on one side, and the wife on the other inside the family. Two different standpoints to look at the term 'father' gives the possibility to accept or reject and enter into the clash and to create disharmony. This specific term 'THE FATHER' is totally different and opposite from the worldly term 'father and mother' and totally opposite to the specific term 'MOTHER ENERGY'. The total opposite term for ENERGY is 'SPACE', which is not energy. Creation is the mixture where energy is playing the role and appears as creator, producer, mother, Earth; while Space within and outside is the real creator, supporter and known through opposite terminology to Energy. And one of the terms is the 'father', SPACE.

From the Space point of view, when we look at the term 'father', then it is neither masculine nor feminine because that space exists within both male and female living bodies. The outer layer of 'that space' does not change the nature of space, but the terms used to know the outer layer are different: male and female, man and woman. And because of that space, the reproductive system and organs can function: then it is not a reproduction, it is a birth, with a hesitation to accept that birth as a re-birth.

A space without the female body – is it possible? No. This means that space is a mother also, not only a father – a neutral gender. So, it depends how we look at the terms, and how we react and create the clash.

To become the authority, owner, master, proprietor, governor, monitor, regulator, ruler, manipulator, etc., etc., is the wish and will of Energy because, indirectly, these are the roles which have to be played by Space, which means that Energy is obliging Space while playing these roles on behalf of Space (as if like Space) for other Energy forms. Because of the possibility of 'Within, Outside and Beyond', the play is possible for Energy – that is why discrimination (or the distinguishing ability) is needed and required to differentiate the difference between the two which appear as one or, as if like one, in that play of Energy within Space the oneness within the one is because of two, while the other ONE is ONE and not because of two appearing as ONE. Both are as a mirror image for each other as one/ONE.

That's why the feeling comes from within to 'that one' as, "I am the creator and it is my creation"; then it becomes the world within the world of 'that one', and that becomes the illusion – 'that world' for 'that one'. After realizing the existence of the other ONE and one's own position in front of the other ONE, one's own created world becomes phenomena and illusion; then the statement comes 'The world is an illusion but not 'THAT ONE'. This is a profound change in perception and cognition of one's own world which brings a change in behaviour, and then the suffering becomes as if there is no suffering because of the acceptance of THAT ONE which brings down the intensity of the suffering, and then the sufferer doesn't remain as a sufferer but becomes detached from it with this realization. This is a painful process where 'am-ness' remains, and 'I am' – me, my and mine and ego, all as 'one' – doesn't remain.

The 'am-ness' is the natural state of being where the suffering is at zero level, it is not there, the sufferer is absent from the area of suffering.

The CREATOR'S WORLD AS A CREATION is not an illusion because it is an EXTENDED PORTION OF THE CREATOR, and THAT CREATOR is NOT the ILLUSION for

US. So how can the extended world be? It is one's own perception and cognition which leads to the illusion as a world within the world, bubble within the bubble. It can be asked: How many bubbles have to burst so the trapped air can be released properly?

Illusion and ignorance, one is from outside and the other from inside, both are connected and related with that one who is living the life. To live the life materials are provided; to communicate, sound is created; for exchange, behaviour becomes the media for transaction of thought, emotion and material; and for that, ignorance from inside and illusion from outside become the guiding factors for decision and action for the desired achievement.

As long as ignorance (as incomplete knowledge) exists inside and is nurtured and taken care of by the illusion outside, it is like the one who lives life moving with two legs to reach one place to achieve the desired one. As long as seeds of desire are sprouting it is difficult to stop having flowers and fruit which have the seeds within.

And then a question arises: How to avoid the fruit or the result of the action and remain as a constant enjoyer, to have pleasure and fun, enjoyment and entertainment constantly? How is this possible? '-er' and 're-' play a very important role of the one who lives the life: is it possible to be free from that?

Terms like 'climate', 'atmosphere', 'environment' and 'pollution' have their own specific meaning to understand, to know and to distinguish from each other. They all are inside space. The growing inner nature is taken care of and nurtured by them. Pollution and dilution are harming the natural healthy growth of nature. That nature has two types of components: one is living, growing and dying and to appear again; while the non-living does not have the cycle of pro-creation and the reproductive unit within, although there is a transformation and change where the term dead and died is not used as it is used for the living but, to give understanding, the term is used in a common way – for example, when it is said that the telephone is dead, it means not working, not functioning.

This non-living has also a space within and outside: for example, the house has space within and outside. Space within is divided by the walls and the rooms are created to accommodate furniture – that is, not living – and the one that is not the furniture (but is going to use the furniture) is a living being.

The measurement and size of the walls of the rooms and the house can increase or decrease within the main wall of the house. The outer external one is always the bigger one working as a cover, container, box or body. The inner partitions and compartments provide comfortable and convenient accommodation so that the living can conveniently to be together to have fun, pleasure, recreation and enjoyment within the main walls.

The internal space (room to accommodate) is also known as an internal cavity. One who lives and that which exists as non-living within the space are affected by climate, atmosphere, environment, and also pollution. Pollution is again related and connected with the two other terms of hybridization and exploitation. The living beings are more affected than the non-living things. The smallest unit for both is different: one is known as a gene, while the other is known as an atom; both are in one way or another connected and related to the process of heritage and hereditary. This is one side while, on the other side, is environment. The non-living and the living are both surrounded by the environment, and this environment is also surrounded by the environment, because environment is within and environment is outside. The dividing lines are the walls, but these do not necessarily exist or be present as a solid structure all of the time. Until the divider line exists (in any form or way) the terms 'in and out', 'internal and external', 'inner and outer', etc., exist.

The internal environment having pollution within affects the thinker in such a way that the thinking becomes polluted, and that polluted thinking of that thinker (who is not yet polluted) comes under the effect of the pollution and starts supporting the remaining two terms which are known as exploitation and hybridization. The distance between these two terms on one side and, on the other side, the polluted thinking and thinker, are known by the environment in space, and that environment in turn slowly and gradually becomes polluted.

Climate and atmosphere are related and connected with the sun: the fire and the flame. Change in pressures are due to change in heat in the different places in space, and this becomes the cause of constant movement from one side to the other because of the constant revolving and rotating nature of the earth, which gives rise to heat, temperature and more or less of it, and the pressure changes because of that – the positive and the negative.

Again the two are cause of the movement that is one movement: one is the SUN (the cause of constant heat and temperature), while the other is the revolving and rotating state of the Earth. And the movement is due to (because of) these TWO. So, how many are they?

Sun is on one side, Earth is on the other side; each has their own energy which gives rise to movement that is considered also as an energy and because of energy. The sun is the producer and creator of the Earth and other planets; in the same way, Earth and other planets also become the creator and producer of their own moons, which only move around their producer and creator, the life sustainers and maintainers, because they provide security. The movement of living and non-living is because of pressure changes on one side while, on the other side, because of the gravitational forces which pull towards the centre of gravitation. The horizontal movement is maintained and sustained by the gravitational pull which forces the movement to move and turn around; it gives the bending effect to the flow of movement, and then the shape of curvature takes place.

The movement in the form of diagonal, crossing, and spiral, is the mixture of the two whose directions are both up and down.

Now up and down become relative terms with reference to the Earth; in the same way, east and west are also relative terms with reference to the Earth. As and when the reference point is changed, the relativity and connectivity of the terms toward the reference also gets changed. Just consider and accept the Sun as your reference point, and then tell and show where does the up and down exist, where does east and west exist? The relative terms do not appear again because the common point, the Sun, becomes the reference point. Then arise the difficulties and problems in communication, identification, elocution and elucidation, because these require specific relative terms to differentiate, and keep separate, and not allow them to become mixed up, so that it gives the possibility to distinguish separately. Then comes the discrimination which is more related and concerned with relativity, and that type of discrimination which one is supposed to have from that apple tree which is forbidden. Because that discrimination (which belongs to relativity) is going to become the cause of pleasure and pain, good and bad, beautiful and ugly, exposed and hidden, fair and unfair, just and unjust, and is different in each living being – it is not the standard common discrimination that distinguishes the material as material, the spiritual as spiritual, centre as the centre, periphery as the periphery. This can help to avoid downfall and to develop resistance towards the gravitational pull of the material. So, under the name of 'discrimination', the living being is more concerned about pleasure, beauty, goodness and hiding the secret of the business, the transactions, through exposing the maximum and hiding the minimum. After this comes the rebellious nature and rebellious thinking, and action which exposes everything. Does it mean that it does not hide anything?

When the minimum becomes 'too much', then the need comes to expose totally: does it mean that the hiding tendency is also exposed and gone away? Whatever is exposed, hidden and covered is part of the surface of the cover as a body. To hide is because of that discrimination which doesn't allow one to remain totally exposed, it brings restriction and develops fear, so the act of hiding and covering remains more intense but the gravitational pull has pulled down the intensity, and from intense it becomes moderate and mild until it disappears in a natural way. Does this mean that the state of being is the same as before eating the apple? The need, necessity and requirement to hide and to cover up the minimum goes away and the total exposure of the surface takes place. Does it mean that this state of being is the same state of being, is the same as before eating the apple? When the answer is no, then that source – the innocent-ness – is not re-established. Innocent was the child, and the child becomes the adult having a childhood problem within, and childhood without the innocent-ness. The lack of innocent-ness in that childhood related problem inside the adult is indicating innocence again through accepting and forgiving like a child. So, to forget is possible, that painful happening is possible to overcome, the memories of the pain which constantly pinched and pained like a 'shoe bite' can disappear.

Along with acceptance and forgiveness, to give up is also necessary: not to hold, not to cling on, not to clench – to be ready to lose, to be ready to release the grip, to decrease the force and strength and power to hold and to possess and to keep: all these give more relief and lightness as and when the process of evacuation starts.

Again space appears, the inner environment becomes free from pollution and then the thinker's thinking is free from relativity. Do we have thinking which is free from relativity? If not, then how can we have freedom from pleasure and pain, good and bad, right and wrong, beauty and ugly, order and chaos, and so forth?

The void, the vacuum and negative pressure as a suction power (the strength and ability to suck) means that what is sucked is different from the suction power, the negative pressure and the void, the vacuum and the emptiness. The object is different from that.

Now comes the preservation: the sucked object is well preserved in a good vacuum pack, container, that is the space which has a big place to accommodate the object. To swallow is one action while to suck is another action. The movement of the object from outside to inside is similar. The cause of that movement is the change in the pressure – positive or negative – for the swallowing or sucking. Although the movements are two, having two different causes, known by two different terms, the movement takes place in space. There is a gap between the two, a distance between the two: to evaluate and look from the space point of view; to evaluate and look from the movement point of view; and to evaluate and look from the positive and negative point of view, the void, vacuum, emptiness point of view. On one side is space, on the other side is movement, and the cause is the pressure and the changes in it. Or we can say, space is on one side and energy is on the other side.

While you are Energy you can't say this! That's why the question – Who are you? You are opposite, or are you opposite of the opposite? And to communicate the opposite of the two opposites, the opposite terms and terminology came into existence. Along with the terminology, one more variety of terms and terminology came into existence which does not belong to either of the first two varieties and so becomes the third variety, which is neutral.

These three varieties can be used as synonyms for that ONE and, for the other one, it can indicate or create difference, opposition and similarity. Now a choice: to accept or reject the terms and terminology. Looking to the source: who has coined the term? Or for what has it been coined? And are the synonyms going to fulfil the purpose with the other equivalent terms? Or did the one who coined the term coin it because of having a different intention or purpose behind coining the new term, to make it popular, or to clarify the object for which the term is coined? For instance, terms such as 'flame', 'fire', 'burning', 'warm', 'fuel', 'smoke', etc., are specific as well as common and popular.

To logic and reasoning (the property of the intellect – Energy), is it possible to provide, to accept, to reject, to refuse, to deny, for fulfilling the purpose and intention, the rejection and acceptance? Is it possible for Space characteristics and quality to deny, to reject or to refuse? So, who are you – Energy or Space? The TRUTH is different and opposite from the established facts.

The writings inside will raise these questions repeatedly to make you think and realize where your standpoint is. The questions: Where are you? Who are you? Why do you have to be in a particular role or way? How long is it possible – is it changeable or unchangeable? Why does it become necessary (and required very often and frequently) to change the role? Is it not indicating a better way to use discrimination which is within relativity and not free from it, and not allowing freedom from it also?

We develop the habit to look at and observe the photograph taken by a camera, while very rarely (only few times) do we prefer to look at the photos belonging to the x-rays of our nearest and dearest ones. Maybe this work of changing requires x-ray photography of life, rather than a colourful photographic representation of it.

So, will there be life representation in a colourful, picturesque way or in the harsh reality of an x-ray?

One life is different from others to the one who lives the life; lives are also different from the place where they are. Place is the space which accommodates many inside, while space as a place – how many are inside in one space? (When we look, then we can see).

It is peaceful or not peaceful because, in the spectrum of disturbance, on one side it is intense of the INTENSE and on the other mild of the MILD: two extreme ends of the linear dimension of the spectrum. The linear dimension with two extreme end points becomes a circular dimension, and the gap between the two extreme end points (that is the intense of the INTENSE, the mild of the MILD) comes so close that they meet with each other like two sides of one coin. The inseparable appears inseparable in the circular dimension, and appears as separate in a linear dimension with two extreme end points which are totally separate. Then, the pieces of the lines are connected with each other and appear as one big, long and continuous railway line without having a break or separation. To avoid and prevent the sound and jerk while moving along it from one end to the other (beginning or start) the connections are done in such a way that they appear as if they are one.

So, when the linear pieces are connected, does it mean that circular peace is achieved? Peace is a relative term because when coming down or back from intense disturbance towards the moderate and mild disturbance, the milder it becomes from intense, the less the disturbance remains intense. The less appears as more peace, because more is the absence of disturbance and less remains as though it is fewer disturbances. And although there are fewer disturbances they do not disturb and appear as if there is no potency to disturb – the 'more' side of the established peace is the absence of disturbance. This is the finite phase of that infinite peace. Is it not the pieces of the peace? Because the dividing line has divided and created more and less out of that one, it has created many out of ONE.

The finite phase helps to develop intense systems which are accompanied by specific terms and terminology along with perceptual evidence. Altogether they become the guiding force and appear as a guide, coach, trainer, teacher or tutor to 'that' pupil. After that, the time for movement is supplied by the potency of the wish, will and desire. And the last requirement to move is the path which is provided by space/SPACE which is infinite/INFINITE.

Knowledge is a relative term because it is related with more and less, good and bad, known and unknown, complete and incomplete, finite and infinite. It is the other side of ignorance and illusion. It is knowledge on one side and, on the other side, it is a piece of information: what is given is knowledge, what is received is information to develop knowledge within.

Academic education and qualification has given more emphasis and stress to that knowledge which is relative and finite, and helps to increase the result. The results of the results are suffering. The presence of suffering becomes intense from mildness; with this intensity comes an equal need and requirement for the absence of suffering on the other side.

The wish, will and desire to live and survive becomes stronger and more intense, it tries to cling to life because of the intensity of suffering which threatens the loss of life. One who lives the life has the knowledge "I am immortal, I am not going to die" and, from the academic point of view, the learned scholar tries to cling to life because of the fear of death. Is it ignorance or knowledge?

Taste is the cause of binding, and taste also helps to be free from the binding of the previous taste. The change of taste, instead of aiding freedom and obtaining relief from the binding, increases the layers of binding. Taste becomes the guiding factor in acceptance and rejection, because the object is tasty and not tasty. The 'tongue' is one, while the taste buds on it are many and the combination of the many 'buds' as a one becomes the guiding factor for that one who likes the life.

From the perceptual, finite evidence of taste and its tastiness – which works like a glue and attracts like a magnet – taste helps develop the knowledge within through the finite inference system that taste is not up to the tongue but is more related and connected to other organs, systems, and functions of the body. It becomes a relative term – the taste – while other terms and terminology help to get relief from the binding of this taste when they are interpreted and understood in a proper, correct and right way. When the change of a taste becomes tastier, the taste (the previous one) becomes tasteless, and then it is possible to give up that object which provided the taste now that it has become tasteless.

The taste of the worldly materialistic life becomes tasteless because of the change in taste. 'Taste' is a common term: one is the cause of binding and the other is more related and connected with the tongue and taste buds. Looking to this, similes are used to provide specific terminology, for example 'flesh and blood', while the popular and accepted terminology of this is 'bread and wine', which indicates the power and strength of taste to relieve the binding of worldly materialistic taste.

The taste of ONE overpowers the taste of the other one which is developed by the combination and mixture of many different ones. The glue principle of materialistic taste (and the magnetic pull and attraction of this material taste) does not function well in front of impressions of the taste of THAT ONE. How many times do we have to develop the taste of THAT ONE? One time is not enough to change the impressions of the previous time. If it is not, then why?

Silence is the absence of sound, while peace is the absence of disturbance. To have the peaceful state of space within, to experience it, for this, this prologue is provided to have a dialogue within.

As long as the two are there the dialogue will go on continuously. Who has to shut-up and keep quiet? Who will decide in that internal dialogue?

Before any one of them decides, it is better to say it's enough for the Prologue that the one who has a dialogue within has to decide. Who will stop from within and for how long? It's a test. Is it not better to have the taste of the test instead of giving up the taste of the taste because of fear of the existence of I, me, my and mine?

Salutation to THE PEACE.
Salutation to the different forms of THE PEACE.
Salutation to the removal of disturbances.

The remover is SPACE.

What is removed is the disturbance – that is an object.

Through the pressure changes within, the disturbance as an object is removed and peace within is re- established.

Disturbance is one form of Energy. Presence of it is to create the need and necessity for the absence of it.

To evaluate the value of the absence, intensity of the presence is fluctuating from mild to moderate to intense until one can establish THE PEACE within, along with the disturbance.

So, salutation to the PEACE, and PEACE, and PEACE.

The Text

ONE is residing in the other One, Oneness is established. Dualness distinguishing the difference is to be known, to be recognized. The other One is to give up being different, the other One is not to possess, the other One is not to be in ownership, the other One is just to ignore, to neglect, not to covet (ANY) ONE'S wealth.

THAT ONE IS: here and there at the same time, this and that, now and then, some and all, everything and nothing, in and out, nothing and everything, hot and cold, only and also, solution and problem, light of the day and night, with and without, same time and different places, complementary and contradictory, an envelope for all and all in the envelope.

Dual state of BEING, dual approach to it. Dual is the duality, dualness is the cause, duality is the appearance, appearance is not real, not real is unreal.

'This' is an experience, 'that' is an inference. 'This' is made by 'two' as 'One', 'THAT' 'ONE' is not made by 'two', 'Two' belong to 'ONE', 'One' belongs to Two, One belongs to 'ONE' directly, One belongs to 'ONE' indirectly. Two has two approaches to ONE. Two are opposite: brightness and darkness, day and night, belong to the SUN.

- Presence of light means brightness and heat,
  absence of light means darkness and cold.

- Presence of light in darkness means
  absence of heat, full moon, moonlight at night.

- Absence of heat when the light is not absent.
  Presence of darkness, present is not the day!

- Earth is experience of existence,
  SUN is the cause of it.

- SUN is bright and illuminating,

Earth is not like that!
Fire is within the Earth,
FIRE ITSELF IS THE SUN.

O Lord Fire, lead us from within on a right path, burn all our crooked, wicked and cunning ways as fuel and at last what remains is the Bright-Body, the illuminating-body of a FIRE within – FIRE OUTSIDE. Similarities between two suggest a qualitative one-ness. Potentially an atom is also destructive although it is small in size and shape!

- To deprive from one side,
  To feed from the other side,
  Turn to connect, to unite, to join,
  Turn again to disconnect, to separate.
  Killing is the forceful turning to join.

Force and pressure to stop, to cut, to turn, to deprive, leads to an end, apparently a death, known as suicide. It is and it is not suicide because it is a forced and pressurised end just like a full stop '(.)' abruptly to a sentence.

Better not to become an editor to a human script written by an AUTHOR, and not to delete own sound or phoneme or letter from the SCRIPT. It goes into a dustbin, or a garbage box; it's a dark place, a storehouse for re-cycling.

Turn has come and gone! Wait for next turn. Turn came and again turning took place by force and pressure of the developed habit. Being inhabitant of this habitation, the habit is developed through continually turning and waiting for turn to turn again!

So, O Lord Fire, burn all this, purify and put us on a right path to move, to burn, to illuminate!

OM Shanti, Shanti, Shanti

Life on Earth depends on the life of the Earth; it also depends on the LIFE OF A SUN!

To be independent to live like a SUN, to become a creator like a SUN, to become supporter, protector, etc., etc., like a SUN is an inherited quality, which is mixed up with the other that is not the SUN! For example, all planets other than the SUN.

A living being has a body also living composed with five Elements. The lifespan of this living being, and of Earth and SUN, is quite different. To know that the difference makes the different, and through similarity the recognition can be made of how similar these two different living beings that exist at the same time are. Because of composition, the mix up of all in one form, homogeneously being together, adjusting, with each other, adopting the qualities of each other, in a such a way that to recognize their original identity becomes difficult because of association, joint, connection, union with the other side, i.e. with the five elements.

Vicious circle
Perfect and imperfect are from 'PERFECT'.
Now, perfectly-perfect and perfectly-imperfect,
imperfect wants to become PERFECT.

Regular and irregular are from 'REGULAR'.
Now, regularly regular and regularly irregular!
Irregular wants to become REGULAR.

Discipline and indiscipline are from 'DISCIPLINE'.
Now, in a disciplined way discipline, disciplined way indiscipline. Indiscipline wants to become DISCIPLINE.

Like this: clearly unclear, specifically unspecific.

- Moon belongs to the Earth, Earth belongs to the SUN.
  Living beings belong to both, SUN and Earth.

  Towards belonging, SUN never shows ownership,
  human beings worship the SUN,

with the ownership to own belonging!
Do not covet the wealth of (belonging of) anyone!

This means to give up even the desire to possess and enjoy the belonging of ANYONE/anyone, because all belong to THAT SUN, including the life energy; then what remains for the living being to possess? Better to give up the right to possess, to have it, to be the owner, to be the master, etc! Individual as a possessor has to recognize the ABSOLUTE POSSESSOR and humbly become the possession of THAT ONE! Means "possessor becomes the possession" once more!

Before this turn or change,
the possession becomes the possessor,
creation becomes the creator,
servant becomes the master!
student becomes the teacher/professor,
a copy becomes the original,
Avidya (incomplete knowledge) becomes *Vidya* (knowledge),
Asambhuti (unmanifest) becomes *Sambhuti* (manifest).

- SUN is ONE and rays are many.
  SUN without rays, is it possible?
  Is ONE without a second possible?
  Rays are waves or particles?
  Rays are in which state of being?

- Rays are spreading everywhere or SUN is everywhere?
  Rainwater is everywhere or ocean is everywhere?
  ONE remains at one place and spreads?

Considering SUN and sunrays are one, rainwater and ocean (the source) as one, the centre's expansion up to the periphery and realization of one's own self gives recognition and acceptance to every other self as one and the same, then the one-ness is established. At this moment, what happens to that dual aspect of one – as an object of enjoyment?

The cause of the result and its result is action, and its cause is decision > thinking > idea and imagination: actions (for enjoyment) are dependent on this process. Change in the processor brings change to the whole process!

The effect and the result of perception is one. The cause of perception is projection > by a projector(s) wants and likes. Accordingly, perception becomes the cause of pain and pleasure, hate and affection.

Information of the object, interpretation of the information, understanding out of interpretation – the starting of this process depends on the nature of the object and the way it is conveyed, transferred and, accordingly, transformation or conversion takes place in further development and growth, concluding at one point or place. The return journey of that processed energy is in a 'role-less role' or in a specific, particular, role. Real change of and in role is from role to role-less role; all other change is un-real and repetitious, which can be proved by the same results again and again in the form of mild, moderate, and intense, until the 'real' change takes place!

Until that time, the process recycles and each time allows THAT HEAT, LIGHT, RAYS, FIRE, SUN to do its WORK. It becomes the worship. The doer, worker, becomes the worshipper! Leader becomes the follower of THAT AGNI (fire)!

So, who is who?
Mountain is mountain, river is river,
father is father, son is son!
Both are one and also two,
it depends on how one looks, perceives, and conveys.

- SUN is ONE and rays are many,
  ocean is one and clouds are many,
  ray is ONE and colours are many,
  cloud is one and raindrops are many,

Earth is one and many are on it,
land is one and many are the sea shores,
land is one and many are on it.

ABSOLUTE,
SPACE is ONE and many are in it,
SPACE is ONE and many are around it.
Around is One and many are in it.
ABSOLUTE is ONE and related are more than one.
ABSOLUTE is Absolutely ONE,
related is absolutely more than one,
absolutely related with ABSOLUTE ONE.

SPACE is ONE and related are many.
ENVELOPE is ONE and letters are many in it.
SOUND is ONE and phonemes are many,
Together many become the One,
Separate they Remain THE ONE.

One is the name, form and appearance.
ONE has the name, form and appearance.
ONE by itself, on its OWN, becomes the Incarnation.
ONE is getting by others and becomes related.
Being related tries to be free from it.
That is relativity and to become ABSOLUTE.

SPACE is ONE,
SKY is ONE,
AKASH (space) is ONE.
Two it becomes,
WITHOUT PARTICLES, ONE,
with particles the other ONE.

ONE is ABSOLUTE,
ONE is related with particles.
Particles are in and around ONE.
They are reflectors, they give reflection,
we consider reflection as reflector.

Clouds are bright and shining, clouds are dark and grey. In summer, monsoon and winter, the colour of clouds changes. Clouds get acceptance and appreciation as change takes place. Dark and grey becomes the cause of depression and frustration because it is cold and not warm.

Ocean is the one source,
SUN is the other ONE CAUSE,
summer, monsoon and winter,
because of the SUN.
Though it is NATURE,
It's governed and ruled by the SUN:
clouds are clouds,
colours are colours.
Learn to accept,
learn to recognize, the work
of the other ONE, and
learn to appreciate that.

Not ready and able to accept, recognize and appreciate starts the struggle, becomes confused, frustrated and depressed. It's a struggle, a fight, between the two: Ego and ego! What to do? Struggle and fight between the two or friendship between the two? Why not? One is single, one is double, one is dual, ONE is Non-Dual. Until movement is constant, the OTHER ONE, the ABSOLUTE ONE, remains constantly movement-less, for constant movement.

Now,

1) movement-less state of being;
2) state of being in movement;
3) movement is energy, ultimate, and ultimately energy is at the end;
4) movement (energy) appears, looks like, seems to be, a movement-less state of being (known as quasi-steady state of Energy – in astrophysics).

Whole having 'hole' inside, and that 'hole' is the Space, as an ULTIMATE BACKGROUND. Bright and shining SUN on DARK BLACK BACKGROUND as an ABSOLUTE OR ULTIMATE. Another form of envelope for all letters!

An individual, one, can know and recognize the Non-Dual from own existential experience which comes from Duality. Once the point of Non-Dual is reached, one can start to play that "Role-less-Role". Existence of a living being remains without giving importance to life-experience. Here, two are living: one without giving importance, the other with giving importance to life-experiences.

To get or to take life-experience and to give or to get it back to give, the life-experiences start with specific, particular, action.

Action with interest and effort are preserved in the memory. A two-way process of action and action-related results: 1) remain outside, 2) inside, up to memory. Fixation of preserved memory is dependent on mild, moderate, intense intention, purpose, interest and effort.

These memories are stored and kept in the storehouse. Special care, with extra-effort, was taken to maintain the storehouse memories. What was preserved, that is possible to remember, and what is possible to remember easily, that shows the nature of interest and how much the effort or type of effort for those actions and the action-related results existed at the time of doing or performing the action!

To pretend, to demonstrate, to cheat, to appear or honestly to be, with loyalty to be, etc., whatever the case may be, action (to remember it, those memories) means to start the process to know one's own self through checking and evaluating.

The reflection of the self, the nature of the self, reflector as a self, and A SELF as a BACKGROUND, all are difficult to distinguish because they are not two! OR they are more than one!

That's why remembering what was done, and what has to be done, will be clear along with its result which is PEACE and the experience of BLISS, Happiness.

A time provided for action is going to finish, the process of decomposition will start soon, and the Eternal Principle will remain UNAFFECTED.

Life is a conjunction; it's a provided and limited time from unlimited time, infinite time, to be together, to remain just together with a minimum gap in-between the two. This minimum gap, once overlooked, ignored, neglected, not considered, not noticed, distinguished or not recognized, the two do not remain as two, but appear as one! Development of oneness, through association and identification, adjustment and adaptation, becomes one out of two or more than one!

Formation of this 'one' and the one which appears are similar. Similarities in this one and that one again become the cause to become one, to feel one, and to experience oneness. Here, similar goes with similar, and similarities develop oneness. This is as long as the difference remains, while it is maintained it creates a difference to become different and not to be similar nor have similarities. This also appears for the time-being because, as a chameleon changes its colour, these two (similar and different ones) change their state at their convenience and comfort. Similar one and different one show the dual dualness in one and one.

Description of the two is available in the scriptures. ONE is described and explained with the help of Another One. As a learner or student, these two principles are known separately as well: as 'two' as a 'one' and opposite of this state of being, 'two as a one'. 'ONE as a ONE without the two' is also learnt and studied by a learner and student. To equalize the concept of 'that two', another 'two' is also included, and this has made it easy to show how ONE is covered by the other one and becomes ONE. Again, the difference has made them different from the level of individual to the Universal.

Difference is removed, different they will not be, similarity will appear, similar they will be! Contradiction will go away, complementary will be there.

World, habitation, is a place, a location for much life. A collection of constant continuation of life of a many-many! It is an eternal place, a location as well as known as an illusory world, where transformation and change is constant. Permanent is impermanent and permanently established impermanency becomes the cause for attraction and distraction. Now, attraction becomes the cause of and for distraction, and the cause of attraction is temptation, while distraction is because of attraction towards the object/objects of the world. Interest is the flow and along with effort it develops contact and then establishes connection. World is the place (location, residence) of many, many lives with various names, forms, shapes, sizes, etc., etc.

ONE, in a different way, is the same as well as similar and different.

1st ONE, ABSOLUTE ONE, is free from relativity. Space is or as a place without particles. SPACE is a totally opposite place. ONE IS ONE.

2nd ONE is a RELATED ONE where Space is or as a place with particles. ONE BECOMES TWO, ONE APPEARS AS TWO as well as ONE and becomes the cause of creation – it looks as if it's covered by the other one, the opposite one. Two layers of ONE ENVELOPE become SPACE with SUN, the source and cause of existence, and an Existential Principle.

3rd ONE is an INCARNATION, a particular, specific form or shape with a name appearing at a fixed time and place for a certain reason and time-period with selected material. This one is totally opposite from the other one and has no choice or option for selection of own performance.

4th one has opposite conditions to the 3rd one. Although it looks similar, it has more and more difference, which makes it totally different. This 4th one also has no choice of selection for own performance.

World (habitation) is the place for or of the performance for 3 and 4.

This 4th one is also covered by the other one, dominantly and prominently, so it gets a form, shape and name for communication.

Again, similar to the 2nd ONE, only the state of being is different to the 2nd ONE. Both the 2nd ONE and the 4th one have their own creation; as creators both are similar, it is the difference in their creation which makes them different. Because the creation of the 4th one is individualized, its creation is inside the CREATION of the 2nd ONE.

4th one is a single one (an individual) with a limited provided time; this one lives and exists along with (and also among) others in the habitation (world) as an inhabitant of the world.

As a creation the world is one, and creation inside the creation (world inside the world) is created, maintained, sustained and transformed or destroyed by the 4th one as a creator, sustainer and destroyer!

A different role is played by each different individual one (4th one) as there are many, many 4th ones! 4th one is similar to the 1st ONE.

SPACE is a place. It is covered by, encircled by, particles in the form of living cells which formulate the living body. Within this living body is a SPACE and it's the place of THAT ONE. Here it's a flame, there it's a SUN: the fire principle is common for both.

5th ONE is at universal level, 5th one is at individual level.

Ultimate provider of material is an unlimited supplier, an infinite stockist and permanent standby. The other one (opposite one) is a contributor for and of life and creation as a partner. It is known as matter, material energy. It has a formless form, constantly moving, changing, transforming, and destroying. It appears as if it is not and also as if it is, both at the same time.

- 5:1 5th one in relation with other ONE. 1st ONE is Non-Dual, ONE Without a Second One; 5th ONE is the Second One, the other one, cause of another one.

- 5:2 2nd ONE is covered by this 5th one and becomes one creator, sustainer, transformer, or destroyer as a one-in-three roles. World (habitation) is their creation: as a sustainer they sustain it; as a transformer or destroyer they transform it, destroy it, so that the cycle and function of these three keeps the world habitation alive with a pause for death and birth, again and again, to appear as a lively, attractive, beautiful, delightful, pleasurable, enjoyable, and most wanted object. Although it is transitory in nature, it is able to give a glimpse of the opposite nature, and through the inference system it makes a force to search for the permanent ONE, the experience of which is not transitory.

- 5:3 3rd ONE as an incarnation just selects whatever is needed for a performance to play a role from the 5th one's storehouse. Once the performance is over, whatever is taken goes back to its original place in the storehouse. This 3rd one is similar to (looks like) the 4th one, but it is different also from the freedom to select point of view.

- 5:4 4th one, although in the lineage of the 1st and 2nd ONE, on one side, prefers to be with the 5th one, considering it to be the cause of life experience. The formation of 'I', 'me' 'my' and 'mine' in order to express and communicate on behalf of the 'Ego' takes place with and through the 5th one. One-ness is established on the other side, to acquire and to enjoy, to rule, to govern, to become the same as the 2nd ONE. At this junction, the 4th one has a choice to remain in connection, in relation with the 5th one and to become an enjoyer of pleasure and pain, and to have the experience of death and birth again and again as a result of the enjoyment. 5th One is the provider of the objects of enjoyment and the 4th one starts to give importance and values, honour and respect, to the '5th one'.

In worldly terminology, the 5th one is considered, recognized and perceived as a mother, a female principle. 4th one, with this understanding, starts worshipping, adoring and offering to HER for more and more achievement and also, with intensity and effort, tries to become the same as the 5th ONE! MOTHER keeps smiling towards the innocent child (the 4th One) who wants all and everything from the 5th One. Actually, the 5th One is a part, is incomplete and not whole; the 4th One is just collecting and accumulating as many PARTS as possible. 99.99 is the maximum number of PARTS, but it's not complete because it's not 100%. The figure 0.01 is highly negligible, highly insignificant, very small in size and number, but becomes the cause of incompleteness. To become complete, total, full, whole, to add this 0.01, the most valuable-value, the 4th one has to know the PRINCIPLE.

There are two types of 4th Ones: one who knows the value and lives accordingly; and the other one who doesn't know and lives accordingly with the other values, the values of the 5th One because it gives more: pleasure, fun and enjoyment, challenges and delightful experiences.

There are two sides to the 5th ONE, and either side can be selected to connect by the 4th One. A coin has two sides. The size of the two sides is the same, no difference;

they are the same size with different impressions on them. It can be fake, false and wrong but looks very similar to give the impression that it is true, not fake, false and wrong. Also it gets the equivalent value to purchase or sell.

True currency (coin, paper or note) has also two different things together on it. The truthfulness is possible to check, test, examine and certify. It has its own validity and acceptance, and is recognized as money in a different denomination. It is constantly moving but not by itself on its own! It is a means to purchase and a goal to achieve. It is possible to collect, accumulate, store and preserve for various uses and purposes. It has a rise and fall, ups and downs; it makes rich and poor, higher and lower, royal and common and gives status and dignity. In itself it's 50%, but that 50% gives the impression of 100%. Because the two sides are perfectly matched with each other, supporting each other, the two together are recognized as one (100%), made by two halves (50% + 50%) as 'two complete'.

Currency is a life-energy (*prana*) in the body of a country and nation. To keep everything alive in a working condition, this money energy has to move inside the body. As energy it's a constant moving principle; but in the form and status of money, it is not ready to move by itself on its own. It requires the movers and the 4th One plays the role of a 'mover', taking care of the constant movement, towards the rise and ups, and also takes care to avoid falls and down in comparison (relation) to other countries' currency flow and movement.

The 4th One becomes the mover on one side and, on the other side, loses control over its own movement (the energy movement inside its own body).

The existence of the 5th ONE – at a different level with a different name, form, size, shape and function – is from PURE to impure, from good to bad and evil. The major contribution, the share in the creation of the world (habitation), is by the 5th ONE. THE ABSOLUTE ONE has played the ROLE OF A TWO and become the ABSOLUTE CAUSE OF CREATION.

5th ONE is appearing as the ONE having two opposite sides. Actually, the 5th ONE is opposite, now it has opposite (two) sides. The dual aspect of duality is because of that dual-ness in ONE, but now the dual aspect of duality tries to develop oneness in duality! For this oneness, two opposite sides have to become One, they have to keep and maintain the opposition while trying to become One. Because of this opposition, the oneness disappears and two opposite sides appear. This shows the strong hold of the 5th ONE.

4th ONE has the possibility of using the 5th ONE as an opposite, to go back to its opposite that is the 2nd ONE, with proper and right use of its opposition. The oneness which develops between the 4th and the 2nd is with the help of (and through) the use of the 5th ONE'S means to become separate from the so-called oneness in duality, through transforming in order to transcend the pain of separation. To get over this pain, the 4th ONE has to properly and rightly use the dual aspect of the 5th ONE.

Misuse and abuse will give another result of which there is no doubt. This is in relation to the 5th ONE and as it is opposite to the 2nd ONE, to be in balance the 4th ONE has to be with the 2nd ONE and establish inseparable oneness where separation and its pain doesn't exist through correctly and properly using the true dual aspects of the 2nd ONE; which are very similar to the 5th ONE.

It's possible to differentiate the difference between the two inside the one, as one or similar. To perceive, to recognize the difference, then to differentiate the two as 'appearing as One', as well as showing, demonstrating oneness. Then, these two different ones can be put together to keep, to arrange, to store, to collect together and then to properly connect, bind, join, and unite together.

The 4th ONE has to do this process again, in a very similar way, to get, to achieve, the opposite result from the previous or earlier process. That's why 're' process, re-arrange, re-manage, re-collect, etc., etc. With 're' to re-unite, the 4th ONE has to be separate from the 5th ONE. This separation is temporary or permanent, ultimate and final from the 5th ONE.

4th ONE has to decide whom to be with: the 5th ONE, the 2nd ONE, or both? If both, then in which way, because 2nd ONE is also together with 5th ONE, while 4th ONE has to change the relation with the 5th ONE.

Unless and until there is attachment – want and like – for the 5th ONE, and full security and protection in being with the 5th ONE, is the desire of the 4th ONE. Then the 5th ONE becomes the object of worship. Although the 5th ONE is the 5th ONE it is similar and different!

Because of the difference in 4th and 5th ONE, the 5th ONE is different for both of them. 5th ONE has many roles and functions and their names are also many, because 4th ONE is many, many more than ONE. ALL are connected and related with the 5th ONE in many different ways. Each one has different desires, so on one side of the 5th ONE is ONLY the 2nd ONE, and on the other side are many, many 4th ONEs. 2nd ONE is JUST together, while the 4th ONE is (doing) adjusting to be together with the 5th ONE because of the fear of losing contact. This develops greater attachment, holding, possession tendencies to the other ONE – it starts to run after the running ONE, the 5th ONE.

2nd ONE as Space, and place having a space, is all the time available, constantly together with the 4th ONE. On this ground of constant availability, 5th ONE appears as available and not available; automatically, the value of the 5th ONE becomes more than the 2nd one, constantly available. Naturally, the 4th ONE cleverly makes an effort to have the 'not available' side of the 5th ONE because what one doesn't have and other's are having develops hate, as well as the feeling of missing and "I don't have" etc., etc. The 4th ONE is not ready to accept these two sides of the 5th ONE so remains constantly busy and engaged in achieving one after the other form of the 5th ONE, to make it complete.

How can incomplete be complete?

With hope, desire and expectation, the 4th ONE prefers to remain busy and engaged to make it complete and to have the feeling of complete from incomplete! They say, 'a glass is half full and at the same time half empty', and to just accept it, don't try to fill it up, and don't complain that it's half empty. A glass is a glass, a container; its content is the 5th ONE, for the 4th ONE. It's the quality that makes the difference, not the quantity. That's why size and numbers should not be important.

The quality, characteristics and aspects of the 5th ONE become more and more attractive and increase the cause of attraction for the 4th ONE.

5th ONE, through participation with the 2nd ONE, becomes the ultimate cause of and for CREATION, at that time remaining outside of CREATION. When CREATION becomes the creator, to have its own creation at that time, the same pair of 2nd and 5th ONE play different roles in a very similar way similar to the way a photocopy looks like the original. That's why in astrophysics they use the term quasi-steady state.

Inside CREATION, the same pair (2nd ONE and 5th ONE) is known and 'Be' as the 4th ONE and 5th ONE. The difference in the State of Being of the 2nd ONE as the 4th ONE with the 5th ONE makes a big difference in the appearance of the 5th ONE. The following terms can be used to understand this:

I.	2nd ONE Primary 5th ONE Secondary	Together CREATION
II.	2nd ONE Primary 5th ONE Primary also as a part of the 1st ONE.	Together CREATION

I. State of Being makes and shows the difference in their status.

II. State of Being makes and shows the equality in their status.

This difference between I and II is recognized by the different, different 4th ONE. Each 4th ONE has tried to prove and establish its own theory as the perfect and best theory through showing some lacuna or missing points or link such as, 'Big Fish eats the small fish', or the other way, 'Small fish eaten by the Big Fish'. In this way:

i. 4th ONE and 5th ONE inside CREATION are similar to the 2nd and 5th ONE.

ii. 5th ONE can be two roles,
   a) Secondary
   b) Primary unequal equal.

iii. 4th ONE has responsibility to recognize, to identify, the role of the 5th ONE and accordingly to be with the 5th ONE,

iv. And to be in harmony with the other 4th ONE.

v. 4th ONE, being with the 5th ONE considering its own relation with the 2nd and 1st ONE,
   a) by accepting and respecting the 5th ONE without attachment;
   b) without accepting and respecting the 5th ONE, also without even showing attachment, and neglecting, ignoring and not giving importance to it.

Attachment towards togetherness and 5th ONE gives pain at the end as a result or effect.

To separate, to detach, to be away from for the time being to be ready again, these actions are with or without any reason. Actions are taken by the 4th ONE to react the same, time and time again.

In this case, there is a return to the same point to restart the same and, for this memory function, subtle impressions of each action are preserved in the form of memories; it has its own storehouse and the same 4th ONE is the storekeeper. That's why it is necessary to clean, to purify, that storehouse, which becomes the cause of pain, again and again. The solution is separation, to be separate, to divorce from the 5th ONE. Instead of this way, the 4th ONE prefers the other way, that is to be separate, to divorce, to detach, from the other 4th ONE.

What has to be abandoned is not done and it is done, which means that 4 and 5 make one 4th ONE. Now, how can the 4th ONE be away, separate, divorced, detached, finally, so long as the 4th ONE is engaged, busy, actively active with the other 4th ONE, or with the 5th ONE alone?

Marriage and children is normal between two 4th ONEs as two opposites together with oneness. Both are known as a couple, they become the creator of their own world (habitation) as a creation. This is a commonly known way of being together as a couple and to have a family, their own creation. The two are different, they do the opposite to the other, and do not accept, etc., etc., and this becomes the guideline for the 4th ONE and for the other 4th ONE. Now both are inside this CREATION, world, habitation.

Final Separation of the 4th ONE is death, so it is expressed by the other 4th ONE, as: 'the soul has departed from this body or corpse belonging to that departed soul known by this name _ _ _ _ ' and 'A condolence meeting is for the peace of _ _ _ _.' No joyful mood, only sorrow, sadness, melancholy, grief, pain in expression, in the environment, remain. The same name was given to both together, now the name and actions remain in the memory.

Body without the soul goes back to the Earth. The composed one was living, having its own lifestyle. Now, it's only a body, not a living but dead body as it was before. Now, the 4th ONE as respondent is absent, gone away, separate forever, leaving this beautiful, attractive body behind: the 4th ONE is separated from the 5th ONE's possession. Death becomes the final separation, with pain. To remain alive, to have a life, to be together with body and not ready to leave the body, not ready to die, means this separation is painful. It is against all desires.

Death is inevitable, immortality cannot be provided nor is it possible to achieve through penance: whosoever is born has to die. No one can escape or avoid death, and for this many stories and parables are available.

The difference between the 3rd ONE as incarnation in this CREATION, is that there is no pain of separation, no pain of death, and who at that moment is so peaceful, calm and quiet in facial expression, even at the peak of painful death. The best example for this is Jesus Christ.

4th One in relation to this 3rd ONE is opposite. Normally, out of a great many, very few can be like this 3rd ONE.

The belief in 1st and 2nd ONE by the 4th ONE, which is demonstrated by living and even at the time of death by not to have a wish or desire to do anything particular for that body in which the 4th ONE is existing. After death, the body is 'at your disposal' and the remaining 4th ONE has to decide what to do with it.

Body belonged to the 5th ONE. Whatever is with you as the 4th ONE, is not yours, it does not belong to the 4th ONE; however, it takes possession and assumes ownership of the body. Master of the body, how is it possible? How can you have ownership and copyright, how can you have the patent number, etc?

All belong to the 5th ONE because 1st ONE and 2nd ONE have not shown ownership and not kept any copy rights and patent for any design: that's why to-day, the 4th ONE is reproduced by 4th ONE with the help and support of the 5th ONE. The cause is attachment and too much togetherness for that creation as 're-creation'. Recreation, entertainment, amusement, fun, enjoyment pleasure, comforts and convenience become part of the life of the 4th ONE, but the source is 5th ONE.

4th ONE, totally identified and associated with the 5th ONE in the lifestyle, prominent and dominant is the 5th ONE: 4th ONE is encircled and swallowed by the 5th ONE. Who is 'one' with whom? To separate becomes difficult. The process is also difficult to stop and is like trying to stop sunrise and sunset, to stop spring and autumn. That's why it is told that its happening can never be stopped and is not by or through you. The 4th ONE is the witness or observer of that happening. Nothing can be done to it. This lesson has to be learnt, those who have learnt are changed totally.

Happening is the effect and the cause is different. 2nd and 5th are the CAUSE of the happening. When happening is the cause, then the effect is different and 4th and 5th ONE are affected by the effect of the happening.

When happening becomes effective, as an effect, then the cause becomes the 4th and 5th ONE making it happen in parallel with 2nd and 5th ONE, like a photocopy. Memories work like a motor, a guiding force, as the best preserver and storekeeper; memories are kept for use and when required are used as a ready reckoner by the 4th ONE.

This becomes the cause of the happening by the 4th ONE, through the 4th ONE, and for the 4th ONE, with the help and support of the 5th ONE. The pair of 4th and 5th ONEs is creating in the same way; it looks like their own creation similar to what the 2nd and 5th One have done in the PAST. After all, 4th and 5th ONE (in the form of further creation) have all the responsibility to carry on, to continue their work! So, they do it with full passion, showing more and more interest to be better than THE BEST! They remain all the time busy, engaged, indulgent, and passionate in this task to sustain and maintain creation, which transforms, changes, dies and destroys continuously.

Originally, it was the work, product, result of the ONE PAIR, the 2nd and 5th ONE. Now it is the work of many, many pairs of the 4th and 5th ONE to maintain, sustain, to carry on creation as a creator. Because of the sense of responsibility, liability, they carry the heavy load of the work as a duty, as a task given by the parents.

4th ONE is caught: it making effort all the time, attempting to be on the extreme side (one side or the other), but not to be stuck in the middle, not to remain in-between while, at the same time, desires to be at the centre, to control, to have all the powers to manage, so creating conflicts and trouble in deciding: what to do?

This state of being develops 'I am ness': associations, identifications, relations and partnership with the other, same, like, similar, can easily be with the similar! Consciousness is the ground for 'I am ness' to develop, to grow and spread around!

Pain is the result just as long as the 'I' is not separate from or with 'am ness', from or with that so-called totality, the 'I am ness'. Here 'I' indicates (stands for) the material ego side, otherwise the expression is 'I AM THAT' or 'THAT I AM', with a proper and right connection, union. That's why it is said: learn to die a 'death'! A constant, continuous process of dying, changing, transforming, which the 4th ONE has to go through to overcome, (as it were) like crossing a river, and what remains as a balance, the outcome of the process of dying, separating, and transforming, is the essence of the 2nd and 1st ONE.

Life becomes 'just to live' without interest, disinterested in all activity, and effortlessly doing it to live the life. This becomes NORMAL, NATURAL, SIMPLE, ORIGINAL, in living. As it becomes so simple, it becomes so easy to live as an observer, witness, seer; but for the other, 'so simple' is 'so difficult', 'not so easy', because of the developed habit of not living simply. 'Not as simple' becomes 'so easy' through everyday practice.

Education is from simple to complex. For highly educated people, the 4th ONE is very difficult to accept, to understand, to adopt and to be simple again in life, along with normal, natural and original. The other group of the 4th ONE maintains and sustains all the opposites to this and is in the majority, and majority rules in democracy. This means 4th ONE becomes closer to the 5th ONE and very much less in connection with the 2nd ONE, or 1st ONE.

Failure, no success, depression and frustration, the 4th One prefers to die and finish its own life because there is no way to be rescued, to remain: the last solution is to finish one's self (this step is second). The first step to finish own self was taken as a 4th ONE; took a turn, made a disconnection, kept no contact and was fully involved with faith, belief, and trust, also with full interest and readiness to do for, in and with the 5th ONE. As a result this occurred in the life of the 4th ONE.

To play the role of a reporter – to report about the object of something that happened to another – is easy, it helps to get the expected thing against the report and for this the 4th ONE (who becomes the observer for its own selfish purpose to report) becomes the reporter from being the observer. Because of the difficulty in withholding and not passing onto others the details of that observation, the object of observation, temptation, or greediness to have more in exchange for the observed material or details, the 4th ONE changes role immediately or at a conveniently suitable time.

In this way, 4th ONE is reporting to the 4th ONE as another 4th ONE, a different ONE, who is not as the same! A new witness is doing the recording as a recorder and is able to play again and again what was recorded. A selfish purpose is behind the reason to change the role from witness to recorder or photographer. It is the 4th ONE who becomes the witness but finds it is difficult (not possible) to keep withholding and not conveying, expressing, reproducing, the detail. So, at a certain time and place, the 4th ONE vomits out all recorded things from within and gets relief from the burden of carrying the information.

For both the roles, use of memory function is very good by the 4th ONE. These two roles look very simple but are very, very difficult to maintain for a long time without changing the role.

To be in one role continually means BEING, thereby not becoming one after the other role players as 'I am ness' in connection with the 5th ONE. BEING is 'am ness' without the 'I'.

Either the 4th ONE or 5th ONE can 'just be' without any relation or connection with any other to see, to perceive and to enjoy the object without changing to become the enjoyer from the seer. The process of seeing, of perceiving, by the seer and not becoming passionate towards an object, not using the function of memory, just being the seer for a long time, is also very difficult work for the 4th ONE. This 4th ONE has to switch off the memory function, which isn't possible. So the habit is to change the role, to have no allowance to be in one role without change, and therefore the 4th ONE is able to give appropriate justification for changing the role and is also able to convince the other 4th ONE why a change of role is necessary. Believing this, following this, the 4th ONE doesn't feel bad or wrong in changing the role.

The happening, event or object can be the same or similar, but the status of Being of the 4th ONE is different and known by different terms: witness, observer, seer, and enjoyer. In relation to the object, the 4th ONE 'becomes' and with this difference changes the term and status accordingly.

To remain as presence, just BEING, with or without involvement by the 4th ONE, and to use this later on as primary evidence, that is to use own presence as proof through becoming a witness instead of 'just being there', 'Being-ness', 'am-ness', presence at the time of happening, is the other way the 4th One becomes. This shows no intention or specific purpose to be there at the time of a happening, as if it is presented or just kept in front to see the reaction (response) to that ongoing action, performance for or in that happening or event. The 4th ONE becomes the witness, is used as a witness by the other 4th ONE as proof. The other meaning of 'witness' is to allow it to happen, to have control over the response and reactions, development of resistance and confidence, as well as maintaining distance and, further, without comments or criticism on that happening or event. Not to become the evidence to prove good or bad, wrong or right, etc., etc., means not to interfere in the ongoing activity of the 5th ONE, in any way.

How easy is it to be the 'Witness'?

In day-to-day life, the 4th ONE, being a witness, avoids becoming evidence because of threat and fear of death, which means swallowing and then digesting the happening or event without getting any side or after effects!

Is this easy for the 4th ONE?

Then it comes out in the form of books and articles related to the particular past, related to specific happenings and events. Because, now in the presence that fear doesn't remain, courage comes back and boldness returns again to get rid of (to get relief from) that witnessing point. To feel light and free, the 4th ONE brings out the part from memory, through remembering each detail, which was recorded as a witness!

So is it easy to be the witness or to become the reporter or informer?

In the same way, the observer turns to be a reporter and makes a change in the role from the previous one to become the seer and also become the enjoyer, analyser, and synthesiser. The character plays role after role by changing clothes (maintaining the dress-code) and conducting programmes one after the other. Instead of remaining in one role, the preference is to transform rather than transcend. The pain in transcending, the pain in separating, is avoided by painkillers, by creating a gap in communication between the two, by turning again to the other side, dimension and direction and transformation remaining transformed without transcending.

If at the start there is the witness, observer, and seer, then to be ready not to change and not to be in any other role or position, to be indifferent within, then the process of pain stops as it starts. This is popularly known term as death, the death of many, many roles. Dying is the role, leaving survival behind as a balance. Survival (balance) is and is not the witness, observer and seer!

As log as there is function, form, shape, purpose, etc., it is ENERGY, not Space!

It is possible to start the journey to SPACE AS A PLACE, but there can be difficulties 'in landing', so there is a return to the mother-base (home-base) from where the journey started.

It's coming back as new with a new appearance, or is it return in another way? Is it a case of being happy to be back rather than having become lost in SPACE, searching for a place the same as or similar to the starting one? Driver is Energy, vehicle is Energy, the path is Energy, is the destination ENERGY? Or is it SPACE? In searching for land, being on LAND, searching the LAND it is possible and easy to find out, get, achieve, what is not LAND!

To prove 'I am' the powerful, the superior, the best in strength, to collect and refine the matter, material and information, is important and the need of the day. Shrewd, cunning, wicked, informer was witness, observer, seer, in the form of data collection, collected by the collector, passed by the processor, analyser, synthesiser, developer, etc., moving through, becoming and changing the format from that of information on one side, and education and knowledge on the other side: it becomes the tool to earn for the student and academic. The best utilization is the other side of the worst utilization, according to relativity. Extreme use of money, material and manpower (human energy) is the goal of management. It has its own academic institutions to promote, upgrade the product, its quality and utility value. Maximum use of these: money, material and manpower, for the best product, the best production unit, has the minimum of wastage.

ENERGY in the form of money, material, and manpower is used by, handled and managed by, the rule of administration done by Energy. ENERGY in the form of a human being, 'the 4th ONE', is considered as resource material. The material is used by 'A Material' for material production in a material world. That's why today there are Human Resource (or HR) departments, ministries, as well as schools and colleges for its education. All are concerned and related to 'HR', even thinkers and educationalists, academics, etc., are all involved in the evolution of the knowledge of HR.

This is where the human being is treated as raw material, a consumable energy, and good quality food for the production unit. The well planned purchase with agreement, contract, and hours of work in and for the production. Out of 24 hours, certain hours are given against certain payment, to spend in a particular, specific place for the work. Change of status is for the time being. Selling of own time (Energy) is against money, payment or any type of cash-in-kind. This is how binding and bondage starts. Later on as time passes, that eaten food (consumed Energy) has been fully and totally sucked-out to make the best product; the remaining portion of that food Energy is kept outside of the production unit, as a used one, consumed one, with a title of 'ex So and So', to maintain given status and dignity in order that an identity crisis does not take place.

As time passes, the green, fresh fruit becomes rotten and uneatable (unconsumable) for the HR unit or for a certain body. Energy remains as energy with change in form and status, birth and death, by ENERGY. Energy wants to be energetic to show (demonstrate) its performance, its show, so it has its own showrooms. Where these shows are going on others become participants or witnesses, observers, seers of this big show in the showroom: What is their goal, target, aim? Accordingly, the others make a collection or achievement or, with reference to the show, evaluate their own position on the map, to know in which direction and in which way to move, to use, to be, etc. This evaluation becomes the guideline for thinking and action for further results and means that purification, which is a process of refining Energy, is going on continuously.

Is it possible to call and know this purified Energy as Holy Energy, Sacred Energy, not evil or the devil's energy, Divine Energy? Is it unnecessary to have Holiness, Sacredness, or Piousness in that purified Energy? Or is Energy solely Energy having nothing to do with all these things? It is ULTIMATE and ULTIMATELY IT IS ENERGY!

Then, what about SPACE? Is it Energy? Does it have relativity? To divide, to give shape and form, to cover and encircle, to be a point or centre – all is by and through and for ENERGY. The balance is SPACE.

Surrendering to survive is done by the lower to the higher, the weaker to stronger, to feel secure and sure for its own life. Energy is in two forms with a common term 'Ego' and 'I'. Two forms, two different statuses, one surrounding the other and finally it's a play of Energy as two opponents who are the components of the play, unending and endless: an infinite play by these two opponents (imprint and impressions, old becomes outdated, new is fresh and lively).

'To become that' becomes the driving force, with interest and effort, trying 'to be that' Energy or is it SPACE?

Energy is the best actor and player, it appears like Space in its act, play or performance, and adds one more opponent and component to the play.

How can Energy become Space? It can demonstrate as a demonstrator just like space. The ULTIMATE BACKGROUND IS DARK BLACK!

In relation to this, others are background and can be a background, and can appear as, look like, seem to be, a background, but it basically wants (would like to be) in front, on top, first, and to have all the importance, respect, honour, recognition, acceptance that is Energy. Although Energy has all these, it always demands from its other form a status, and to fulfil the demand all tact and techniques are used. The nature of Energy is the means to acquire, posses, to have, what belongs to the other!

He, she, it, they, Energy can try and try and can acquire, posses, have all the time, infinitely, forever and still remain unsatisfied, discontented and disturbed; it also can't totally cover up Space. It is possible and easy to do with its own other form and state and along with difficulties it can manage through various techniques, even manipulation. The result is that it looks as if Space is possessed by Energy or that Energy has acquired Space: it looks like a false satisfaction. That's why it is suggested, advised, that it is better not to try to have what belongs to the other, that is Space!

Even if it is considered that Space is possessed, that it is acquired, it's better to give up all rights to it and be happy and enjoy the happiness which develops out of it, out of giving up. Be wise and do the activity with this wisdom; which means to allow things to happen by or on their own, using it's own flows of energy, and take own position with a little distance that allows all the possibilities to move with full freedom and, because of that little distance, the result will not affect or reach to that position. In this case, a little less is better than a little more.

A constant struggle, desire, and conflict to be on or at which place, back or front? Looking to the advantage and benefit of both places, there are preferences although it's better not to loose one but to keep it and the opposite one (side) at the same time. However, it is possible through cleverly putting one's own other form as apparently another one for many, many others (who are not able to distinguish the difference between the two) to see and consider 'two as two', while the clever one out of the two enjoys the benefit of both positions while being at one position. The set up structure and design look very simple and common (normal) and at the same time it has a specific way flow of its own energy alone with the other also.

Although it is one Energy, it has many, many forms and states, so it takes care to remain behind at the back and also ready to be in front to attract, to achieve, even to fight as a warrior, to prove its strength and power and to bring the other energy under its rule in a specific order (discipline) to make it more beautiful and attractive. Is it a fisherman's net or a trap? Anyhow, that Energy becomes the enjoyer as a ruler of both places, at the back as well as in front, in two different ways. It's an illusion and it's not an illusion. It is and it is not!

Energy cannot compete with TRUTH, which is ONE. So, what to do? Many, many FACTS can be established so that Energy appears as TRUTH on the principle that 'many makes ONE' (in the same way as a duplicate or a photocopy) with endorsement and affidavit, so that it's possible to believe and accept on behalf of the ORIGINAL. The ORIGINAL is one and its photocopy is possible to distribute to many, many. Possessing the photocopy, accepting it as an original, keeping it on record as evidence provided by the other Energy! This one who has accepted, is also energy, possessing its own original copy but remains unhappy and dissatisfied – dis–satisfaction becomes the mother of invention. Even being in constant contact with Space (the ORIGINAL, the TRUTH) Energy needs to depend on its own established facts This shows the independent nature of Energy: meaning that it is dependent inside in its own system but shows independence outside. When many facts are all together trying to appear as truth for a short period, as time passes that so-called truth also passes away, along with Time.

How can time carry away that truth? The answer is because it was and it was not, at that time it appeared and also disappeared as a truth: present converted into absence. This means that in ETERNAL TRUTH, PRESENCE and Related TRUTH, presence is different: or it can be described as BACKGROUND and related back to the front. The nature, type, function, of the back is the same (common), while the front is different.

On one side it is accepted without any opposition that ENERGY is ULTIMATE and the ULTIMATE IS ENERGY. Energy has many, many FORMS, functions, systems, structures, flows, results, effects, etc., and each one has its own terms for communication, to come to an understanding. Different questions give different answers to clear up its image (picture) for better use by and for each other's energy in any form. It has its own state and status, which becomes the base for further changes and consequences. The form is conform to Energy's role for priority, which means that to avoid, to neglect, not to take care, to let it be, becomes more important. Because importance was already given to that priority, what happens is that, efficiently and skilfully, Energy moves towards its decided destination. For this, on one side, more greed and, on the other side, very controlled disciplined to hide (to cover up) the strong temptation and attraction towards the other side of Energy's form. According to achievement (a decided destination), the priority becomes according to the priority, selection becomes according to the selection, achievement becomes!

'To avoid' becomes the priority. According to it, selection to achieve that 'to avoid' is through becoming busier, more engaged and involved on the other side of 'to avoid'. Achievement on both the sides and 'to avoid' is avoided. As well as involvement, engagement has also brought achievement 'in the form of' results of selection and action.

Even having a two-sided achievement-'plus', one is constantly pinching to bring awareness about what was done, what happened in the past, so it becomes necessary and important to avoid. Importance was given to the mechanism to avoid and as a result its technique becomes important for engagement, involvement, and to remain busy, having brought appreciation, recognition and acceptance to that Energy in its concerned field, which is inside The Main FIELD of ENERGY.

'Avoid to avoid' means not ready to face, to go through, to have any responsibility as binding, not willing to lose freedom, and better to avoid, to escape, to run away, to keep a distance, to be 'cold' rather than 'cool', is on top of the list as a priority along with the other list of achievements. That's why there is preference to have more and more space to move, to meet and to be in contact and in touch with the other form so to avoid knowing its own form; then it is the other form, where attraction, temptation, and greediness can work and keep busy, engaging, involving and indulging in each other, because two opposites are two and complementary while also becoming one.

Energy, although it is formless, gets as many forms as can be possible through its own formation. No other can imagine or count the number of forms! Countless, uncountable forms; what remains in balance out of formation is also an Energy and so it is within the form (outside also) as formless, shapeless, etc. Form has its own format and function. Its specific purpose is to be in that particular form, that particular energy. Why does it prefer this?

The reasoning behind, the logic behind, the forms is not that easy to know or comprehend by the other Energy;

although both are Energy, and in the form of Energy, even after that one is exposing the other! One is trying to catch the other! One is trying to pull down the other, in many different ways all of the time. Everywhere this play by the two opponent players is going on continuously. It has its own rules, regulations, code of conduct and manners, values and ethics etc., and all are related but bound to relativity. All the players on the playground compose, arrange and manage with skill and efficiency, which becomes informative and educative through its presentation.

Then how can it be illusion, delusion, and ignorance? It is a one-sided expression to a two-sided happening! To cover up every way and all perspectives, it is expressed as that the total world is illusion, delusion, and ignorance: all are adjectives for Energy. Is it by and through Energy? SPACE has no other way but to accept what is and whatever is going on, without any comment or criticism!

To indulge or not to indulge: is it a choice, option or alternative action? As long as it is Energy and energetic (functions maybe in many forms) sure it can be good or bad, acceptable or discard, refuse the form, functions and results in any permutation or combination, from any point of view. Creation, World, habitation, has a form of Energy where specific form is and is not, are many points of view that are different for each other.

As an inhabitant of that habitation, having an inborn habit to move and to be together, it gives or makes it easy (possible) to become. 'To be' is all the time the goal, aim or target for Energy but not for Space, which is all the time indestructible. It's Energy that gives form, shape and even carries space with a covering, encircling like a body or box. Space is divided by Energy, and also Energy is divided by Energy. Space creates fear, gives the challenge, permeates more freely, allows one to be, provides all the directions and remains broad and open. On the contrary, Energy makes threats, takes risks, creates obstacles and hindrances, wants to become, to select one direction, and often changes from one to the other, broad to narrow, open to closed, etc., with repeating action, again and again.

Energy being one but becoming many, tries to have oneness and equality with the opposite, it wants to be harmonious, demanding trust yet remaining doubtful, it is in search of security and gives surety. Because it is in many forms, shapes fragments, pieces, particles, and atoms, between the two a space appears and disappears; in the same way, Energy comes and goes. Being unlimited and free, Energy becomes the provider and controller in and with a limit to other forms of Energy. That's why a question arises: Why and for what purpose am I here in this world, habitation? What is my task?

One is the tree, the other is fruit and flower,
One is on the tree, the other on the ground,
  separated.
One is branch and leaf, moving towards the open sky
  to get sunlight.
The other is root, underground, moving towards the
  source of water and food!
Tree was and is in the seed,
Seed will be the tree?
That tree will it give flower and fruit?

Future related questions easily arise and remain without answers. The sprout wants to come out of the seed and the seed doesn't want to break. The same as the chicken that wants to remain in the egg because it's so comfortable and convenient, protected from all, yet wants to have a glance at the world, to see inhabitants of that habitation.

How long is it possible?

In the case of the seed, roasting or by over-heating the possibility of a sprout for further creation is annihilated and the seed now becomes ready and remains for another use!

Egg is broken, worldly person has looked at it and decided what to do!

Mathematically, the full point (.) has no value. It can change the value of 1, as 0.1, or 1.0, just by being on the left or right side. Zero to start, zero to finish! Point to point connection is only one out of 360 degrees, so an opening is required. This means 359 degrees remain unused all the time; so it gets its connection from the other side and has multi-connections for multi-functions and results. It has maximum use in minimum time and Space (place); it becomes compact, tiny, and little, yet makes a big performance. The more it is concentrated, the more it becomes narrow to pinpoint the focus. Naturally avoidance happens side by side, or it is purposefully concentrated to avoid the other?

All numbers start to appear from the '(.) point'; all letters of the alphabet, phonemes, appear from sound. These are the two forms of Energy, while Space is beyond these two forms. Availability of knowing 'how to be' becomes less and less, while knowledge in the form of information is available in plenty for knowing 'how to become'. There is a big difference between 'born' and 'made'; today as per demand, something is made to fit, to suit the demand, and maker becomes supplier (provider) to get back what was invested in the beginning to try to gain a little more than the previous investment and, for this, it becomes the calculator, to have, to all the time get back in return more than was spent, invested and given.

Finally, all belongs to Energy. Instead of increasing possessions and having false satisfaction about the result, it's better not to try in the first place; giving up is the solution rather than concentrating on getting it back, either in this way or that. This is because Energy is continually and energetically doing calculations and remaining fresh: it becomes refreshed again and again. That joy, pleasure and achievement, one after the other, together with changes of status, standards of living and lifestyle, is how Energy tries to appear, giving the impression that it was Space, superior to all. Is it possible?

Yes it is and no it is not possible. Inside creation it is possible to have a higher position. Actually, higher and lower is itself a part of creation, as bigger and smaller Energy in two different forms, thereby becoming enjoyer and sufferer!

Space is already at the two opposite end points of highest and lowest, at the maximum of maximum out and above and the minimum of minimum in and under.

Being in-between, caught in-between, to be in-between, to be like the other one and to be either/or any end point becomes the goal, the aim of all movements of Energy – and up to a certain extent Energy achieves it.

Being a constant moving principle, ENERGY (in any shape or form) keeps its own movement, then it becomes reformed or transformed and even this change (movement) becomes the cause of conversion and it converts from one to the other one.

Although remaining the same yet appearing to be different, are the previous one and the present one two, or is it that with the difference they appear as two? They are two and they are not two. For a very, very few they are not two, it's a delusion, pleasure and pain. Even in relation to that ABSOLUTE ONE, this one again becomes delusion, pleasure and pain all in one.

Finally (ultimately), what remains as balance is that ABSOLUTE BALANCE, there is an ABSOLUTE BALANCE SHEET where a two-sided performance is shown. As it is a balance sheet it has two sides and each side has to be balanced, not unbalanced. What is shown is very different from what is seen, or is what is seen shown? Then, each and every one has seen the same and not different. Where does the difference exist?

What is shown is shown to each and every one the same, that's why it is known as world, habitat, creation, child, etc., etc., and what is seen is not the same, not similar, it is different because each one is different from each other. That's why there are two sides: majority and minority. There are very, very few who are different, who are in the minority, they are not in connection to what is shown. They are disinterested and even have no willingness to see what is shown, they consider and accept them as a part of a 'shown' so that the other can distinguish the difference between the two parts as shown and seen. This process (analysis) helps to locate their own position, known as localization, which means 'where is/are', and 'how is/are' are shown and seen in relation to each one's position. From the positional point of view, the two (both) are on (at) different positions, 'shown by' and 'seen by'.

To have a position, to take a position 'to see and show', means:

a. show and seen
b. see and show, again,
c. shown and seen by and further
d. seen is shown by how many?

At least two minimum in this process or game played by two as different, although both belong to the ONE, either a CREATOR or CREATION. So a question: what is shown is seen by many or by one (shown by one or many and seen by one or many)? Now, one or many is shown by one seen, seen by many! The same appears as different because of the difference in each one's position and background.

Newspaper is one, readers are many. Many are readers who give importance to the news; a few just read it as a newspaper without giving importance to it. Where does the delusion and illusion come? Who is responsible for what? Newspaper is a creation and is read by a reader! How? In which way? It depends.

The position of the ONE can be one without changing the position to be 'seen'. Whatever is shown can change its position. Whatever is seen is in the past and therefore not the whole. Many have seen and not been in the same position, but everyone has seen a part of that whole show. It is 'taken for granted' that each and every one has seen the same show. Although the show is the same, it is seen as a part assuming it's the whole. Whatever is taken for granted is avoided in presentation, and this means reading can be line by line but there is also more that can be read between the lines. There are two ways to convey a message: what is written is to be read and what is not written is to be understood without reading (the readable writings).

Assumption, presumption and taking something for granted helps to develop the logical structure with the help of the inference system to prove what is provable. The statement made by another who has seen the same show becomes a limited, narrow, or small sphere in comparison with the other's statement and conclusion. The approach to become small, little, narrow or individualised is just an appearance in comparison to the other bigger, higher, taller, broader, wider or universalised approach.

There are two types of logical structure and two types of presentation: first, seen by the individual and second, presented taking a different position; although these are principally the same they take different positions to become different and not to be similar or look-alike.

Without disturbing the show, whatever is shown is either part or whole, it is seen from the very beginning until the end, or just a portion is seen and a conclusion is made about the whole. That also becomes and works as evidence to prove and to support the logical structure.

The story of the blind men and the elephant is popularly known. How the whole is presented and known is by parts together with evidence supported by past impressions, imprints (of information as knowledge) as worked as a reference to context, to interpret the present show from the evidential proofs (the ear, trunk, foot, etc.). Examination of a part as if it were the whole is done totally perfectly, accurately, and precisely by each individual, but what happened in the end was that their statements differed, as the parts differed to that of the whole, although the whole (elephant) was, is, and will be the same.

How can a single individual see the total, complete elephant as a whale? From which position, very near, very far, from where? To see clearly, how much distance should one have from the object as a scene? The show (as an object) is seen by different individuals with different positions and distance. To consider the presentation and statements about the elephant without knowing and considering their position (as a cause of their supporting statements), how can it be known in which way the statements are made different from the previous one?

A statement is a FORM of Energy. Energy is the show as a whole and in part; the show is seen by Energy as an Individual and in a different-different Form appears as a statement where Energy (also as a former Form) becomes a comparative statement to prove the efficacy of one to the others. Energy to Energy, how can they be compared when each form is a form of Energy? The conclusion is Energy is ONE and just so long as it is different, difference is maintained, to compare, to prove, with evidence of proof, that KNOWLEDGE IS ONE. How is it that the statements are different? It is because the parts of the whole were taken for granted and out of the many a few were used, utilized for the presentation of 'seen', to show again in a limited scope – even if it is a telescope it can help to see what is far away! Statements from this position are certain to be different from the former form of Energy as a statement.

The one individual line appeared; other lines appeared, were drawn, and kept with it; the maximum bigger line became the Universal approach. Finally, both are or were lines and will continue to be lines. From the size point of view, it is possible to compare the two lines, the individual and Universal. From the line point of view, both lines start from (begin) with the same sized point of origination.

Each one has given importance to considering the other part equally important and they have taken it for granted that what is shown by them is enough proof. But what happened? The same portion, which was not covered up (taken for granted) becomes evidence and proof to prove that which is considered as enough is not being considered as enough, and that here is further presentation of that whole show.

In this way, everyone has shown, giving the maximum from their position and point of view. The given (the shown) has the scope to add or deduct because it is a play of Energy to hide, to cover up and then to expose, to open up. The size of the space becomes smaller or bigger with and through Energy and its different-different forms.

What is the occupation of Energy? It is to occupy, to posses, to have, to become owner and authority, and to be self-sufficient.

What is Energy going to occupy, possess, to have? Energy has its own different, different FORMS and functions, and their results.

From this point of view, why does Energy have to run after its own form, function and its results?

Why does Energy need to prove itself, and why does it expect and accept recognition and appreciation from Energy as other's Energy? Why does Energy have difficulty to recognize, to distinguish, and to discriminate? Is it not that its nature is itself an obstacle to this process? Why is it easier to be heated rather than cool, why is there preference to be cold or hot? How can we talk about the attraction towards this type and nature of Energy by another Energy in a different-different form?

Either this tendency (the attitude to have, to possess, to occupy etc., etc.) has to be given up, or it's better not to posses that which already belongs to the other (meaning possessed by the other, occupied by the other, that is SPACE) and make a choice or selection according to one's own convenience and comforts for happiness.

Being Energy is to be on the bright side rather than the dark, black side where the absence of SUN Light (Energy as brightness) is not there. Each single form of Energy has a choice to be recharged again and again, or not.

Consumption is because of the connection, recharging it is reconnection, reunion to its mother unit (recharging unit). Consumption leads to death (separation), because the consumer consumes it.

The individual, itself as a unit of Energy, is used and consumed by a big machine, an individual, for the production of the other form of Energy, and the consumed

Energy unit does not remain for further consumption because of its limit and provision. So, it becomes used Energy, consumed Energy. As its utility value finishes, the asset becomes a disposable item, a liability, which no one takes. Then again it starts moving and rolling as before, after being properly sucked out, consumed.

As a unit of Energy with less power and strength to carry the load, the unit shows reduced functioning and creativity as another phase. Where the energetic part of Energy becomes less sparkling and twinkling, it withdraws, takes less interest and the tortoise-syndrome starts conservation for prolongation. What was possessed is not ready to be lost and instead of becoming ready to give up, the unit prepares to hold on.

What has to be held is given up, and what has not to be held is held. Now a struggle between the two: one has to hold and not give up, while the other has to take it away. That holder becomes householder – house is transforming and the holder has to be out of it at any time.

How can a holder hold a Space? Or is SPACE THE HOLDER of the Holder? Then, what is held has not to be held again because it is a waste of strength to hold again what is held. It's better to give up, enjoy the happiness and conserve Energy: a two-way approach to happiness for a long term solution.

Today, opposite of this happiness (satisfaction) is short term, repeated again and again. How important is continuity? The longer duration remains at the level of expectation and desire to have more and more, with greed as a force and pressure behind for movement and achievement after achievement and then conversion of it into the other. This makes it bigger, larger, many, but also smaller, little, less than the previous one in comparison: although the size becomes smaller, the value of it increases – the case was taken, the calculation was done precisely and accurately to gain more in another form. The goal is to increase strength and power, so first collection and accumulation, then press and compress to make it more compact, solid, and heavy, bright and clear.

After all, Energy remains an Energy form either in a separate-separate form distinct and different from each other, or it's collected and united, combined and suppressed, compacted and solidified with an attractive shape and curvature. Energy has built the Energy level, a sphere, an area, then starts encroaching, moving further and further to acquire, to posses the maximum from all directions. For this, various activities are done by collectiveness, becoming, forming a group, an energy unit, which forms a system and starts its own functions to survive, because it's survival of the fittest – the unit is not ready to die, yet keen to kill.

Activities done by Energy have made an impression and imprint, also a seed to grow as a result of (effect of) action, which becomes the cause of binding for that Energy. So there is the desire to enjoy, not to have any binding and to remain free from all bondage. Even for that strong desire there is a burning desire to remain all the time freshly energetic, to enjoy the maximum, more than all other forms of Energy. How it is possible for that Energy? That's why it is mentioned in such a way: Who can desire to live longer and be free from the binding of the actions and performance and activities?

Indirectly, it is advice to that Energy form that has decided to live another way. So one form can have a wish, the desire to live for one hundred years, to survive; and the other form, who doesn't follow the advice of giving up considers (assumes) that everything is 'mine' and all different forms belong to 'me', 'I am' in it, as well as 'my' rules of order are controlling them. 'I am right', 'I am best', 'I am the highest, superior and perfect of them'. No one is equal to me. To become and remain powerful and stronger, that is the action, or orientation, nothing else.

A technique, a method, is given to live longer without binding, then what to do and how to live! Without mentioning spirituality, how can terminology be used in such a way that it becomes easy to understand? What does it mean, what does it want to say to us as an Energy form?

One who keeps away and lives in enjoyment, moving away from the brighter side, avoiding the clear sunlight (Energy), takes shelter behind, hides and covers its own self with a blanket of actions, performances, and activities considering that no one knows about it, and that Energy never prefers to be exposed in light. Flashlight for photography is OK; later on in darkness, x-rays make a clear diagnosis. So how much should one avoid the light?

The maximum way to keep away means to kill one's own self, to keep away from that particular, specific field, away from access to or of light, using a thick shield, a cover. Good logic and reasoning never allows a light to enter in the theatre where one's own play is going on, in its own light. Changing the lifestyle to a totally different way to live, one becomes different, transforming, and considers that as progress and development, but in which direction: downward, upward, towards hell or heaven, towards the SUN or away from the SUN? According to the reference point, one can talk about the position and destination looking to the direction of the movement of Energy and its forms.

Where will they be? How will they be? And why will they be in that way? Who can do the mathematical calculation? One who knows this mathematics, that one can tell us. What will happen? It will be a prediction on the basis of calculations, with permutations, considering the possibilities and probabilities; the conclusion comes up from the churning process of either in or out. That in relation to time becomes or is known as a prediction where the analysis and synthesis is well done. This prediction is in relation to future happening, and the place of the future is inside SPACE, the same SPACE which is inside and outside.

As a tutorial is between the tutor and student or pupil outside; the tuition class and its fees are paid by a pupil (student) outside; and on the basis of that learning or tuition class, the pupil passes the Exam conducted by the Examiner outside! As it is outside, so it is inside, in another form. That pupil knows tuition by THAT TUTOR inside as intuition. Who has to tell the pupil to act inside? The inner one who tells to act inside is the Intellect. It is a part and property of Energy. As a doer, the principle is known as 'I am', 'I am the doer', 'I have done it', and 'I will do it'. Without doing and getting (achieving) the result 'I' can't remain, it's my nature, I know how to do, the needed tools are mine, they belong to me, and for my enjoyment, fun and pleasure 'I am doing it'. It's the reason why I am energetic; I know the value, give the importance and take care of prioritising selection and avoidance. It's a general phenomenal performance.

The more connection to the worldly and material side, the more it requires to consume more energy forms as enjoyer and doer. This is known as being selfish, if not highly selfish; everything is kept personal, giving and taking care of the personality and its image and impression in another form of Energy. It's also known by the other way as 'ego', and its self-esteem goes up and down, ego-boosting, ego-feeding, hurt ego, ego-puncture, ego problem, and egoistic behaviour, etc. Ego is one, it has dualness inside! dualness is the cause of duality outside.

It is a mixture, a combination of two at two levels:

I. Two are
   1) 2nd and 5th – makes ONE
   2) 4th and 5th – makes one

II. Two – level
   1) Out of Creation
   2) Inside Creation

III. Combination – mixture
   1) Higher / super conscious
   2) Lower / common conscious

IV. Known by
   1) 'I' – as EGO
   2) 'i' as ego

V. Known by
   1) SELF
   2) Self

VI. Known by

1) Real
2) Un-Real

First the formation with the help of the two opposites as One; inside this formation, again the opposite has two opposite sides, ends, or parts. These two opposites have one middle, middle centre point, that is the opposite point or centre from the other side of ONE.

Another way to know this is 100% divided in two parts:

1) Becomes 50% + 50% = 100%, again divided and not divided.
2) 25% + 25% +50% = 100%

1) appears as 50% > 100% =
two complete sides $\frac{50\% + 50\%}{100\% \quad 100\%}$

2) 25% becomes 50%
and 50% + 50% = 100% – appears complete
but 50% is ignored, neglected.

In the process of becoming complete, the growth progress and development becomes more important, 25% becomes 50% and tries to have completeness, fullness. How is it possible? Two times 25% = 50% as one part, or one half of the other 50%; but what happened is the transformation of own size from 25%, 25% to 50%, twice,

- and achieved 100%
- or appears as 100%
- or false satisfaction,
- or glass half full as 100% and half empty as 50%,
- that remaining 50% forms the original 100%.

Looking at this mathematically it becomes clear how cheating takes place as the complete appearance looks similar, are two as 25% and 25%, and different also, opposite also.

This (1) 25% + 25% or 50% + 50%, one part of the other belongs to Energy, it has two opposite ends, sides or parts to connect and to have continuity, but on its own there is no continuity! However, continuity can be achieved through connection and combination, and a mixture of the two opposites can become one from it. All effort is futile, without the other half. Real growth, progress, development, transformation and conversion etc., are all related to (connected to) ENERGY and its FORM and FUNCTION. That's why the conclusion can be made: ultimately Energy, and ENERGY IS ULTIMATE; It is and It is not.

Because SPACE is beyond, the Real transcends from one side to the OTHER. Conversion of the Real means ENERGY, which converts into ABSOLUTE SPACE or becomes SPACE (that is it returns to its ORIGINAL STATE from where it came before becoming Energy), which means the complete loss of identity as Energy and its energetical nature in all forms and functions.

This process is painful. That ego, 'I am-ness', prefers to be the enjoyer, creator, doer, to be ready to play many different roles, to be in various forms and to do many, many functions in different, different ways, to multiply from simple to complex. To remain continuously changing is the nature of ENERGY and to do this in a natural way is its habit! Identification, identify and identity crisis is the expression by 'I' connected to 'I' and the ego. 'I' is the sprout (shoot) of the seed known as ego. Cultivation starts with a sprout (shoot) with lots of vital energy, that's why it is eaten by the other Energy for growth. Growth is eating the growth of the other, two are the growing forms of Energy becoming one for a while and separating afterwards – the 'use and throw', 'hire and fire', by Energy of its form and functions. 'I', in connection to ego, as a sprout, has the choice to choose the direction, destination, and means (tools) to reach or to access.

Nature has set the example: sprout, shoot, growth towards sunlight and the open sky, while always avoiding darkness. Plant has its own intelligence to know, to search, to find out. Root is the other side of the seed and sprout's direction, searching for food and water, moving, to spread for food and water; while the sprout's shoot is growing, spreading towards the open sky and light, sunlight.

'I' came from the seed and goes back to the seed, to come out again and again! It's a cycle and recycle. Seed is one but two-sided: one side is effect and one is cause – effect in the present, then cause in the past. Cause in the present, then effect in the future! From the time point of view, present is related (connected) with the past as its cause and with future as its effect. Force and pressure is exerted to push further, to move ahead and to come-out, to go ahead, but not to go back, step back, give up, and to sit in the side of effect. Connection with the past is also painful and depressive for that 'I'. To remain creative is the solution, otherwise destructiveness will become easy for that 'I'.

So, the choice can be to shift the centre towards the side of the cause to connect, to become the cause, to be responsible for creation, to posses, to have for enjoyment or for better living, for removal of the opposite and opposition, for overall total control and rule. Also to get the credit, appreciation, recognition, acceptance, through becoming the cause rather than the effect! Because of 'Me', 'you' are here!

'Employer-employee relationship, to hire and fire, etc., then strike, rebelliousness, revolt, to be against and in opposition, not to accept, reject and refuse, not to agree etc., becomes spontaneous reflection from each other side to each other; later on, the winner becomes stronger, is the winner; the looser is also an Energy, 'I', 'Ego'. To get back what is lost is the vow and vote in a collection of strength and power, to show 'Who am I'. To give or to get (to take) the reward, gift, honour, credit, etc. – 'I, me, my and mine' avoids punishment: the idea of being punished never appears on the screen of the doer, the programmer.

But however, 'ready to punish' waits for the opportunity to take revenge and for that, analysis of 'why and how' is going on constantly to become more precise and accurate for the result of that (for) that action or performance. A well-planned, well-cooked and served properly, decently food item of revenge and punishment, in a very delicate manner and style, makes a more delicious appearance of the food items that only the one who eats can know and no other can recognize. So, no other can prove what happened, how it happened, why it happened, and unanswerable questions remain for the other form of Energy! After all it's a play of Energy, play of the big ego, bigger than the other ego!

In this way, through its forms and functions, its results and effects, Energy seems to be different from all points of view by maintaining a proper imbalance, in a balanced way, for its flow. This Ego, as a seed, is one with two sides (as effect and cause potency), is itself a mixture of the two, either 2nd and 5th, or 4th and 5th. It is just like the shadow and light together, or contrasting. Existence of the existential principle, along with its contrast or shadow, is dual-ness in one, and for that the term 'ego' has four inter-related terms, 'I', 'me' 'my' and 'mine'.

At two levels, higher and lower, the higher level EGO and lower level ego work in co-ordination all the time, cooperating together for the result and effect, while one is able to put the blame onto the other and make efforts to attempt to have a larger portion from the result, a bigger share and credit in any form, again and again, and not just once. To become praiseworthy is the goal, the aim for that ego, and also to be surrounded by the beggar in a decent form, who knows how to beg in a decent way (manner) as per the standard code of conduct: the behavioural norms are fixed for the varieties of beggars, all with different connotations. Again it is a game, a play, played by two egos, a pair of egos, but sometimes (because of corruption) here also the match is fixed between the two opponents. The crooked, wicked and cunning has proved 'I am not that', 'I am honest', 'clean and clear' through providing evidence as proof, so it is proved to become the contrary.

Is it possible for Energy to become Space? Or is it possible to be like, seeming to be, appearing as Space? It's a fight or struggle between the established facts of whom or which one is the TRUTH? TRUTH is TRUTH; it doesn't require anyone to prove its own existence. It is there and not there, so it has to be searched for, no one says that they search the facts! They say they are searching the TRUTH that is there and here: all the time, on that GROUND, searching is going on! Very often they find out what is not the truth because it is a fact, and then remain busy proving the factual value more than the other one has through comparison and evaluation in a different way and to make the other realize who is more valuable. For this, a constant new formation or deformation process is going on to change in the value-system, and various selfish motives try to have faith, belief and trust from the other similar forms of Energy. It's a clearly unclear manipulation!

Who is the manipulator? Not Space, but Energy and its forms, for status and Image in others and among them. It looks like a dance, a play, a game and many other forms of performance where the flow is constant and the movements are continuous. That one, who flows moving along with the movement, to be in the motion, is emotion. Existence or the existential principle in the motion is known as emotion. A motionless picture is not attractive because it doesn't show life or liveliness; it stands still, but how long? Dead it becomes, or dead it is declared, no one wishes to look at it.

The last respects, regard and homage are paid to that one who died a moment before! All the collections in the form of memory are preserved and kept well, to carry forward; the audited account of clean and clear actions has got the due stamp and sign of authority on the balance sheet for preparation of future expenditure and income of Energy in 'budget papers'. These papers are related with a future time period, while the balance sheet shows the past time period. How is the present? The one who lives, that one knows how it is, and why it is.

Facts are outside, truth is within; facts are proved, truth is realized.

The river of death is crossed by dying; in other words, the other side of the means is achieved, or actualised, that is immortality or nectar.

The worshipper is one of the forms of Energy that is busy, engaged and involved in worshipping 'That Energy'. In which way? It needs clear understanding, discrimination, and ability to distinguish the difference, and differentiate the difference between the two types of worship as one worship of Energy. Is it a worship of the form and function of Energy or of the contrary, as a form and function of THAT ABSOLUTE ONE?

Energy worshippers are very many. The worship of ENERGY is for Energy, by Energy through different forms and functions of Energy. One form of Energy is busy arranging and managing its own programme of worship by itself in a decent and discrete way, not rough and rude, however, trying to be polished and posh, fragile and delicate, tasty and delicious, and delightful in appearance so as to attract the other form of Energy for worship, and this becomes their function. A regular function of the worshipper is to worship that particular, specific form for protection, shelter and security, for peaceful living with enjoyment and happiness. Each form is busy with its own functions, as also are other forms. Form of function is itself a container and content, one is inside the other and they exist in hierarchy. This order helps to rule and execute the lower or sub-forms and their own formation.

A hierarchical structure is everywhere, all the time, in various ways. It is like a ladder, a staircase, and steps to move up and down on. Today, to save energy and time, the elevator is available. Just stand there and be transported means that one form of Energy is carrying another form of Energy. The non-living form is carrying the living form inside, managed and operated by the living form of Energy.

What Energy busy for? Why is it engaged? Why does it have to prove its own exclusive rights to be in power and to be alone, having the monopoly to use it without restriction, binding, limit, or boundary around its own movement? Being Energy, it is observing its own form, function, structure and system, their results and effects, and attaining continuously in two opposite ways the one result (effect), all the time alone and together. Energy being always alone in its own form, has its own way, with its own results and effects on one side; on the other side it all the time together. Here on this side it is as 50%, while there on the other side it is 100% originating from 50% and developing an imitative photocopy (mirror image) of its own reflection as another 50% to become 100%.

How can there be two pairs of 100%? First, the basic original was made by two 50%s as original or basic; second, one half played the role of betrayer and formed its own party from its own portion of 50%, and by becoming duplicate it attains that 100% state, as the previous one.

In this way, two pairs have achieved and become 100% in two different ways – dual dual-ness becomes the cause of the dual duality. This has given a possibility of permutation and combination between the forms, functions, systems and structures and their results and effects:

1) Both are together.

2) Both combine together, binding together.

3) Both growing together, sharing the result (effect) of togetherness.

4) Being together, becoming one from togetherness through developing oneness in togetherness, proper blending, unification, and appearance of one from that union or combining of two together.

It is a third one and not.
It is the middle one and not.
It is the effect and cause and not.
It is the life to live and not.
It is the process of death and not.
It is to love to enjoy or to die a death and not.

It depends; it has departed from two ends, both applicable to the One. It is two-ways to access the One, or two-ways to escape, to avoid the one, to be away from the One! That's why there exist alternatives and options with many choices of and for selection, having substitutes, dummies, and then problems and confusion to select the best out of the best, the excellent out of the excellent! To say 'It depends' is the product and function of the Intellect, which provides the convenient and suitable logic and reasoning in argument, justification, clarification, notification etc., etc., and also decides and supports what is decided (and even helps to decide), so that the 'I' can be an executor of the decision. Actually, intellect is the property of ENERGY. It has a sharpness and brightness appearing as cleverness and brilliantness for better functions and results.

As this property, the intellect, remains unclaimed by its original proprietor (ENERGY), it gives a chance for the other one to demonstrate its own right to become intellectual and become proprietor of that ego who has to carry out many functions through 'I', 'me', 'my' and 'mine'.

Being innocent, like a child to that MOTHER, the other one becomes more and more clever and then becomes an idiot, foolish or stupid because of the result, not because of the performance, during the time of the performance. Cleverness and brilliancy was there, that did the work of knitting the binding so that it appeared as freedom! This was done cleverly and in an excellent way so that it becomes difficult to prove who has done it? Who is the Doer? This is cleverly arranged and managed so that it appears as 'I am not the Doer'. Then who has done this? Destiny!? How and through whom? Why is there difficulty in accepting the responsibility of pain and suffering along with credit and appreciation?

How can one escape and avoid the two together?

The easy method (technique) is to be with one of them out of the two. Automatically this process (mechanism) looks like a play or dance, a constant movement to attain, to achieve the other end, the opposite end, without transcending. It is not possible. That 'I' became the intellectual, it became the owner cum proprietor of the intellect, and this acquired possession (ownership) has compelled, forced and pushed it to be in further usage of it. In the same way, 'I' became emotional and started flowing along with the flow. No need to teach the fish to swim, the bird to fly, or the deer to run, and ENERGY to move.

As one became intellectual, another one became emotional. One can use logic and reasoning while one has to manage the flow, handle the flow. This means that both have difficulties from the other side. This is known as faculty, it belongs to the one 'I', one ego, oneness. The developed personality is like a special dress, uniform or mask of that persona who has identified and become one with it and developed its own identity.

Then, identity crisis: swimmer can enjoy swimming in deep water, knows how to swim and has no fear of water, then ask the swimmer to walk into the water until it covers the head, to walk in the water and not to swim, not to lift the legs, not to change the position, is it possible?

Try it and see the response and reaction of that 'I', the ego. To have maximum enjoyment without being or getting lost (disconnected with time and space and place) very, very few can do. Yet some have done it.

How can a swimmer be a controller of the flow, a manipulator of the flow? To do the manipulation in the flow is different from manipulating the flow itself. The swimmer can do one of these, not two; however, the swimmer tries to manipulate. At that time the swimmer is not a swimmer, not in the flow and flowing with it. For a moment the swimmer had changed the role and that 'I' again became the expert and excellent swimmer to die in the water.

What is that water and its flow? It's a term for that form and function of Energy, also a result and an effect.

To be strong and hard, the emotional one becomes cold rather than cool! One who becomes cold, an extreme opposite can become, extremely hot with anger. Depolarisation and swinging from one to the other extreme points to hold own status and being-ness, that is Energy. If it becomes too energetic it burns too much to have the expected, desired and calculated result. Although it is a loss against the gain, the gain is highlighted while the loss is ignored, neglected, considered as negligible. The gain becomes the guiding factor; instead of getting a lesson from the loss, learning from the loss, concentration and attention was given more to the gain, again and again! The growth of one side has simultaneously grown the other side as well and together both sides become enlarged.

The energetic form of Energy prefers to handle, manage, control, rule and manipulate both together from either side of both of them. It is possible to do this and for that one has to attain, to achieve, to be in the centre, to come in-between the two and take a position (to be established in it). To sustain and maintain that acquired position one has to work hard. Devotion, dedication, honesty and loyalty are shown to that hard work, which is a function of Energy. What is done will give the result, and the past will appear in the future. The form, function and appearance will be the same as the past; however, it is new and fresh from the future.

To be in-between and to be caught in-between are different situations. The first position is pleasurable; the second becomes painful, which is a later development of the first. What can be done if caught by the two? How can an escape be made and freedom gained?

One, who is caught in-between, is a form and function of Energy, as two is also a form and function of Energy. They are different, similar, the same, and opposite. As the size of the form and function changes, its type and nature changes, the hierarchical order also changes. As relativity and connectivity change, again it brings change. It is not change only once, it is all the time and in all different, different ways. Change is one of the terms for Energy. Energy brings change. Change is a temporary state, and changes appear on the surface one after the other. There is change in the sequential order, a changing order!

As a drawing with many colours looks beautiful, also Energy with all its colourful forms and functions looks fresher, more beautiful and attractive. However, the start and finish, beginning and end, is also noticed and recorded by the other form and functions of Energy. The worship and worshipper, the object of worship and its purpose, all are different components of Energy. Method, technique and materials differ for each one, because each one tries to show uniqueness, which is not in the other's action or performance. So, in a unique way, being one Energy and becoming many (different), it appears as many different energies and compels (forces) the other to believe and accept with trust and confidence each one in a different way.

Naturally, the availability of choice, options, and alternatives are there for selection, because to do something a decision is required (needed). To decide, to select, in and for that choice, the options (alternatives, etc.) give a selection with priority, thus neglecting, ignoring, not considering, the remaining after selection. Because the purpose is clear, the motive to move is clear, an answer is given to that question: Why is it done or decided?

The inner one doesn't appear outside, and the outer one is an appearance of that inner one in connection (in relation), so it is and it is not.

Through the outer appearance of performance how can the motive behind that performer be known? How can the difference be distinguished between the

- performance and the performer?
- worship and worshipper?
- doing and doer?

Are they one because of the identification or oneness in togetherness, or are they two separate but they appear together? One selects (the other neglects, ignores, does not consider) and moves further with the help of selection. The result shows whether the selection was right or wrong.

Intellect being the property of Energy remains unclaimed by the proprietor (owner). The other one who just has it for use (and it is provided for use) is always with that 'I'. From birth onwards that 'I' (intellect) was there. For the first few years it remains in a sleeping state, or a dormant state, not active in helping and supporting the decisions of that 'I'. Those few years are known as the childhood of that 'I', who is adult now, and then that 'I' is considered as if it has its own intellect and becomes intellectual, starting to living intellectually in a stylish way to be unique in its own lifestyle! It becomes exclusive and distinct from any other formation of style of ENERGY!

Naturally, Mother Energy smiles at that smartness in the unique lifestyle of that 'I' (of that ego) who is also one of many forms, functions and results of the Energy Mother. For each mother, a stupid, idiot, foolish child is not an idiot, stupid and foolish child. She considers the child as contrary, opposite, and is encouraging to it all the time, saying you are my best child. Then the child starts believing it and considers that others should also treat him or her as the best child among others!

Being an adult and knowing well about relativity, knowing that good has bad on the other side is forgotten (just as best has worst on the other side is forgotten)! Being busy and engaged all the time is why there is avoidance to look at that side as it is!

The best use of intellectuality is to avoid it successfully; now and then it becomes difficult with change, because what has to be avoided can arise very often: to face one's own ugly face means face to face in a calm and quiet position. The doer, the 'I', the ego, has decided not to 'do', which means it has cut off the connection and connectivity for the time being. What happens?

On one side it was disconnected, on the other side a connection and connectivity took place. What was avoided, neglected, ignored and not taken care of, starts appearing in a different form and format. Force and pressure is utilized by this form and format to make a confrontation, to show it again, once again.

There is a challenge by its own Energy to itself; 'own' is in two different ways. Energy as a doer is done in doing that with energy the doer: energy has faced the challenge to be confronted by a part and portion its of own energy, which starts to oppose, and create obstacles on the path. First in a mild way as an interrupter doing the interruption frequently (very often) in an ongoing activity or performance. The performer who is able to continue, even with interruption, is considered the winner; while the defeated interrupter has changed strategy to become stronger from mild and moderate. Now interrupter with revenge and anger (either rude and rough or decent and discrete) becomes a distracter and distracts the doer, gets success to throw out (put away) and outstrip the performer who was considered a winner in front of the interrupter but now becomes the looser because of own energy play.

How can Energy be a winner and be defeated by Energy? One form is the winner; the other form is the loser. One side has the joy of victory, and the other side has the pain and agony of defeat, of losing. While connection and connectivity (relation and relativity) exist, takes place or happens, two appearances appear and two opponents oppose during the effort and attempt to see the difference, to create the difference, to remain differentiated, so that one has the advantage of selection and being able to avoid moving making the other appear (look like) it's not moving, although both are moving!

For as long as this situation lasts, the identity, image, status, personality, position, authoritative power, ownership, etc., etc., terms and conditions exist for the use of Energy, and Energy remains energetic, like a mother with male children who is always ready to take care and show sympathy and compassion. Because it is needed, it is required, and so it is provided. For this purpose it becomes two opposite objects so that each one can gain satisfaction from its own performance and both can have a common aim or goal. This aim, goal, or target, is achieved (attained) singly, or one after the other, or only one and not by the other. In a way, the two opposites remain attractive, contradictory, and also complementary to each other to be complete and having completeness, so both try to be complete and fit and well for the other one.

How can an incomplete be a complete without help? How can 50% become 100%? That's why it's important to know and accept the other 50% as together and separate at the same time. Is it not a balanced state in imbalance, a state in-between with equal distance or proper distance from all sides? Being inside and remaining unaffected by the result is achieved through indifference towards the state of in-between. That's why there needs to be equality and equanimity to avoid the pain and its cause both together.

And for that, fraternity, although it looks like a male term (fatherhood, male culture, male dominancy, ruling, etc., etc.) as it is opposite to the female term in its appearance, culture, and behaviour, this fraternal side is considered and presented in a totally unclear way, and then the advantageous becomes stronger and more powerful to rule. This is the flipside of Energy, a SPACE, a 50% of the other 50%, of that 100%, which is two as one and the opposite one also.

Terms are coined because of the form, according to the form and also according to the function. Two are opposite terms and the connotations are connected (related) to so many different forms, functions, systems, structures and the results and effects to make it complete the cycle.

Now the terms SPACE and ENERGY: the two are opposite as it has been described before and together as a complete one, as well as separate, as two different entities that are opposite to each other. Although they both appear to look different and opposite to each other, the front side and back side are common, not different: even the background is common and not different for those two different ones?

The question is:

Child belongs to whom?
Flame belongs to whom, the candle, wax or thread, or all together?
How can one decide?

Then light and warm both belong to the flame; how can one belong to one portion of the candle and the other belong to the other portion of the candle – is it a whole or part? It's better not to mix up having an advantage in the confusion and unclear understanding of this terminology, which has its own world separated and together with the other world, when ENERGY has the known popular term of Mother, known as Divine MOTHER. Then, opposite to this term, Father is applied to SPACE, and that's why there is the expression 'Father is in Heaven', meaning in SPACE!

Fraternity is indicating SPACE, which is totally different from Energy. The intellect, as one of the forms of the property of Energy and its proprietor, has used for its own benefit the connected, related, twisted meaning of the term to achieve and attain its own calculated motive (purpose). A mother can play the role of a father and can demonstrate fatherhood while remaining as mother or female. In the same way, a father can play the role of a mother, can show motherhood, and can remain as a father or male. The principles both have the form, function, system, structure, results and effect, and point of view. Both are different, they identify two separate terminologies, divisions, apartments, compartments, to show the difference so that they remain different to play their own provided role. From the role point of view, these are forms and their role, while the principles are common in each one of them.

Which role to play, when and how and why: who decides? And in relation to what principle? If it can be any role, it means there is freedom to select the role and act! If it has to fit the form and function of the role, then it is specific and particular. This means that freedom within the role remains, not the freedom to select any role at any time that is convenient and suitable.

Which one is the guiding force and pressure? The outer Energy or the Energy within? Who has provided the convincing logic and reasoning to whom?

Finally, attraction and temptation toward the opposite has made them play opposite roles through accepting the challenge and also through getting encouragement and support to play a particular role. Who has decided the plan and programme and offered it to whom, in which way is it presented and treated, who are these two? Or is it ONE Energy?

The term 'connection' is cause of the confusing or unclear way to clear understanding and it is the effect because its cause is different than the term. The term is given, applied and provided in order to know, to identify, and to communicate with the other, to convey certain specifics in a particular way or manner. Thereby it became necessary to coin the term, considering it to be unique and exclusive. Later on, what will happen?

In a unique way, that unique term is used again and again to gain! The inventor of the term is not the creator of the object of the term applied and given to it. So, a term was coined and invented, later on it becomes popular. Now, there are two groups, one using the popular term and the other using the popularity of the term. Both are right and perfectly accurate in their way. That's why, as evidence and proof in the dictionary defined word or term, there are many different meanings in its application and use. The dictionary has collected and presented many, many words, in alphabetical order so that it is easy to find one specific and particular word out of many! Ocean is the diction and diction is becoming the ocean – it becomes the cause of addiction and intoxication. Even for prediction one has to use diction! It has its own importance and value. It reflects and connects, and it helps and supports the structure and construction, established with its own popularity and usage.

Inventor is inventing and happy with the invention. Another is happy because of inventing how to use, misuse, abuse, properly use, the invention! The other one has also become happy because of the availability of two types of invention. In this simple way, the simple becomes complex by losing its simplicity, it's as if simple becomes the simpleton! This is because it is considered, believed and accepted with confidence and trust that the:

photocopy is an original,
artificial is natural,
abnormal or not normal is normal,
unhygienic is hygienic,
temporary is permanent,
pain is pleasure,
periphery is centre,
round is square, and

square is round!

What is seen is according to one's own projection, perception and cognition! In this condition, use of the right term in one's own correct way gives understanding rather than having to understand. Both are communicating and using popular terms to try to convey their part of understanding in a particular way. After becoming popular, the invented unique term slowly comes into common use. What happens to its uniqueness and exclusiveness in relation to (connection to) what the term was originally coined for? No one is able to make the link because the server is not working and a link is not possible: the message is tried again after some time!

What is forgotten is dead and what is in the memory becomes immortal because it remains alive in that state, condition, or form – after all it is ENERGY. How can a death have a death, or how can a death die?

How can Energy stop moving? As long as SPACE is available Energy is allowed to move and roam without any charge: this special facility is provided by Space! So, how can ENERGY stop moving? Who can stop it?

To stop movement, one has to take a position and fix it on the ground becoming steady and then it may be possible to stop it, but when SPACE is fixed and STEADY GROUND allows and permits movement, then against this condition, which is the better one?

This means that ENERGY has to MOVE and remain in a constant moving condition or state. Then it is not possible to stop the movement, which in turn means that there can be no death, so making Energy immutable and immortal. That's why ENERGY is accepted as ULTIMATE and ULTIMATELY ENERGY. Energy remains at the last.

Then whose death is it? Who dies? How, when and why are related questions to the other conditions. But death as Energy never dies or stops.

Once the link (connection) is broken and re-established as a new connection or as a renewal of the old connection, it takes time to get acceptance in a new way to that old ONE. Here the term is FATHER (PATERNITY and FRATERNITY); a grammarian has connect-ed it with the male gender and treated it as masculine against the female gender and feminine term.

A simple question: who introduces a father to a new born child or whom does the child know first, the mother or father? Or whom does the child recognize first, the mother or father? Or how and in which way (through whom) does the child come to know and recognize the father?

All the time the answer is a Mother, and opposite to this form, function, shape, structure, system, is a Father who has opposite qualities, characteristics, aspects, and nature. A very popular and known term is 'mother and child relation', where the mother is considered to be the creator and producer in a different expression, while the child is considered both as a creation and as a product. World habitant is a creation, a child, a product and, as a single individual, connection is first and not last with Mother ENERGY (Mother Nature). An inhabitant is a product, is a creation, inside creation or as a part of creation (relation) and at the last, the ULTIMATELY LAST, there is SPACE. No one has yet found out what if anything comes after that.

That's why the opposite term to ENERGY is SPACE. ENERGY as MOTHER shows (introduces) SPACE as FATHER, an opposite term, a PRINCIPLE, which is beyond the grasping and compass. The appearance of SPACE creates curiosity to know about its appearance, and curiosity of the child is satisfied with the help of Energy: a mother's answer to the child's question 'Who is he?' and the role explanation also. Very honestly, as a 50%, ENERGY has introduced the other 50% as a contributor (shareholder) in the creation of a child as a FATHER, a SPACE.

Is it not true that Space exists inside each one, each individual? As it is outside, so it is inside. The divider is Energy – material, matter, particles and its forms, functions, structures, systems, results and effects – and for as long as it is there, 'in and out' will remain. For as long as the point, position or reference is there, 'in and out' will be in use. So, both are in-between each other up to a certain extent or limit, after that ONE REMAINS – ONLY ONE, A SPACE WITHOUT PARTICLES, DARK BLACK – ABSOLUTE.

Even the SUN, which is so big in size, looks like a bright spot on that BLACK BACKGROUND! On the other side, the same bright spot – a SUN – is the centre of our Mother EARTH, which (along with many other planets) moves around the SUN, around the centre. So how big is the centre? A BRIGHT SPOT?

The position (location) of the CREATOR of creation, of a world or habitat, is THAT PLACE known as SPACE. SPACE IS ITSELF A PLACE FOR THE CREATOR. So, it is outside (remains outside) and is known as OUTER SPACE. Inner Space is ONE, it is the envelope (cover) that the other one is covered by! Inside the envelope can be described as where the COVER is covered by (hidden by) – and just appears as if it is smaller than – the cover! So THE COVER is smaller than the cover! For what? Why is this?

When it has been accepted that the particular, specific cover is a cover, then there is the appearance of 'in and out' of the cover. Really, 'the cover' is able to cover, precisely, accurately, totally, completely and fully, THAT COVER.

Never, never! It appears, as if it is and it is not, also!

Now in this situation, that 'I', with 'me, my and mine' as a sprout of the seed of ego potency, has a choice to be or not to be and what and in which way to be or not to be. Why and for how long is it for that 'I' to be or not to be?

Because of better use of the intellect, there arise many questions, problems and dilemmas, conflicts, and confusion as a result of the best utilization of the property of the intellect that is logic and reasoning, all the while knowing very well the notion about the proper way to live that what belongs to the other should not be possessed, not coveted, not owned. Then, how one can show, demonstrate, exhibit, one's own possession? Each one is waiting and watching for an opportunity and chance to pounce; up to that time, they become witness, observer, seer, as if praying for prey and then paying for it. Here the position of that sprouted 'I' is energetic, highly active and enthusiastic doing and performing to show that it can multiply the seed potency and strength of the seed, the ego!

It belongs to whom? Is it not a reflection, a mirror image of the other one, the higher and superior one? The image in the mirror and the mirror for the images, whatever the case may be, both are showing THE ORIGINAL, means:

The original image in the ORIGINAL MIRROR!
Same as the original image in the original mirror!
Which is inside the MIRROR.
MIRROR is ENERGY,
image reflection is considered as image production!
Then,
why not be the producer of that so-called production, that is the images!
So, being a reflector, becomes a projector and producer;
then, becomes perceiver, witness, observer, seer,
of that projection (production).
In this way, MIRROR is ONE and mirrors are many,
many mirrors show many, many images in each mirror,
which are original images, in an original way of communication.

THE ONE ORIGINAL IN ITS OWN POSITION becomes and appears as many originals, in many mirrors, because they are in the opposite position with each other.

As a mirror it is one.

As an image it is one.

As a reflection it is one.

As a placement it becomes many because each one is opposite to each one. They are similar and different with the same image of THAT ONE inside the mirror!! That's why, it becomes many from one, to indicate, connectivity, relativity, and dual duality.

If the mirror is damaged and broken, what happens to the image reflected in it?

Identified image is broken.
Identified reflection is broken.

Identity of entity remains as it is outside the mirror.

THAT ENTITY has nothing to do with the condition of the mirror.

The living mirror is in front of the non-living mirror!

Beauty is beautiful and chaos is in order being arranged and managed in a systematic way to have beautiful results out of it. This entails the recycling of garbage in different machinery: a living machine can transform garbage in a better way than a non-living machine, which transforms the garbage in a useful way. Both are complementary to each other while the garbage and producer are working for better living in a chaotic condition in a beautiful way! Why not try it?

Freedom and choice allows one to try and try and try! And it allows one to cry like a child from birth onward. Crying is known and familiar, it's a part of life and result of enjoyment, the starting of another process.

In the beginning is crying.

In the middle is crying.

At the end is crying.

It's a crying Energy!

As it is laughing and angry!

Biological mother provided the DNA Test. Test tube baby (child) has a mother and father. The donor has made the donation, but does this mean it's a donated child?

It is a process of happening and the result is a child. Through (and with the help of) the DNA, it's possible for that child to know (to recognize) its own mother and father as parents.

What about the Divine Mother, how can a child do a DNA Test? Which type of test is (or will) be called a DNA test because the child has to establish a relation with its own mother and not with a look-alike mother!! So, it's better to distinguish the difference between the two in one.

Divine ENERGY, Divine MOTHER: once it is accepted, automatically the OPPOSITE TERM TO THAT

ENTITY known as SPACE or FATHER is given, applied or allotted for better and smoother communication. The use of the common, popular, well known, well-established and accepted familiar family terms show family relation (connection) to and with THAT PRINCIPLE as MOTHER and FATHER. It has nothing to do with any gender, form or function, nor structure, system and result of that. The fixed notions, ideas, imagination on one side, transform and transform again and again, refine and refine, change and change, but this does not mean it has transcended, it has changed Absolutely.

As Divine Mother (Divine Energy) is common and one for all, so also is ENERGY, or ABSOLUTE ENERGY, or any other related term. As it is perceived and recognized by a child, that child has adopted the term to establish the relation (connection) in a very, very particular way, a specific way. Being a child and having its own child, praying and calling like a child, worshipping like a child – TO THAT MOTHER. As this relation is accepted and established, automatically the third/THIRD, Entity/ENTITY appears and gets consideration and acceptance side-by-side; it's all the time together and separate, one and two: one having many inside or many having one inside. As 'It' becomes 'TWO' opposite to each other, difficulties are created to understand, to realize, to recognize, to know, to accept, and appreciate, etc.,

TWO as a TWO, and
TWO as a ONE, and
ONE as a TWO, and
ONE as a ONE and
ONE with and without ONE.

The only one without any joint, is ONE without any joint, and that is SPACE. It has a joint, which appears as a joint: it is and it is not the joint with Energy.

Dark black is the background on which are many bright spots to illuminate the dark black background. Both remain as they are without change. The SUN is one of the bright spots constantly giving (providing) life Energy. It has

FIRE, HEAT and LIGHT ENERGY to provide (distribute) to the other.

EARTH is a planet like other planets having a moon and moving around the centre, the SUN. It is the same as other planets, in as much as it maintains a proper route and distance with each other moving around and around, while at the same time turning round and round on its own axis. It maintains both the speed and movement accurately (precisely) that is measured in units of time, with a fixed reference point of the SUN, or using the SUN as a fixed point. The time period for one round is fixed, and the same is so for one round around the SUN, made with its (the SUN'S own Energy. Both the rounds.

Moon is moving around the Earth and the two move around the SUN. For detailed figures and accurate time it's better to read (to see) the books on astrophysics or astronomy.

Being on the Earth, we are able to see, perceive, and know the SUN'S outer form as the cause of life and death on the Earth; and we can see that the size of the Earth is so big in relation and comparison to the size of the individual.

In a contrary way, we can imagine the size of the Earth to be the same size of the individual and, stretching the imagination further, we can imagine the bigger and larger, broader and wider size of SPACE as a container having small balls in it and, even further, to imagine not one part, not part by part, but to imagine it as a WHOLE and to find out own self 'I', me, my and mine and own big ego inside that SPACE. Is it possible to find out, to locate the position where am I? This is a stretching exercise for the imagination. Imagination gives a push to thinking, it helps decide, this makes it easy to do and to get results.

Results show the cause of it as wrong or right. Earth is alive and has life on it. It has a fire within and fire on it. That fire helps survival and provides life. It gives heat and light, and from a safe distance it's possible to reduce it and become warm with less heat, becoming cold from cool. Then the other way: less heat to warmer, move closer to increase it until it burns, then automatically move back, turn around to bring to the other cold side to the front, towards the heat, the SUN.

There are two types of Energy: one belongs to the Earth and the other belongs to the SUN. To which does your individual Energy belong? It works in two opposite ways. Two are meeting constantly, to affect the third one who is on the Earth. No need to go for night and day as it will come to your place, even in Spring and Fall. All the seasons will come one by one: just be there, or is it possible to live in daylight all the time? To achieve this, how much does one have to move, how fast and in which direction?

Light is a light from the SUN with heat, without heat it becomes moonlight, a reflection. As long as there is light a shadow is there! How big is the shadow? As the night changes, the density of darkness in the shadow changes. Natural light is different from man-made or unnatural light.

Light is equal to clarity in perception,
warm is equal to love and affection.
Both belong to the flame,
which is inside,
and a large size fire is outside
that is the SUN.

Flame belongs to us and gives life. Love and wisdom together is philosophy: which is belonging to and for life? What to do to maintain warmth so that there is no need to search and get it from another? What needs to be done to have good, clear light so that it is possible to distinguish and select without making a mistake?

There are two factors:

1. Cold.
2. Darkness.

Two are again belonging to one!

These can be handled (managed) in two ways:

1. One against one.
2. Two against two, i and ii,

This means to separately handle, manage, tackle, or to solve the problem, disturbance and or questions related to both of them, either one by one or together as per need, requirement and necessity.

As long as one flame is working in the same place (position), how can the other flame be? Naturally, to wait and watch with acceptance, patience and tolerance the performance or works and their result and effect may be best. Looking to this point, the results and effects, that is the pain and suffering, miseries, sadness, sorrows, melancholy, problems and disturbances, no ease, no peace etc., etc., it is suggested (advised), that it's better keep off that flame known as ego and ego related performances, results and effects so that the other flame can appear and be there in the place, position of the previous flame. That's why it is popular to keep off the burning flame, which burns and becomes the cause of pain suffering, etc. Even the fumes are not hygienic; the emission of light, heat and energy is to over-power the other flame and its performances: rivalry, or rivalry having a friendship blanket.

Dark, black, void, cold, has a sucking power, an absorbing capacity; it is opposite to heat and temperature as a measuring unit of heat and cold, as opposite to it.

Health is maintained because body temperature is not more and not less. Temperature regulation is done by its own system to take care of health related activities of the body. Fever by any cause is the example of an increase of temperature known as disease leading to restlessness! Head has to remain cool and legs to be warm: this is a good sign of health.

In the function of an inner life, when the flame starts diminishing it means it's time to say goodbye. The warmness starts reducing, this means the heat inside the body is indicating that the responsible flame is not able to burn and provide enough heat as well as light; clarity also reduces. The result is that the appearance or manifestation of mistakes, loss of memory, deterioration, slowing down, loss of willingness and interest etc., etc., is like withdrawing, shrinking, or being back to the starting position that is zero aging process, etc.

Flame is the symbol and as a symbol it is kept outside on that particular place (space) where the previous one was functioning and working; however, that particular, specific one flame is absent, is not there, meaning here it is not, and there somewhere it is! To indicate this (mention this) the other flame is kept as a replacement so the other should know the present whom was in the form of flame is absent and now remains as a corps, a dead body (which was a living body) and now this dead body and flame becomes two separate entities.

Name was given to whom? It was given for communication, and then what happened? Dead body remains, name remains as it was given. That existential principle does not remain, it does not exist in that body but is separate from it, so a living body becomes a dead body and is declared dead. That person, who was living inside by and with that given name, having a record of birth, time and place of expiration, became dead and is given the record to keep and to close that open file or chapter! Now, the name and memory remains behind in various forms with functions and ceremony and celebrations to remember the past in the present time.

It is by Energy, for Energy, through Energy of that Energy! Not Space!! How can SPACE celebrate SPACE? How can that ENERGY have died? Is it stopped, or has that particular, specific form stopped giving any response. Was that check-up done before declaring it dead (the cornea reflex test), along with other checking to be accurate in making the declaration? The response-giver does not remain, it is not there in that body, and so it became cold and known as dead.

Decomposition starts after the departure of that principle. The existential principle just being inside with its presence, all activity was going on in a composed state. That principle worked like a catalyst or catalytic Agent inside as the cause of changes, and at the same time remains unaffected as long as the identification (association) is not developed. This developed identification in relation to the changes is the cause of binding and is expressed (communicated) as "I was Patient, and I was not happy. I was very, very, unhappy, having pain, suffering, miseries, sorrows and sadness, etc., etc."

Really, that who has to be a catalyst (a catalytic agent) has to take all these things and even has to try to take credit for positive changes, to be bound by positive, good results and be once again in that pot, an earthen pot with fluid and many other things! Is it possible to bake and cook SPACE? Or is it possible to do it with Energy, to Energy and for Energy?

An earthen pot has to hold water, so it has to be baked and cooked to transform it from raw to ripe so that it can hold the water and have the possibility to break changed because of its hardness. The change in consistency it gives a change in sound response, meaning that response to the stimuli becomes different as it changes from raw to ripe. That's why puberty is one phase, maturity is another phase, and to be wise is the next phase: to achieve wisdom and becoming wise does not mean being only intellectual. Being innocent has to become wise, otherwise becomes over-wise or stupid, idiot or foolish, the opposite of wise and wisdom!

It is that clear light belonging to a FLAME that also has warmness.

How is it that an intellectual can be emotional at the same time?

Both are states identified (associated with) becoming one with that, 'I' conscious. It says "I am intellectual", "I am emotional", my activity (performance) is the same as that, that field or area is mine, all the properties and qualities are mine. Me, my, and 'I', that ego expresses energy, shows its own ruling, power and strength in and at all places, even in and at Space also.

In this way, the manifestation of the predominant (or dominant) nature is possible to recognize, to know, to find out, to locate etc. As Energy is working through different forms and their functions, structures and systems, it then gets, obtains, attains, achieves, the results and effects, before they manifest. That Energy has done the prediction, has formulated the hypothesis, has developed the prognosis and has even done a projection of that which has not yet happened, is not yet existing (meaning a future state is present in the present time) and on this basis it has taken for granted that further calculation, analysis, and discussion is started by ENERGY!

Being in-between and among Energy, it becomes the enjoyer of Energy and gets pain and disturbance at the end from Energy by Energy. Then where is SPACE? What happened to SPACE? It remains AS IT IS, unaffected, unrelated, unconcerned, indifferent, totally to the other state, opposite of opposite!

Energy is the doer, not SPACE. The doer gets it done through Energy. It seems like effect and cause, or cause and effect, which are two sides of one coin; one without the other is not there in the same way. Happening and doing or doing and happening: happening is there, means that doing is there and the doer' is there behind. The doer is doing continuously, non-stop, which means that happenings are also non-stop and continuous. Why and for what are this and that, here and there, happening? A question remains unanswered to that intellect or 'I' because how can a limited intellect grasp all the different, different happenings?

Even that individual is not able to know how happening is going on inside (how life is going on) and the individual considers that it's going on because of a well-planned programme and organisation with its own will, wish and effort. That's why it is considered that 'I' am the doer and it is because of me it's mine, and the good (best) result comes to me and my relatives and kin; bad is because of you, and it's yours. Once the taste of power is tasted, then all the time is the desire to have that taste and the doer uses strength in any way to achieve it. However, it is done skilfully in such a way that it appears as "I am not the doer" of the happening, it is not because of me and it is because of me also! Which one is and which one is not?

Whosoever distinguishes has to prove the answer with evidence and proof. Finally, is it Energy that is the winner against Energy,

or is Energy the looser against Energy,

or is Energy defeated by Energy?

No one knows because of doing or happening how this result comes about. Is it two Energies, or it is one Energy in two? What is it?

Space research does not mean it is in search of a Space or for a Space. It is taken for granted that Space is, so there's no need to search again and again. It is taken for granted that research is in Space. It is inside Space; then what is it for? It is very clear that what has to be found out is different and opposite to Space; who can see (perceive) far beyond to find an object becomes and remains a challenge even today. Many scientists have tried to find out the cause of the Universe, many have been awarded the Nobel Prize, but not the CAUSE! Their conclusion is: ENERGY IS ULTIMATE and ULTIMATELY ENERGY. It has a quasi-steady state.

As Space is taken for granted in Outer Space Research, it is in the same way that Inner Space is also taken for granted by modern medicine. What is more, this is the same in modern science where the law of gravitation is applicable to the EARTH. It is because of the Earth that a big pull, a tremendous pull, needs (requires) push to go, to move against, to remain and maintain without affecting the gravitational pull; and for that happen it has to burn lots of Energy, against the Energy, in search of ENERGY!

The pull of the body as an EARTH is tremendous; an individual body is equal to the Earth, as it will go back from where it came, from ashes to ashes, earth to earth. This is the cause of the attraction (temptation); it's the same as the big pull of gravitation, that's why levitation is against gravitation, principle is against principle and action is against action. Or is it power and strength against power and strength, Energy against Energy? Then where is SPACE? What is not Energy? Why is it ignored and neglected?

Because SPACE is the SAME IN ALL (common in all), the difference is important to show and prove through evidence how different each one is from the other, and for that importance is given to make it more important, to appear as more important. So, what is common is avoided as it is in mathematics. The common is kept it aside because it becomes easier to calculate further, to work with the difficult. In this way, keep aside the COMMON and be ready for difficult!

Then come achievement, success and failure. For that expectation, desire and ambition are needed to solve the more difficult, to move towards the complex from the simple, and again that complex becomes simple and then the next complex. Higher and higher it goes until that height is reached where the balloon is going to burst, burn out on its own, by itself, with its own auto-programme! Burn out, torn out, by Energy for Energy and of Energy!

Again, as an avoidance, the common moves from simple to complex and makes (converts) complex into simple; moving further, complex becomes the Simpleton, as simple – ton collected the same as metric – ton. Heavyweight of simple-ton because being a simple, normal, natural, original child, having a childlike curiosity to know and for that to move, to collect, to have information and to grow, develop, progress, in a concerned, related field, leaving the simplicity behind in a normal natural way, originality was shown in duplicity, imitation and photocopy; talent, skill, and efficiency, along with creativity, all these were used as the best, but became worst side of the best!

That becomes the cause of surprise: as it was given, so it came back the other way. To give a surprise and to get or receive a surprise are two different processes. The one who was simple (in a simple way) crossed simplicity and landed in complexity by adding ton, tone and tune to the term, form and functions, and becomes simpleton with good tone-up, form, tuning the functions and appearing as beautiful.

Using the intellect one can become wise and have wisdom, living with the minimum, minimum of pain, suffering, disturbances and problems in life. Instead of this, the contrary maximum is achieved: showing off one's own intellectual performance and this becomes opposite of wise, showing (demonstrating) the opposite to wisdom! Also, approving, supporting and taking care of the opposition's forms, functions, structures, systems and their results and effects as much as possible, is done so that opposition to the wisdom and wise can remain continuous. Is it not an action taken by Energy against SPACE?

Childlike curiosity tries to know more about Energy, to have the strength and power to execute and to enjoy, and for that the child has approached the SOURCE of ENERGY through prayer and worship in many different ways. To please, to make it happy, to get it back, or to have more and more material, strength and power, the offerings were made and kept for that ENERGY. Whatever ENERGY can do, can give, is done and given maximum to the worshipper to satisfy; instead of giving immortality he asks to prepare and provide any conditions in any type, number, form etc., to avoid death, to prevent death, to live, to rule and enjoy as much as possible, and the worshipper formulates conditions to avoid, to prevent death by any way. Formulation, preparation of conditions, was done by the intellect, which is a property of Energy.

Now, this Energy on one side looks as if it is complete and total, or whole, because 50% appears and is considered and accepted as 100%. As well as being 50% (a better half), it is also considered to be another half of 50% and incomplete, and a part of 100% at the same time. Two opposite appearances of one Energy, and the Intellect being the property of that Energy, has made an effort and attempt to prepare, to construct, to have the best conditions to avoid, to prevent death as far as possible through making it more and more difficult (impossible) to perform that action which can become a cause of death! Even at that time loopholes existed! Death was possible, the conditions were all fulfilled and what was to be avoided (prevented) was not possible to avoid and prevent, so it became clear that death is inevitable for that one who is born! After birth it is definite, the time depends, sure it will come.

One who is not complete, how can that one provide the complete condition without having any loopholes? How is it possible for the intellect?

A big challenge is accepted to protect the 'I', 'me', 'my' and 'mine', with the ego, but it was not possible. This means that always, all of the time, there is scope to make another – smaller, bigger or equal – line through, or making or preparing a second parallel line, a line-to-line, not for alignment or to be in one line without the second. The second line all the time has the advantage of the first line, as it is past, or history, or a record, or reference, or a previous one, which has two possibilities in it, either to join and continue the line (tradition), or to draw a new line, and to start a tradition with some change and modification to the previous one, to show, to prove the better utility, applicability, and practicability through providing the same in a different, modified and better way, to prove superiority.

History is the record of events and happenings. Short stories and tell-tales are also passing from ear to ear and year to year and survive years together in many different forms. These have many different terminologies, events and incidents, to say, to depict, to narrate the characters, personalities with different attributes, different for every person, to make it clearer, to understand each aspect of ENERGY and SPACE, separately and together!

This is in our own literature. It's a storehouse, a record of references, all written, spoken or told, belonging to the literature. It has many varieties of books of and for knowledge. The books of law recording cases and judgement are common and accepted by both parties of Lawyers. Judge has to listen and decide, according to those books, even after this common, what is uncommon? There is a lower court, higher court and Supreme Court, three levels to deal with different types, natures and classes of cases. Here, performer and performance is by the intellect for that doer who has done wrong in the eyes of the law.

The books of law are one portion of literature, which is just like an ocean full of knowledge. There is also much more information, which floats on the surface and moves here and there with a little push, having no substance, it moves quickly from ear to ear, like rumours spreading as a virus. This is not good for the health and hygiene of a computer. This everyone knows. The computer has anti-virus programmes for that, but not for one's own inner computer! No anti-virus programme, so the healthy thinking, analysis, and processing is interrupted by a virus. Instead of being healthy it now it becomes unhealthy thinking, analysis, and processing; nothing changes, all the functions are going on well and fit, but in an unhealthy condition. Hygiene at a physiological level, but polluted thinking has taken charge to decide and do properly! Sensory filters become corrupt, or the fitting arrangement is done in a contrary way: inside was kept outside, and what had to remain outside came inside in a perfect and accurate way. The crude oil after passing through the refinery became pure but in which category? Energy remains Energy even after refinement, and again refine!

SPACE is opposite. How to refine and refine outer Space as a place? Pollution is at and in that inner Space and place is the cause of polluted thinking. Then what can the thinker can do? Thinker becomes the executor of polluted decisions! Who gets the result? Everyone shares equally more or less?

Knowledge is given (provided) in the form of information against cash or kind. This is done very honestly as a part of life; the other parts of life remain apart from this (like a compartment, department or faculty) to have their own separate existence and manifestation because the flame is one, the light is one and has the spectrum of colours, even in the rainbow it appears (manifests).

This does not mean that a flame is colourful and can live life in a very colourful way! A flame has to burn to provide light, one light, not colourful lights; one flame after the other has to give warmth, a mild heat, because it's a flame not a fire! It has to burn steadily, without shaking in the flow of the wind; it's better to protect it from big gusts of wind that can put out the flame, and then the light can be available to all others.

Today, the work place, teaching place is permanent, but not the workers or teachers who come and go; they are changed and replaced as per the choice, function and result. Also, desire and expectation have to match with each other, then they combine together, grow together, as long as the selfish motives are not fulfilled. When they are, separation happens without developing hate and vengeance in each other, and with proper ceremony and appreciation, the conclusion is done and title allotted as 'ex_ _ '. Time brings the axe down on continuity; it is cut and separated from one end and connected again from the other side with another activity, as a doer.

How is it possible to stop whatever has already been done that has changed the form and doing? That's why it is asked (remembered) now it's time to remember. What is done? For whom is it done? Just see clearly in the diminishing light before it goes off.

A retrospect, a revision, a reflection, a re-analysis, a re-checking, a re-evaluation of what was done has to be done by the doer! This shows how the doer lived the life until today! How many roles were played, responsibilities taken, ownership and authorization developed and got, and how much encroachment was done to acquire, to posses, to have what belonged to the other without showing covertness or becoming covert, as if it came by itself, of its own towards 'me'. What can 'I' do to oblige? 'I' am accepting, not as an obligation 'to me', 'I' took care of it.

Doer is Energy, and doer gets it done by Energy. At the same time, that not doer was highly busy, engaged, involved in the planning and programming to prove that the evidence, clue, was kept behind to prove the other way, and for that ease, precautions were taken at various levels and in different ways to appear on the screen of society, family, country, or any organizational set up, presenting that image in a clean, clear way as if it was not done by that doer, and whatever is done is by the other doer. That one is not the culprit but is innocent and knows nothing about the happening; at that time that doer was not present, its absence was recorded so proving that 'I' am not the doer! The brain centre, nervous system and peripheral movement are all connected (linked together) with the help of other organs, systems and their functions and work in co-operation, becoming complementary to get the share of the result in the result!

Where is that 'I' consciousness, where is that ego?

A command is given by a commander, the inner one who tells the intellect to act is one part of a doer, the other part is an ego, a very good partner! Then, as the result of that doing it appears, manifests and its result is also experienced and noticed.

Then, who is the doer? Who has done it? Did the brain centre work for it? Was it the nervous system that played the role to carry the impulses to and fro using peripheral movement? Which part of the body played the role in relation to (connection to) the actual happening, to achieve the result?

The doer has one form, but it is not necessary to have one body, it can be a collection, because one doer-unit of a collected intellect or ego becomes a good partner and can work and appear as one doer made by (formed by) many doers, or many has made one! Each one has information and memory in the past connecting to the other concerned related part.

Where does totality exist? Is it inside one or many? All are the forms, functions, systems, results and effects of that ENERGY and its appearances. These appear using the term 'multi' as a prefix to any word instead of much, more and many. Much, more and many has no limit; once the limit is crossed, it becomes too much of excess, it's harmful, known and accepted by all.

So, on one side to show, to demonstrate "I am not the doer"; on the other side, life can be lived giving the impression of not being the doer, rather than getting or having the impression. This means that the student is learning to teach, and the teacher is also learning to teach more clearly and efficiently, imparting knowledge in the form of information and that is considered and taken for granted as education by Energy, to Energy, in an energetic way for Energy.

What do you think about SPACE? How to educate? How can Space educate Space? Which way? Or is Space the teacher of that student, Energy. How will teaching be?

What the doer is doing, the other doer does not do and does not follow. Whatever is taught has to be learnt to pass the exam, to teach again, to carry out that noble work as a profession! That's why a frame, boundary, limit, boarder, fencing is built to keep inside, to remain inside and taken for granted. The acceptance of this limit is by each doer because it is artistry of the other doer to prepare while the other one has to take care, like a security watchman in a different way at various levels. So, the syllabus of the course is prepared and proposed to teach, to carry on that noble work. Both are busy and engaged along with both, many, or others who are also engaged and busy, as they have involved themselves to teach with different motives and purpose. In this way, it becomes the world of knowledge-cum-information technology. A single doer and a group of doers (as a single unit) starts functioning because it's an ENERGY and has enough space to do, to move, to create! Then to sustain and maintain!! Then to transform, to convert, to destroy!!! Then, what remains is ENERGY. From the beginning right up to the end, the play of Energy takes place on the stage of SPACE.

Doer' is living in the world of knowledge through knowledge and information! Another doer doesn't want to follow the previous one, so has to find out, invent, and prepare its own path to move, as if that knowledge is belonging to that doer's intellect! In this way, cracks, break-up, separation, starts appearing and make it look as if it is different; the difference is created by intellectual ENERGY!

The other world also exists for the existence of the doer who gave preferences and priority not to knowledge but to existence itself, because it is the manifestation, which helps it to live, to survive.

The doer has a choice, an option to have alternatives to select according to own preference, priority and value system, and prefers to live (to survive) in connection (relation) to those worlds. Although the WORLD (habitat) is one CREATION or CHILD, it has different worlds in it, where the inhabitant prefers to live comfortably and conveniently. ENERGY as MOTHER is ready to nurture the culture in its own way so that it is flourishing and nourishing and becoming attractive, and creating the temptation to have it and enjoy it, to possess it, to rule and command it. The use of knowledge by that doer is to fulfil a curiosity to know and now is able to say, "I know", "Don't teach me how to use tissue-paper"! Although the doer knows how to use tissue-paper, the doer very proudly stops, blocks, and cuts the communication and is not ready to know more (because of any reason) and very strongly expresses "I know, I know", with repetition, giving stress and emphasis to the knowing. Up to this point it is perfect, accurate, partial, 50%; relatively perfect and accurate is the other side of imperfect and inaccurate as well as to know and not to know, or the unknown.

Unknown is more than known, it brings about fear, stress, and anxiety; because known is manageable, unknown is "How do I do it?" "What will happen to me, my and mine?" Questions remain unanswered. There is no security and guarantee, so there is insecurity because of not knowing how to distinguish the difference between the two. Paper is paper, cleaning is cleaning, then why not use sandpaper replacing tissue paper and tissue paper replacing sandpaper? What will happen?

So, from the argument point of view, the intellect can provide any logic and reasoning, but this doesn't mean the result of the action or performance will be any good! Then, why did use become misuse, wrong use, and abuse? This was because of not knowing how to use 'I know', and that it has to be used. How? Why should it be used?

Does the doer know in detail or is there no time to know in detail because of so many commitments and responsibilities and the limited time for each activity and performance. The doer (as a provider) provides limited time from the given day and night for each and every action, activity and performance. By its nature, Energy being a child of an energetic mama, child as a doer, knows how to increase and decrease the speed, to be fast and slow or a normal speed. When it is not normal this normal becomes abnormal, further this normal as a normal is accepted in a very normal and natural way. Where is that original normal? Who knows?

Everyone knows with one or other reference what is normal and what is not normal: both exist at the same time, because relativity exists, duality exists, and ultimately energy exists! That's why logic and reasoning, arguments, justification, and clarification, are given, demanded, and have arisen, between the two which are different and similar and opposite! Doer has no time, so doer is in a hurry, worrying and spoiling the taste of the curry of life! Being a cook, a chef, keeps all rights to decide and do the cooking of own self: perfect boiling, swimming in its own prepared soup and waiting for help, to welcome it! After checking and evaluating it, then to select and accept the assistantship to oblige the other! This acceptance of assistantship of that assistant (helper) is binding, obliging the other way, because one who is in the 'soup' can come out of the soup the way they entered or find a way through own efforts and attempts.

Being generous and kind to the other shows kindness in acceptance, otherwise being independent, free and alone, it's possible to do without the helper and assistant. Doing two things at the same time is impossible, for example eating and speaking are two different flows of energy, one eating from outside to inside, the other speaking from inside to outside. Similarly, to work here and there is not possible to do at the same time, that's why the doer prefers to select one out of the two according to own preference, priority and choice, and at the same time oblige the other through acceptance and being generous, as well as demonstrating own ability and willingness to do what the other doer can do, is ready to do, and to encourage, to motivate the other doer. And in a contrary way, expressing and showing the gesture for refusing, not giving importance to that offer of help, work, or assistantship, makes it negligible and very small so that it is possible to remain free from being bound to pay it back. This is considered as service to a higher one, by a lower one, to a master by a subordinate and assistant or helper!

This appears as a duty with responsibility and that doer who became lower to the higher, subordinate and assistant to the master (owner, authority) becomes humble and polite, honest and dedicated to do that duty with devotion and affection. The work is considered as worship without any expectation in doing or performing the duty and knowing well about the Law of Action where the result of that performed duty to that Lord of power and strength is sure to come when the deity becomes happy and pleased by the services of that doer (worker, worshipper, helper, assistant and subordinate).

It is the management and organization of ENERGY, POWER and STRENGTH, where all the roles are played by Energy to ENERGY. How and why does SPACE have to pray? How can SPACE worship SPACE as a worshipper? How does it become smaller and bigger, higher and lower, in and out?

Isn't the answer because ENERGY and its form, functions, structure, system, together with its results and effects of 'I am-ness', 'I consciousness', ego and own self, becomes the reference point and divider to make two, to create two, to have two, out of one! Because divide and rule is easier than to unite and control!

As long as the divider exists, division of the division, dividing after dividing, breaking after breaking, is continuously going on! The break-up process is functioning at all different levels in its own way! What happens after that? Reformation, transformation, cutting and pasting, tailor-made, ready-made, production is carried out on a large scale, for the masses, the multiplicity. Then the dealers distribute and supply to the consumer, the one who uses it again and again, consumes it and becomes the consumer of that ENERGY with many, many identities and roles to play.

ENERGY becomes the giver and receiver; giving and to receiving is the natural and normal function. In two movements it is clear that the giver is giving and the receiver is receiving, it's a very simple and easy-going flow of Energy occurring in a very smooth and harmonious way. In these two types of opposite movement both are happy, and happiness reflects and reflects, again and again!

This was the way of living in ancient times! Cult and culture was there, civilization developed later on and the individual became civilized, the old system of exchange, known as the barter system, changed with the introduction of currency and money. This was against the material change in the value system because from time to time the evaluators changed their own values to be better than before. Very cleverly and cunningly, one term has replaced or removed the other term.

The old pair of two terms, give and receive, has a new appearance because these two terms are two sides of one coin, and one coin has one value, while the other coin has either more or less value, so there are many coins with different values. In the same way, give and giver, and receive and receiver becomes one coin: giver is the receiver and receiver is the giver. Which action has to be first and second is not important, because give to receive, or receive to give, means that the flow and coin play their role properly. Later on, the giver prefers not to receive because it is binding, it is an obligation and, once it is received, then to give becomes a duty and responsibility.

How can this binding, this obligation, this responsibility and duty be avoided? How is it possible to remain free of this mechanism? The one who becomes free from this mechanism has no responsibility and duty to give back, because it does not come under that category of being received. To check and control, to regulate the flow, it is insisted that the receiver should give a receipt and the giver should posses and show the receipt, produce the receipt, to prove that it was given. The giver is ready to give without becoming a receiver of a receipt.

For the giver, giving is a pleasurable act, while to become a receiver is painful. It's painful, it's binding, and binding never gives freedom, it's holding back to give back because it is received. At the same time, the expectation is there on the other side from the one who has given, or who is the giver! Each one being the giver on one side enjoys the status of giver and the process of giving. Each giver highlights the list of given and also develops the skill and efficiency in giving without becoming the receiver against the giver. So, it is shown (demonstrated) that the given is given; actually it is not, because against that given the giver has received, and now doesn't know that the emptiness (voidness) still remains even after that process of giving with ease and paying full attention to the movement, becoming fully aware about the maximum to give honestly, so much so that the other can have maximum!

Are both the giver, or has the other played the role of a receiver? Then why has that one not given enough? In which role was that one? Instead of investigating, checking one's own role in that movement, the movement is to start enquiring and checking up on the other side, which it is easy. The difficulty is to know (to find out) one's own role in that moment and movement?

That is the cause of pain, disturbance and problems, because cleverly that term of receive and receiver is replaced by another similar term, so that receiver does not remain, the binding is not there, obligation, duty, and responsibility, are avoided carefully by accepting, installing, and establishing that term in the place of a receive and receiver! It becomes a very useful term; later on it becomes popular and established and has been proved technically fit for the replacement and it's why two pairs (two coins) can be used by anyone. The choice of which one (coin or pair) is suitable, comfortable, and convenient can be made.

Justification was also given for replacement; it was that waiting is unnecessary for the giver to give?

The ego of the receiver becomes beggar?

Begging is not preferable. The beggar waits to receive and watches how much others are getting and how the giver is playing with the receiver. The giver tests the beggar's patience by trying to develop irritation and anger through becoming impatient; the receiver may turn as a patient who has no patience and doesn't know any other option, or is not ready for any other option, because of own set-up of do's and don'ts in a particular lifestyle.

Giver becomes the observer and enjoyer, enjoying the disturbance and restlessness of how the receiver is caught in-between the conditions! Status in danger, no problem! Receiver becomes ready to sacrifice (suffer) and becomes the patient because of suppressing the revolt (the rebel) and not becoming the other option. For that this one spends lots of energy, consoling and justifying the act not to become the other option.

Is it correct or not, who can say?

The root and seed of violence, strike, rebellion, revolt and break-up is towards the established and so-called good order of the so-called givers who give to get back more than they have given. Once this becomes known, the anger of the receiver who waits and waits and waits to receive what the giver has given becomes zero-tolerable, then spark, flame and fire to burn (to destroy) in revenge and punishment for not being given. Or not received?

It's a fight, a struggle, a conflict and arguments (court cases) occur between the two coins, two pairs, between one who has not changed the term and one who has changed the term and status! Through the replacement and the chain reaction of replacement after replacing that term, relationship begins again (starts) at a different level in a different way, slowly and gradually the numbers and percentage of replaced terms becomes more and more, even skilfully and efficiently the replaced term (the new one) appears the same as the old one! The one who knows manipulation at a higher level expends much less strength through using tricks of the trade and becomes ready to receive as a receiver, to demonstrate acceptance, patience and tolerance, to appreciate the giver because both have recognized each other's pseudo role!

It is pseudo, false, or a copy and both know each other, so without any problems and difficulties both are ready to accept and appreciate immediately after the recognition. Being honest, loyal and dedicated to that role from time to time, which is played so perfectly and accurately that they match with each other, it creates a pattern from a single unit:

The pattern is constructed,
The fashion is designed,
The demand is created.

Then the transaction (exchange) is possible between the two. Who are these two? Exchange of what? What is moving? From which direction to where? How much time does it take? With change of time and place, finally what happens? It is consumed! It is transformed!

What was invested doesn't remain as it is, it comes outside as a profit with interest! No loss! Helpers are ready to help with their knowledge and experience to establish or rescue, to exchange the places of demand as supply, to modify the transaction places with new theories for better results.

The two ends, 'plus +', and 'minus - ', are the cause of the movement. This movement has many terms, or has been known by many terms. It appears as a flow as well as an exchange, both together and separate. It is inside each and every action, activity, and performance.

Analysis can be made: how it is, how has it been used, and what is the result?

Again this can be divided into two: 1. experience and 2. observed. It has own way of communication, which means simple to complex, clear becomes unclear but with more and more effort and attempt to make it clear! The idea can be given up to make it more clear and useful in a normal, natural way. There are two possibilities: either it moves from plus to minus or it moves from minus to plus. Plus has excess so it moves, minus has less so it moves.

Who has to move first?

Plus when it moves acts as a distributor to the minus, minus has to search, has to find out, has to be with disturbance, it gives the urge and push to do, to move, to create, to invent, to search and research again and again. That's why a good company mentions in their advertisement that 'dissatisfaction is the mother of invention', and with this they introduce a newly invented product to their customer! This advertisement is good for both the buyer and seller of the product. Two are getting the benefit through the effort of one! The effort of THAT ONE is beneficial for the two – all the time to know THAT ONE and to express "Thank You" for the effort, so we too are beneficial or benefited!

There is a constant effort to remain in the position of plus and to avoid that position of minus. Technical difficulty is solved by the technician through providing a proper term 'replacement'; the old has gone, the new has become more popular and established and is accepted by all. Even the thinker has done the thinking to develop the concept, to prove the theories and it is used for achievement. Minus is not to be the receiver, there is no need to be in that position, it's negative, not good: think how to be positive, be in that position of plus, and then learn, get education.

How to manage this and how can it be organized? How can it be handled, how can it be worked out, and how to obtain and keep a plus position all of the time?

It's a temptation, an attraction and then distraction. Later on the result shows that minus has all the time followed the plus! The bigger the plus, the bigger the minus. Living in reality, believing in relativity and avoiding the minus, trying to be only the plus with all clever and efficient ways it is done. At the end what happened: clever becomes idiot because what has to be avoided was not possible to avoid. A question remained over what was avoided at that time because in the pain of that minus, the negative appeared again because it was all the time following that plus like a shadow.

Pain has got access through the minus, negative or through the replaced term! Total development has shifted the area from the middle, it moves towards one side more, the other side less and in this way, minus (negative) is avoided: this shows a shifting of the central or middle line. The movement was done because a decision was taken and to that decision proper logic and reasoning has given support. This means that the supporter becomes the intellect and the 'I' becomes the intellectual. The decision was taken intellectually and action was taken perfectly accurately, so it's a responsibility to justify, explain, defend, and argue for how and why that decision was taken, which becomes the cause of pain today!

To be clean and clear, the 'I' need not defend and not accept responsibility for that failure, the minus (negative) result which gives pain rather than pleasure! Looking back at the pattern and phenomena, the cause, one out of many appears as the maximum use of the replaced term and change of status and image!

Energy has plus and minus; without this, it is not Energy! This is the cause of the movement either at the higher, super or lower, common, general level.

Although it is one, Energy becomes the distributor and donor to whom? To Energy, who is the receiver when it is done by two different, opposite flows, circuits, cycles, circles, when complete connection, etc., takes place, and binding takes place.

It is an instinct to catch, to meet, like the dog tries to catch its tail through maximum bending, moving towards, the pushed object that is the tail. The effort is divided into two, concentration and attention, and it becomes a game, fun and pleasure, and a challenge to catch what is difficult. It is just in front, not far away, so why to give up, why not to try again and again and, at the end, fatigue, exhaustion, energy loss, no gain!

In this way, energetic Energy fixes the goal to catch its own tail-like object, which is not very far and also not very near to access, to reach, to catch, immediately, in other words it's just like the proverbial carrot, which becomes the cause of all effort and movement and remains all the time fresh, lively, and reachable. Is it a dreamer of the day who sleeps and is not awake, that intellect who doesn't know whom to tell to act, and when and why. The listener is also the part and partner to decide and to do, to have credit and appreciation. That's why the object of attraction is fixed in such a way that it creates temptation. This is just as in the case of Dr Pavlov's dogs and saliva, where instinct in animals was proved and how it works. Here, understanding is one step further that is how energy works through energy, becoming more and more energetic on one side and dull on the other side, active on one side, passive on the other, plus on one side, minus on the other, positive on one side and negative on the other.

One with two sides is how many?

Although it is one with two sides, it has a gap in-between, distance is the other name of the gap, which provides freedom to move and to be free!

In the other way, freedom is the gap between the two; separation is the increase of distance from or of a gap. The gap was created by a crack, and demanding nature has increased the gap for more freedom, becoming separate, apart, by part, and distance is maintained by their ego.

Together they were,
One they became, now,
Separate they are
to become one again!

It is a complete part. It is 100% from 50%.
It is full from that half.
It is break-up and not, it is separate and not.
It is full and not, it is 100% OR NOT,
It is two and also not!

Then what is it?

Now, here, it is this.

What is it? What is this?

'This' is taken for granted,

and 'that' is to know and prove,

and to recognize.

Now 'that' is known, it is proved by logic and reasoning!

That becomes the cause and this becomes the effect, the result of that. Now because of that, this is here, it is proved and accepted, which was taken for granted! What occurs is that which was taken for granted, is now proved and verified!

What?

ENERGY is, was and will be,

or

SPACE was, is and will be'.

Which one was taken for granted?

Or was it the two together?

The base line (starting point) is changing, shifting as and when it is taken for granted!

Is it common and general for all the base lines, starting points, or does it differ? So explanation, justification, arguments, clarification, and presentation also differs, this creates the difference, and through this difference each one becomes different. It means, being one and the same becomes different, to live in a different way, creating more and more difference and distance, to remain separate to have own area, territory, to move freely. The urge and demand for freedom causes Energy to become the supplier, the provider of the freedom of movement, the controller and regulator of that movement, and becomes the monitor and governor of the movement. This means that movement is by Energy and Energy is (has) movement in it, or itself is a moving principle!

Then, there are various roles played by Energy outside and inside. The external and internal are different: many roles are played by one outside, externally, while one has to play many roles in relation to the object, each time they are different, different.

Does this mean that One is inside the many, or does it mean that many are inside the One?

The measuring unit of the movement of ENERGY is known as time. Time is infinite because Energy is infinite! The measurer is finite!! Because provided time and energy is limited, means that it becomes finite, to limit the form, function, structure, system and their results and effects, just like a bubble or balloon. Or 'I' in the saloon! Bubble, balloon, or saloon, shows the limitations of the form and formation. This form can be many, many and separate from each other; constant formation of these forms on one side and on the other side a change of form, new formation, transformation or destruction of that form! This is also going on constantly and the phase between the two formations is known as the life of that form, which is measured in a time unit with a number of years or age from the date, month and year of birth, or in the case of a product, the sell-by date so that its possible to know how old things are and how old others are?

Knower is Energy, the object of knowledge is also Energy, and the process, a link between the two, the bridge, is also Energy. These three different forms of one Energy are a whole, and three belong to this One, as a whole, and are known as a component or part of the whole. That's why Ultimately ENERGY, and ENERGY is ULTIMATE. Although it is, even after that it is not possible to cover SPACE totally! SPACE appears in-between forms because they are different and separate; not ONE FORM, many forms and formations. There are two possible ways to cover up space: either to become very small, little and tiny, to spread and fill up the hole of the whole, because WHOLE has HOLE inside! Or another option is to become bigger and larger through uniting, binding, joining together, one by one, part by part, not to remain apart or separate, so that all are combined together to become one, to look like one, appear as One!

And what happens, just see. A frog came out of the lake and observed a buffalo near the water of the lake and tried to become bigger than that buffalo. What happens, it either bursts or blasts! It will never reach up to that size! The story indicates that the formation of different forms are up to a certain fixed limit, after that the next process starts automatically, just like the change of gear in a manual or automatic car.

The SUN and other planets and stars are not enough to cover SPACE or to even make it bright. DARK BLACK still EXISTS, and will EXIST, and was EXISTING also, as a BACK GROUND for all.

Who is it that can go beyond that BACK GROUND, what is there?

That is why it is considered and accepted, and recognized as well as appreciated, as an ENVELOPE for ALL! BRIGHT SPOTS are THAT SUN and STARS.

Earth is the product of the SUN. Earth is the producer of many. As a producer, and being a product, Earth has done lots of production with its own Energy! This Earth Energy is never allowed to go away, it pulls back, it has a FIRE within, a flame within! So, it is alive, and gives life! It provides a place to live and to survive. That's why it is known as Mother Earth. The body belongs to it and goes back to it.

SUN is the source and resource of ENERGY on Earth, from Earth, and to and for the Earth, and to those who are living on and in it.

Although SPACE is a common BACK GROUND for all, Earth becomes the ground for all those who are on the Earth. That ground becomes the place, a piece of ground, or a piece of land, important for all to live and to survive.

Earth is a constant receiver,
SUN is a constant giver.
Giver remains as a giver,
while receiver becomes the giver as well as being the receiver.

In this way, Earth has changed the status of being and becomes useful and helpful to all those who are there on it. The receiver means to be in minus, not plus in a general, normal, natural position. However, with inner strength and power, force and pressure, with the help of that FIRE which Belongs to the SUN and within the limit it works, and with limitations does all the functions and gets results or achievements, within a limit. This limit is difficult to accept because the fire (flame) within is burning constantly. As a result it demands, and for that the supply has to be constant.

Now a question to that Energy can be asked.

In which role is it to be or not to be, and how long to remain without change of role from one to another? How to maintain control and regulate the fire or flame within? Excess use, too much utilization, means consumption of the fuel or stock within results in burn out, exhaustion. Because goals are very high, not only one, but a list of things to achieve is ready one after the other, step by step, even side by side, trying to fulfil needs and desires, wishes and ambition, simple to complex, higher to highest, has fixed the limit the sky and the expression becomes, the sky is the limit for that limited one!

How a can a limited one fix the limit beyond capacity and ability? Is it an act and decision of a wise or over-wise one? Otherwise what!

Sky is the other term of SPACE! Infinite! How can there be a limit? Even though limit is defined, and kept as the sky, what to do? What it indicates is that the doer will not be the one but many will try to reach it, but after that limit no one, not a single doer, can reach to that limit. Is it a direction or a destination?

When the role is played and changed very often, then a question arises to that 'I': in which role do I have to be or not to be? Who am I? Is it this identity in this role, or that identity in that role?

That 'I' in a mirror image or reflection identifies either with the fire and flame, or with that Earth known as body, container of fire (flame). The question to inquire into shows a state in-between! Whom to and what to accept, whom and what to reject? It becomes difficult to know to whom that 'I' belongs: is it fire and flame or Earth? As long as it is within, inside, how is it possible and in which way is it possible to avoid Earth?

Actually, both belong to the SUN and are because of the SUN, having a common BACK GROUND of SPACE! Ultimate and Ultimately SPACE! Space research means research in and inside space. It does not mean research of Space! It is taken for granted that SPACE is an ORIGINAL STEADY STATE. That is why quasi-steady state is the given, known, expression for Energy! Although ENERGY is Ultimate and Ultimately Energy, it has been proved again and again by all in different ways, from different, different fields, that time, it was taken for Granted.

SPACE is, and for that there is no dispute. Even in this situation, condition, ENERGY has found out its own way to prove, to establish, and to show, through its own property, the intellect and, on that accepted and non-disputable ground, it has created the dispute, dialogue, controversy and contradictions, quarrels and fight, conflicts and struggle to prove its own strength and power. It even has changed the role and replaced the term, to deceive, to cheat and become a copy, a look-alike. It provides possibilities to evaluate, count and compare, to judge and conclude, through creating, maintaining and transforming the differences from time to time and place to place, between each other, so that each one can have its own importance and struggle for acceptance, recognition and appreciation, constantly. Finally, Energy has achieved this, and for this achievement the use of cunningness, shrewdness, wickedness was done, just like 'salt in the soup'. This is considered as a sacrifice for ENERGY by Energy with different ways and means.

Achievements, along with all the different skills and talents, have increased the value of the achievements. Because: "Mine is better than yours"! "I am superior because of that"! "I am on a higher stand, place, than you, and I am living a higher quality and standard of lifestyle!" "The description and narration of all attraction which you know that I am having"! "I am here, you are there, my place and surrounding is far better than yours"! "I can help you, don't hesitate to ask"! These and many others like them are because of achievements after changing, replacing the term, change of role and status and image, they are now able to say, express, and to show their own capacity, strength and power, ENERGY to ENERGY!

Because SPACE doesn't care for this is why Energy has picked up the expression "who cares! The answer is that Energy cares, not Space!

Who are you?

What are you taking care of?

Why and for what?

From the Earth's point of view, it never expresses, never plays a game of obliging and obligation, it is just there as it is, in a common way for the two opposites, as the deer, cow or goat runs along the ground to save its life from the pursuing wild animal chasing for the kill. Both the killer and the object to be killed are using the same ground, piece of land, Earth, common to the two opposites.

In the same way, Books of Law or Law Books are common for both parties of lawyers: is the stronger one the winner? No, not all the time, the weaker one is not always the looser! Strength and power is on one side, while the tricks of the trade are on the other side, any one of the sides can be the cause of winning and loosing because of different ways of handling the available sides. This raises the question: when to use what?

A constant giver is the Earth, who is constantly receiving and is a constant receiver. This has a sign or a symbol of 'minus', negative and because of this it has changed this very skilfully to become the other, appear as the other, and look different!

SUN is constantly giving, and is a constant giver,

The giver is giving constantly,

The receiver is receiving constantly.

Although it's ONE ENERGY, One is the producer, creator of the other. SUN is the producer, creator of the Earth! Earth is a planet, along with other planets; it came into existence in

Space separately; it became separate from the SUN, or the SUN has delivered the Earth!

SUN is the MOTHER who has delivered many others, not only the Earth! Earth is one of them; everyone knows this and has learnt and studied it.

As Earth is a mother ENERGY, in the same way, this mother is because of that MOTHER SUN! Who delivers, produces, creates, gives birth and takes care, provides and allows to play and enjoyment around own PLACE of EXISTENCE! Through another characteristic, the features and qualities of that mother do not appear as mother, but is now considered as FATHER.

SUN, in this way, is considered, worshipped, expressed, and looked at as FATHER and as MOTHER also. Two together as one means zero, plus and minus together at the same time, so it is also considered as neither Father nor Mother, but as a neutral gender because how can it be expressed. Which form of grammar can be used is the question for linguistic use, not for the SUN!

SUN is SUN, is all the time PLUS;
Earth is Earth, is all the time MINUS;
This is one pair, both are connected, united with the rays, and light.
SUN is a FIRE ITSELF,
Earth HAVING Fire within.
Earth is a body to that FIRE within,
Body as an Earth, having a flame within!
Both are living and having a life!

FIRE ITSELF IS THE BODY OF THE SUN, A GOLDEN DISC, WHICH HAS COVERED THE TRUTH. To look at it, to watch it, that glow has to be removed in order to look behind the GROUND.

Now, a question, simple question, Who are you? How will you answer? Will it be, I am this, or that? I am not this or that!

Flame is a flame, FIRE is a FIRE,
Though both can burn,
this is a similarity, which has a difference also.

Flame is little and smaller in comparison to the fire.
Burning takes place because of the flame, while
Fire consumes, burns and becomes bigger and bigger.
Enlarged form of the flame is fire!
Now it is known as fire, flames of the fire!
It was a flame and has now become fire, Transformation,
Quantity, or measurement point of view different,
Quality, point of view both are the same, so
they are similar and different and the same also.

Their needs and requirement of the fuel and the result is according to their size, capacity and limit. A flame can be extinguished by a strong wind, while the same strong wind co-operates to spread the fire! For a flame, the enemy is the wind; for the fire, the wind is a friend! Stronger is good or bad?

Flame and fire on the Earth have 'on and off' time! Fire within the Earth, at the centre core, keeps it moving, turning, and rotating constantly in one direction, even moving in one direction! Why not two? Why only one? What would happen to it?

Keeping the SUN always in the centre, Earth moves round and round; or because of the SUN'S power at the centre it holds and makes (keeps) the Earth moving round and round: two expressions of one ongoing happening, from two different points of view. In the same way, turning, moving, rotating on its own axis, or bringing the back to face the Sun, or heat of the Sun, or to have a sunlight, or to have a day effect from the effect of the night! Constantly. What is it?

Is it possible to know, to explain, to measure this quality of the Earth? Dedication, devotion to the fire, known as the SUN. Why and how does this happen?

ENERGY IS THE CAUSE,
ENERGY IS THE EFFECT.

In an energetic way it happens! Day has light, it's a plus, a heat; night has darkness, it's a minus, a cold, or minus heat! Day area moves to night or night area moves to day? Plus goes and turns to minus, or minus goes and turns to plus? Is there anybody to stop this? How can an inner fire or flame stop when itself is the cause and effect? How is it possible?

When Earth, along with fire within, belongs to the SUN. How can an individual having a body as an Earth, having a flame, deny the connection with the SUN?

Fire and flame from one side, on the other side, flames of the SUN: the difference is bigger and smaller, and having two types of background, for both of them. The BACK GROUND of THE SUN and the ground of the flame, and the ground of the Earth and its fire, is the common?

Their back is different? Because of the difference it is different, it becomes different from the position of the individual habitat, it becomes front to back, up and down, east and west, etc. The SUN is the fixed reference point or the point we choose or select: can any point be a reference point? It should be a fixed point, how long should it be? As long as your work is going on, not finished, that fixed point has not to change its position or place; that much everyone knows, because it will effect the measurement and calculations and the total or sum will not be correct!

Who cares for that ultimate fixed point? To arrange, manage and organize the lifestyle, which reference point is better, one which changes position from time to time, or an unchanging one? To argue, to stop, to block, it's easy to say, even the SUN is moving, along with all the planets, around the other centre. So how is the SUN the centre?

Good argument, perfect logic and reason to block, to stop, to show, that nothing is fixed and not moving, so all your effort to convince is futile! And that is why our reference points need not change because they are changing their own position, place, from time to time! Is it not a good example of comparison between the two! That's why a question:

Who are you?

Sun?

Who are you?

In which state is the existence?

Existence of the SUN and existence of the individual on the Earth, is it common?

What about the time factors and the time period?

Who needs patience?

Who becomes a patient?

Who has to wait and watch?

Why one individual is not the reference point for the other is that it changes from point to point as the need and necessity (requirement) changes. It means that argument for the sake of argument, to take an opposite stand to argue, so that it's easy to protect, to defend own logic and reasoning for the decision and action, becomes necessary for the common individual. Those who don't know more about the body and its purpose and functions, don't know about the inner flame having any connection or relation with the SUN, or not? And in which way, it is and is not the relation and connection!

Where does that 'I' exist, in which area?

How can a flame say, "I don't require a body, a cover"?

A protection is provided to the flame, or does the flame select?

How much right over the body has the flame?

Are they separate and different, then why is it that they are they together?

For what?

Both are Energy formed in a different way.

Whatever is with you, does it mean it belongs to you?

Is it for you and for your use?

It is taken for granted that whatever is with me is mine and I can use it as much and in any way, at my wish and will!

Is it not projected ownership, extended right of authority, to consider first as 'mine', then to say it's not 'me'!

What is not belonging to you when it is provided to you to use or not to use, how can you say it's not me and mine?

This means it is projected and then refused, not accepted.

The total process is the function or the act of the intellect with perfect logic and reasoning, or it's a process as a result, effect, a ripening, a wisdom from within, from the light of the inner flame. If the Statement is correct, what is the base of the understanding?

Body is the cover, container; if that body, cover, container is so ugly, not good, then what remains without it, one has to accept and to deal with it. To discard one form of the body and not being able to distinguish the other form of the body, although it is the proper understanding about the body and it is not the proper understanding about the body! That's why, this other form of the body becomes the cause of attraction, which becomes the cause of distraction, and the cause of attraction is the temptation towards the body! By force and pressure, suppression of the temptation and desire for and towards the body can be enacted. Later on, that becomes the cause of one's own problem and disturbance, pain and suffering, because what was to be avoided was not avoided properly! Consideration of discarding the living body (decision and action) was done; what about the abstract body, and non-living body, which are different to the subtle body and causal body! As body is equal to the house, in the same way, house becomes the body!

This house as a body, one should not possess, not have ownership over; while house as a property, an individual becomes the proprietor, owner! It is not the house and it is the house because it is known as a place to live, that is house with a specific activity and function to live, and even after that it is not the house. The thought that a family is using the place, means that the idea it is mine and it is not mine develops within and the flame of greed becomes fire of greediness, and greed becomes great! Because Energy has done what it has to do as a doer!

Energy of the Earth is different from the Energy of the SUN, and Energy made and created by the individual is also different to these two! Three different types of Energy formation known by a common term, Energy! From and with which reference can it be understood and described?

Force and pressure is the nature of ENERGY, by force and pressure, or using force and pressure, Energy can achieve Energy! Not SPACE! SPACE appears as it disappears from there!

ENERGY of the EARTH, is divided into two, from the two areas, it becomes:

- Front facing to the SUN: bright, day, plus heat, with light, sunlight, mid-day.
- Back from the front, which is opposite and not facing the SUN: dark night, minus heat, with moonlight, midnight.
- Two adjoining points,
    1. SUN-set, from mid-day towards mid-night, known as evening.
    2. SUN-rise, from mid-night towards mid-day, known as morning.

Although it is ONE Earth, having all possibilities and different sets of timing, temperature, climate, light arrangement, on each different place or piece of land, the experience of the dual state of nature and the divider as 'I', and the position of the 'I' as an individual living being has to be, with duality inside! This is because body is equal to Earth, it is also a flame within, that has fire within! That's why there is a double duality! SUN doesn't have this problem of day and night, its effects are on the Earth, its cause is the SUN and the movement of the Earth together, meaning two become the cause for one happening, which effects many, relates with and connects with many!

Two are saying:

I am the flame, and fire within.
I am not the body and Earth,
I am that SUN, FIRE,
Out of two,
One just repeats and recites,
The other one lives life accordingly!

Energy of the Earth uses the Energy of the Sun and fire within as an excuse to move freely in Space. A big transport agency, Earth transporting, carrying, to show, to enlighten its own habitants, to provide light and to hold them in such a way that it develops the understanding in a contrary way! Mother is holding a child, or is the child holding a mother, or is it both to each other? How long and in which way should one hold the other?

How is SPACE HOLDING The EARTH?

How the Earth as a holder is holding everyone!

How everyone has a holding tendency!

Does it belong to the Earth, Energy or to SPACE?

To increase the grip, to become more and more tight, contracted and then solid and compact, is a functional nature of Energy, which doesn't want to lose or give up (or let go) that which is under its own possession.

The process of holding is of two opposites: Energy has to close and increase the grip and tension, to use strength and to take care that the held one has not slipped out of the grip, or possession, fear, anxiety, worry, etc., also develops. SPACE is opposite to this!

The FIRE and FLAMES of the SUN are different from the flames and fire on and in the Earth, and of Earth as a body, a living body! Earth is one, and Earth as a body and flame within (known as a living body) is not one! There are many, many living bodies, living as an Earth, living and surviving on and in the Earth body! Two together receive and use that light of SUN ENERGY. It's a mixture of the two Energies, SUN and Earth, Space to place and place to Space, a two-way journey: SUN as AMBASADOR of SPACE!

ULTIMATELY SPACE IS THE ULTIMATE BACKGROUND, DARK BLACK. Now to have ONLY THIS BACKGROUND means total blank, void, NOTHINGNESS, on one side; on the other side, everything, world, creation, and individual 'I', a living being; two extreme points, and there is no clue or link to imagine, to think, to develop a hypothesis, between these two extreme points. The SUN is a bright

SPOT, why doesn't it have an existential principle, a cause of our existence, and also of many other planets.

To solve any mathematical problem it is allowed to take a sum of 'x' to proceed further. This sum of 'x' is not fixed and standardized, it can vary from problem to problem, and it is allowed, permitted and accepted by experts of the field to solve, to work out the problem. In scientific investigation, one has to prove with evidence the findings, and then they get acceptance, recognition and appreciation. The cause and effect theory has tried to reach the Ultimate CAUSE, but through research they have reached up to ENERGY and accepted it as the ULTIMATE CAUSE.

Then a question arises about the Energy of the SUN that belongs to the Earth, and that Energy created by individuals in a laboratory: what is the difference and similarity in them. Then comes another question, how is Energy different from SPACE, or is there any difference in them and is Space a synonym of Energy, or is ENERGY the other term and name for SPACE? What is the answer? Then it can be asked, why is SPACE without particles BLACK, DARK BLACK? Why is research in Space and research of SPACE not done?

It is taken for GRANTED, the same as the sum of 'x'. From start to finish in space research, 'SPACE IS' is taken for GRANTED, and other than that everyone wants to find the answers, to search again and again. SUN is an AMBASSADOR, a representative of SPACE as an existential principle. It is source and resource of Energy and life for all living beings, the known cause of our Existence, a centre of movement. It appears as a life-source in a steady state, without having the duality of Earth, with a similar appearance of fire within and life on its surface! It is good for us, this surface, to survive, to be alive and not on the SUN where all is FIRE. That's why it's better to accept the DARK BLACK BACKGROUND as NOTHING and SUN as EVERYTHING, and from that everything, everything is with us here on Earth.

Now start from here, from here and there, or from that point where you are on the Earth. That is the first point. The second is in relation to you; others are the same like you but at different places. The second is similar to the first, and second becomes the Earth, which also has another starting point, as the Earth has a moon, that individual also has a part belonging to that living body as an Earth.

This first and second, along with their moon, are in connection with the SUN, with a distance getting, receiving, enough heat which can give life, and burn also. Moon is reflecting the light, or moon plays the role of a reflector, to reflect the light of the SUN. That light is also SUN light, then what is the difference between the two lights? One is with heat (plus (+) heat) the other is without heat (minus (-) heat). Instead of saying it in this way, better to say it is moonlight, a cooling light from a bright moon!

The established term 'sunlight' has given credit to the other one also (moonlight). The moon considers it as 'my light', which gives a more cooling effect. And people prefer my light (!) forgetting that it is possible to have it during the dark night only! In the daytime, although it is there, it's not visible or effective because of the strong light of the SUN, which is brighter with heat, suppressing the cool!

There is a distance between the individual, Earth and SUN. First, is the individual (living being) along with the non-living also. This is a small unit inside and on the Earth as a second unit, which is quite big and larger than the first one. Both, along with their moon, came into existence from that third unit, the SUN, with a considerable time lag and process of transformation. The first one appears to say it's mine!

To go beyond, to search the cause of the cause, is the nature of Energy, and how can an energetic investigator remain without doing any invention or investigation or research? So, first they found Earth is flat, and with that reference, considering it as a fixed reference to analyse, to check, to evaluate, the movement, found that the SUN is moving, as it is sun-rise and sun-set, on east and west, which was confirmed, well-established and accepted. Later on, the fixed point changed status and became the moving point, and from flat came the appearance, looks like, a round shape. The curvature and its curve, to look, to see and perceive, to think and imagine was not easy for many. Those who had even noticed the curve considered it as the horizon, a meeting point at the end where nothing further was visible. As there is no other horizon possible to catch in the same way, so it was not possible to locate and pin-point the curve, and this made (compelled) them to state that it is flat. Flat and straightforward is how it looked! Finally, flat becomes a round curve appearing at the horizon.

Distance very far away changes the size of the object: flat becomes round, and Earth appears as reflecting and shining like a moon! So, what appears in the distance is not so when appearing close up, contacted, and with a minimum distance! The individual's experience of the Earth while living on it and from perceiving (observing) it from far away makes a big difference, because the reference point is changed! Perception gets changed!

Many changes take place as a consequence of that change in the reference point. Even the evaluation system and cognition get changed because of this and, as a result, expression becomes revised, modified and changed in relation to that object! This happens because the first point, the individual, has changed the position and reference point also, in-between the third point SUN and EARTH as second point or unit, and takes its own position, a position in SPACE between the two. To whom does the individual belong? Earth or SUN? Although they know that they belong to the SUN, they prefer to live on the Earth: life and enjoyment is there, not on the SUN because they say (express) Earth belongs to us, me and my 'I', we, you, all of us belong to the Earth! A BODY!!

The SPACE in-between is one and another is beyond as a background of the SUN and all the planets, it is totally another type of Space; the difference is made by being with and without particles. The fourth point or unit becomes

SPACE, a Dark Black Back Ground as a SPACE. Up to that point (unit), it's all right to argue and to block and to stretch the imagination, and then where to stop? How to stop? How to convert and transcend? What can be done when one does not know? Either get lost or come back to Earth and start to live again on Earth to avoid (prevent) this happening, a bright SPOT, SUN, is selected as a representative of SPACE.

The objection is because of the object. SPACE can be an object as well as particles and Earth and moon can also be objects. Why does one have to be the reference point of the life, why not two? Two together as one is also possible to accept! Here in this way, they are separate, together as one they are not.

Together as one they are:

- Separate they were?
- Separate they are?
- Separate they will be?

SUN and SPACE beyond as Back Ground are two separate entities or can be considered as one and we try to live in a better way with that reference point. What appears is the body of the SUN inside or behind. They try to know, investigate, pray, and to find out that TRUTH, which is covered by the Body. The fire, flames and rays as a part of the body cover up that TRUTH. That's what all are searching for!

As Earth has its own Energy, an individual also has its own Energy. This Energy is a mixture of two Energies: the Energy of the SUN is hidden inside the other, as a one. They are together up to that time period and life is lived; then they become separate and life is over, finished. Death is the term and pain is the result of that separation. It is possible to provide the cause to join (unite), and the cause to separate.

Gravitation and its pull requires anti-gravitational force and pressure against that strong pull, which brings down, keeps up or down and doesn't allow and permit to anything go away. Magnetic forces decide the directions to avoid and prevent; at the same time the force is effortful to meet the opposite end, nature, or side! Knowledge of this is there with them all the time readily available for use. Fear of falling down is stronger and makes them find a support or balance.

When one problem is solved another appears as a balance to maintain and not to have more or less and imbalance; so weight has to be distributed equally on both sides or on all sides equally. This is not enough because movement of ENERGY is there all the time, so it should be in harmony with the other Energy form, function, system, structure, result and effect. This harmony is experienced as health. Of that and from that harmonious movement of all, each different one at one stage have body as an Earth, or Earth as a Body! On it, and in it, Space is a place where there is movement in harmony or disharmony. At any rate, when it's going on in order then it is beauty, and ugly or chaotic when it is not in ORDER.

When an individual is in SPACE, far away from the limit of gravitational pull (or after crossing that limit), it overcomes the fear of falling down; being in Space outside the Earth as a body one is able to walk in Space, move in Space: then where is the up and down reference? Which position is straight and standing? When Earth is as a ground, SPACE is not there, and space as a ground is there, so it is and it is not that GROUND. How can East and West be decided? One is absolute East and West; the other that's on the Earth is related east and west.

When it is asked to that individual, where are you now? "I am in space", is the answer. An individual is inside space! What about the SPACE within? Is it possible for that 'I' to be in that SPACE within? It means to be in one's own inner SPACE and to explore that inner SPACE, to find out, or investigate, or to do research. Is it possible for that individual? It requires some technique to leave Earth and to get away from the gravitational force, to be in the area which is free from gravity and the gravitational forces of the Earth so they are not affecting that area, place, Space!

Against gravitation is levitation, to be away from the ground, to be without contact of Earth and to be totally in

SPACE. Earth as a body needs one type of technique, and body as Earth needs another type of technique. When to do what? When to use which technique? It is easier to be outside in the external space; preparation and practice for this journey requires different materials and knowledge, and there the 'I' remains all the time in contact and connection with the stations, points and towers on the Earth!

What about the inner journey? No contact, connections are cut off, and then it is the body and it is not the body, it is my body and it is not my body, 'I am' different from it. What happens to that individual travelling inside Space, moving further towards the SUN? Life which appears on the screen disappears! So, the programme is to be away from the SUN, not to go in that direction. To explore and measure the heat of the SUN it's better not to have any sample from its surface; the same fear of death arises from within to that 'I', ego, who started the inner journey.

That's why the doer, that 'I', ego, of the individual, first enjoys and appreciates the practices and its results, and later on stops automatically as and when the inner mechanism gives warning signals. That ego energy immediately catches up, picks up and changes the practice programme with proper justification and explanation, ready to clarify in detail why other practices are so important and why no time remains for that practice. Later on that one complains that it is not able to restart that practice, which was so nice and giving good results!

This is also an avoiding technique! The best and maximum use of skill and knowledge to avoid and then prevent becomes the cause of pain, suffering, disturbance and problems. When to avoid and to prevent what? How and why? Energy is avoiding, preventing Energy, means good is preventing (avoiding) bad, plus is preventing avoiding minus, and the scientist wants to grow a banana without a skin or cover!

Knowledge is the cause of pain and suffering, because incomplete knowledge is the cause. In which way and how it is incomplete? The knower has no time to know and find out how it can be complete; instead of that, the knower considers and takes it for granted that that knowledge is enough for decisions and action or execution and performance. The result of this action is one which manifests outside, and the result of the result is the other one, which manifests inside as either pleasure or pain.

Knower becomes the doer, and after deciding and executing becomes the experiencer of the result. Knowledge becomes the cause, in this way, and the other side of the knowledge is information! Information is information, not knowledge, the informer has given (passed on) the information and receiver has received it as a form of knowledge. This knowledge is just like a seed that has the potency to grow and give flowers and fruit, a seed with a cover to take care of that potency, to protect that potency which is inside the seed!

Then a question: what is the seed? Seed is one having potency within, and that potency is the seed. Is this because it is the cause of the flowers and fruit, or is it that without the potency it is not a seed? Then, what is it? It is a seed and it is not a seed! A seed with potency is a seed, without potency it is not a seed! It has the appearance of the seed! It looks like a seed! It is similar, and seems to be a seed! Who knows how to test it? To check the potency the test will destroy the form and one seed will be declared to be with or without potency. What about the other seeds?

In the same way, information has the potency to become knowledge and to give flowers and fruit as a result! How is it possible to grow the roasted seed? The taste of roasted and toasted is special. The one individual who receives the information in the form of a teaching and learning has the responsibility to cultivate to get the flowers and fruit! Nursery is one, garden is another, and park is more than that. All three are having order and a system for a beautiful look and appearance! Forest is opposite to the above three! Before it was a forest now it is a park and avenue culture!

Here language is the ladder or ladder is the language! On the ground of (basis of) information, this ladder is kept fixed, steady and then work starts and the movement to climb up or get down, to be on that step where working or acting becomes easy or comfortable; the fear of falling down doesn't remain at that time of work, action and performance. Language is a means of communication: to be curious to know is first; then negotiation for that curiosity and object of attraction to know, to move or not to move. To act or not to act?

Internal or external guidance and support is to be taken in order to make a decision; mild, moderate or intense, is the nature of curiosity and guidance. The object of curiosity and attraction towards it becomes the winner to distract the curious one through giving more importance to that object of knowledge. So, it becomes important for the curious to start the action and to move carefully, to reach up to the place of the object to know! The object to know is either living or non-living, so what to do and how much to do is taken for granted by that curious one, who becomes the doer; knowing, action and performance is done; checking and investigation is done swiftly, precisely, within a given or limited time, so quickly, along with surprising the fear, keeping it on one side with full confidence and trust in own ability. What was decided to know has now become known and curiosity towards that object is gone along with attraction, interest slowly reduces.

In the case of a non-living object, disconnection has to be within a short period of time and the living object has to make a continual effort and attempt to be the object of attraction and curiosity. That's why the game of surprise is played by Energy! To give surprise means to catch the person (individual) unawares and not awake, giving a shock to the system of the receiver who is not yet ready (prepared) or organised to receive it and who has to become a receiver: a prize is surprise.

The curious one has received the surprise, first from the object to know, then later on becomes the surprise giver rather than receiver. During that time curiosity was reduced to "I know now" it is not new it is old. Then new and fresh, soft and tender, gentle and mild, become the object of attraction and the search starts again. It becomes research of what?

That the curious one knows. After knowing and getting knowledge about the object, now it becomes difficult to keep it within, to preserve and hold within. It needs and requires strength, power, and the capacity to hold, to sustain, and for that the related concerned systems and their functions have to work well to keep it active for a long time. It is not an easy task!

To know the object is one; the knowledge of and about the object to keep within is another; to bring it out again, to get rid of it, to get relief, is the common action (just like to vomit) to get relief of either food or information or knowledge from and of that object, living or non-living! In a sports stadium it is a relay race where the baton completes the round, not the runner! In the same way, the intellectual plays a game of 'hot potato'! On another level, the commercial advantage to have any type of advantage becomes or takes the form of a rumour! The rumour just floats like a piece of garbage, as some precious information and the exchange of it, increasing in value with those precious exchanges! And for that many precautions need to avoid (prevent) the leak of information! Relaxed and normal they are externally; underneath they know it should appear natural and original.

Is it not hard work, a hard task, to have all this, without any physiological disorder? It's a play of Energy to be the best. Is it more efficient than SPACE? OR Energy?

A magnet has two opposite poles, plus and minus. Opposites attract and similar can go together with similar, they can't attract each other. It's possible for them to go together, remain together, to bind and connect, join and develop continuity. Opposite ends have to meet, to join, to connect together and oneness comes into existence or as it appears.

It is a principle accepted by all different communities with different terminologies to communicate, to clear up their concepts and experiences, their theories and practices, etc. This principle gives rules and regulations to the movement of Energy and its flow, which is supposed to give formation or shape to a structure, system or function for the expected result. At a different level, in various ways and means, this movement of Energy is going on and the guiding factors are magnets and the magnetic role played and displayed by Energy.

Now, this current of Energy, the flow of Energy cannot escape or run here and there, it has to move round and around and for that the great helper, puller, holder is the gravitational force. So, on one side, Energy moves to escape, to run away; on the other side, the pull compels it to take, to have a turn and turn after turn and again the turn moving continuously, making connections with its own opposite end. What happens is a vicious circle, regularly irregular: in a balanced way it's imbalanced, in a disciplined way it's ill disciplined!

The circle is completed by that Energy which is not COMPLETE. However, that which is not complete but incomplete has provided (given or created) a complete circle! And that complete circle is round or zero, which is neutral, moderate, or balanced, etc. It becomes an established fact, so the search for truth becomes necessary and important.

Earth is a living body having a big gravitational pull to that magnetic Energy flow. Similarly, the living Body (as an 'Earth') also has the same possibility where individual to individual bind together, keep together, grow together, and form different types of circles (round or wheel) to move, to work, to perform, the decided thoughtful decision. The binding (connections) joining the two have purpose, intention, motives, as a cause and the effect is development of one-ness, identification, association with each other: this also is in different ways and at different levels.

How long will this remain? Separation and break-up is bound occur, cracks appear, gap and distance as a result lead towards that destination with full freedom, with separation to become two again, to have own identity, and for that to remain single, alone, and one becomes necessary, as well as freedom and to be independent, becomes the strong inner urge. Therefore, the individual has developed the skill of management, to achieve, to fulfil this burning desire, on one side; on the other side, interpersonal dependency is because of the structure, system and function. For the result to create the temptation, attraction and compulsion there has to be a combined effort, they have to be all together to achieve that goal, target, or aim which is fixed and decided by the clever one as one of them!

The peak of a mountain is always tiny and small in size compared with the size of its ground base, and it is on the height (or above that base) that the higher and the smaller area is more in contact with Space and open-ness. Where to go: either further into Space, or return back to the ground? It's not possible to collect and accumulate, to receive and pass on to the other; downward is a more easy movement, upward is difficult. That's why the living being, after reaching the peak of the mountain, plants the flag as a representative, a non-living marker to live there because one can't live there, be there for a long time. Today, to reach the peak, to establish a record and break the old established record, creating a new record, becomes the goal, target or aim. So, one is busy breaking either one's own or another's record! To break it is the inner urge, the nature of ENERGY, even a relationship, partnership is broken to have the new.

On one side the search and demand is for the new, fresh and original and, on the other side, to develop and encourage repair, to renew and recycle. In this situation, two has to compromise, adjust and adopt to maintain what? Is it for one's own status and image, own value system and principle? Really, Energy knows and doesn't know what has to be moved. To act, to perform, to have a result, Earth Energy with its own magnetic and gravitational forces has to move, why?

Fire is the cause of union and separation, formation and deformation, composition and life appearance and decomposition and death when life functions disappear. The flame and fire in front of us on Earth gives light and life: that is outside, or is it external?

The living body is because of this flame and fire inside, within, or internal, the living body of a single individual and the living body of the Earth. One is on the Earth with qualities, characteristics, and aspects of the Earth; both have their own nature, which is governed by the SUN. Both belong to the SUN. The size of both the bodies is different, both have connection (relation) with flame and fire. As Earth came from the SUN and later on had its own life: ENERGY OF A SUN, Energy of the Earth, and energy of an individual living being.

Although the three are apparently different, all are working together as three in one and form a small unit, then bigger, and then biggest unit, the SUN. Each form with its formation, function and purpose is different from the other one: three are similar, different, and opposite at the same time. Although these three are one made by two, they have oneness in togetherness. The reason and cause to unite, combine, join is different; they also have to exist separately and for that they have different time duration. To be together and separate, with or without pain, to join, to unite, to combine again and again, or not, is decided by their way of living and being and existing.

From the flame and fire point of view, these three are the same with a different amount, size, and quantity of fire and flame.

From the covering point of view, SPACE is the ultimate cover and ultimately to the SUN.

While the remaining two have their own cover along with Space as a cover, it means they have a double or dual cover!

From the contact point of view, there is direct contact and exposure to SPACE by the fire and flames of the SUN.

While the remaining two have first immediate contact with their own cover, and then to SPACE; their fire and flame has no direct exposure to Space!

From the protection point of view, SPACE ULTIMATE is the protector and provides protection to the exposed fire and flames of the SUN.

While the remaining two have their cover to protect their inner fire and flame, so, for them, the protector is that cover which provides protection not to get exposed, so covers and dresses!

From the function point of view, all the functions of the SUN are going on under the cover of SPACE!

While for the remaining two, all the functions are under their own cover, which is going on as under-cover activity.

From the SPACE point of view, SPACE is an Ultimate Dark Black Back Ground for the SUN, where the SUN is appearing as a Bright SPOT.

While for the remaining two, they have their own Space to move along with their own form as a cover! This is their related Space, from all different ways it is related and connected with them on one side and, on the other side, connected (related) to the SPACE of the SUN, which is ULTIMATE, Dark Black, Back Ground.

From the relation and connection point of view, the ULTIMATE DARK BLACK GROUND is related (connected) to the SUN directly!

While for the remaining two, the ULTIMATE DARK BLACK GROUND as SPACE is connected (related) to SPACE with Space directly and then to that two!

From the connecting link point of view, SPACE is connected with the Space related with the two, through the connecting link between the two on one side as a receiver and giver is the SUN and the link is the SUN'S RAYS!

From the rays point of view, they have a penetrating power, a powerful Energy which belongs to the SUN and is given to all in the form of RAYS. This means 'A POWER-HOUSE SUN', and its RAYS are so many that they work as a cover, a dress! Is it beautiful? So, it is a cover and it is not a cover and because of that, SPACE is a cover to that which isn't a cover!

In the case of the remaining two, their rays have to pass through their own cover first and then to the next object, so the penetrating power is either reduced or becomes polluted, diluted! That's why it becomes important to keep the cover clean so that penetration is good.

From the establishment of connection and relation point of view, all are connected, related and free.

The Earth and individual also have their own Space, they are surrounded by it, and have their own freedom to move and act under cover. Each one is established in its own position and connected (related) with the other as an optional connection. There are many, many optional connections and relations.

From the choice and selection point of view, SUN has no choice, no option, it just has to give and give, and is constantly distributing rays to burn, to have fire and flames. These rays travel up to the two, they are receivers!

From the utility point of view, the SUN has utilized its own surrounding maximum area to spread the heat of the fire and to enlighten other objects in SPACE.

The remaining two have the light of the SUN and try to be enlightened. To utilize its fire, flame and light in their own way, to connect, to relate with other objects and to enlighten them, means to help them and to be useful to them, so their light and rays have been utilized in their way as a result – transactions increase to have benefit and profit.

From the applicability and practicability point of view, the Dark Black Back Ground and Bright SPOT (SUN) on it become the ideal example for the remaining two. As a receiver of that penetrating power in the form of light and rays, with an option and choice they have applied, and through various practices tested its practicability and verified whether to rely on it or not, they have found that doubt and distrust has started functioning from within!

The need to check, to test, to verify, to see and confirm, becomes necessary for the two because that cover created the obstacle of whether to recognize and accept. Only when the object been clarified can appreciation become possible.

From the belief and faith point of view, the SUN on one side shows and gives trust, belief and faith as a binding material, working material, a tool to the remaining two! These two are not ready to believe that what they are receiving is permanent and constant from that SUN. As a result, the holding process start and the fear to loose, not to get again, appears, and doubt, lack of confidence and respect, and honour to own state of being appears. Then a question arises: Why am I here?

How can that cover be discovered and used? Misuse, wrong use and abuse occur frequently, while correct, right and proper use is rare and often by mistake!

From the giver and receiver point of view, the SUN is the GIVER, a CONSTANT GIVER, and the Dark Black Back Ground is allowing it to pass through, permitting the rays (light) to move through, to reach to the object that has taken objection! This objection is an obstacle on the other side to divert the flow, the movement. Through hitting each other, heat increases, sparks comes out of that, ignition takes place and the other one catches the spark, turns into fire and flame and starts functioning by itself as if help and support are not required So, it is neglected (ignored) and care was not taken for that afterwards because it says, “Now I am on my feet, self-sufficient and independent, help and support is not needed, now I can give, provide, the help and support!”

After getting ignition, the ignited one starts showing and paying gratitude to that IGNITOR who provided the first spark and spoke to the wheel and to the motor engine.

Who cared for it?

The receiver has changed the term and title and prefers to be the giver to have credit, respect and appreciation through giving. Now a problem arises and becomes intense, from mild to moderate to intense. This means a long process is over, givers have become many and receivers become less and less, day by day! Givers are so-called because they make a big show of giving to get back more than was given! So, a new way of calculation and calculators came into use: how to get back more, becomes the problem. Various ways and means at different levels and for different purposes become available for each giver who is not a receiver on one side, and planning and programming takes place to get it back from the other side without becoming a receiver, without having any obligation from the other, ready to oblige the other!

From the clash and conflict point of view, the SUN as giver has given light, heat, and rays; the object took objection and the first clash diverted the flow and brought change in the movement. Movement remains and is going on non-stop; at the same time, clash has produced many changes in direction (of the movement). It looks like play and becomes a game of entertainment, and the one who moves along with the movement, and swims along with the flow, starts losing interest in the clash again and again. So, that one tries to avoid particular clashes, which become the cause of diversion and distraction from own path of movement. The need and necessity to move freely becomes more and more. The shortage of a receiver on one side, while on the other side plenty of givers, has changed the ratio and proportion, has changed the picture of transaction, which means its nature and type has also changed.

Wilful giver and forceful receiver, because willingness is not there to receive, then how does it work?

The receiver has received without willingness and wilful effort, without paying any more attention and interest in receiving; then easy to forget, or not to remember, that which was received, as awareness was low on that side of receiving because at the same time, the other position of awareness, attention, and interest etc., was engaged, involved, invested, so that proportion is and was changed. This has indicated that there is a shifting of the central, middle line where the 'I' has to be, the line of position shifts because the value system is changed along with change in the role, that is not to be in the provided role, not to accept the role of receiver and to become the giver to get it back! This means that to take through choice, with own selection, taking the advantage and benefit from the situation and circumstances, becomes normal and natural. Originality and uniqueness starts developing from within, just like a sprout from that seed of the ego! The opportunity is to take and remain free from any obligation that is binding: as it is provided so it is taken! When it is offered it is taken to oblige the provider who has offered, to bring happiness, to please, to satisfy, to show courtesy and manners, and so forth. Justification, clarification and explanation are given to prove that the one who has taken has carried out the correct and right action.

Why was it provided? Why was it offered?

It is necessary to become curious to know the purpose behind something, and to know is one thing and to do, to act accordingly, is another. That action has a dual purpose to provide and offer, so that freedom (along with the right) remains safe to decide and to select and then to act and do accordingly. It's freedom to make a mis-take, because what to take and what not to take, how can it be known? How can avoidance and resistance or control for taking or not taking be decided? Once it is taken, then how can the responsibilities and related results be avoided?

Very often, fear develops because of those mistakes and their results, they start shaking confidence and creating doubt in one's own decision-making and selection. When an evaluation and judgement, or a conclusion, was made and subsequently a decision was taken and action and performance was carried out by that doer, 'I', the ego, to show, superiority was demonstrate. That was given the go-ahead only to prove and establish all the time that it's not the same because of fluctuating attention, diverted concentration, and movement transfer to automatic by the controller of the movement. The habit of neglecting and ignoring had a chance to interfere, apparently, and the movement remains continuous, on-going until the monitor, regulator and governor of the movement (the doer, the 'I', the ego) becomes suddenly aware of the strange, uncommon, unnatural response, reaction, or result. In comparison with the previous one, correct and right type, this becomes incorrect, becomes a wrong one!

Who got it? Who has received it? Who has confirmed it and recognized it as a mistake? The one who was taking liberties and advantage has taken that which has not to be taken, so the expression happened by mistake! It was not the intention, idea, thought or plan by the doer!

A sudden interruption, welcomed without any resistance, as a swinging rope used by the doer to shift the focus of attention and awareness from the ongoing movement transferring to automatic, and starts thinking, analysing, doing side by side, as per habit, to save time and do two things at once! Can speaking and eating take place at the same time?

Means two opposite natures of movement (activity) create the clash, accident, surprise happening, result, response or reaction from the other side of the doer. Now the doer is the receiver and has received the surprise gift that was given, provided, offered by nature through that sudden interruption. The engagement and involvement with keeping aside the on-going movement and picking up, selecting, welcoming that which has not to be, not to do, creates the question, what to do?

The blame game starts. Who is responsible for this wrong and improper movement has to be punished. How can a brain, brain centre and its function receive punishment? Naturally, no one can reach directly to that as there is no direct access, so the covering part (obeying part) which is directly engaged and involved with those parts get the punishment, or reward. The 'I', the ego, the self knows how to disconnect, how to and when to withdraw, so what it is, is there and it is not there, that 'I', ego, self. So the punished is the one who gets the punishment; the one who managed and arranged not to get or have it, then how can that punishment work as a reforming system, how can it give reformation, re-correction, re-structuring to the movement done by the doer?

What has to be corrected? Where is correction needed (required)? To the movement, or to who is doing the movement, or to the source and support given to the movement, or to those or this or that who played the role of an observer, witness, and seer of the movement? Or the given punishment is accepted? Or does it mean that the change will appear as per the expectation of the giver of that punishment?

So, not to give or get the punishment but only the reward is the solution. Or nothing, neither punishment nor reward, neither hell nor heaven, experience neither stick nor carrot. Because of equality, equanimity, and fraternity, this situation should not occur, or it is a necessary occurrence as a tool to achieve all these three terms in experience in daily life!

From the two different opposite movement's point of view, the sun has the strongest one-sided movement from the centre to the periphery. Just as waves and tides of the ocean move toward the land, encroaching it and then giving it up! Two directions, out-going and incoming or returning; with a fixed point of reference (the land) it's possible to notice that waves are coming in and going back! As expansion and contraction, as inhalation and exhalation, as in and out, from the fixed point it's possible to find out the type and nature of the movement. Here, in the case of the SUN, it's the waves and tides of the fire and flames, their light and rays. How long do they have to travel in SPACE? Is it until they meet with an object? This does not mean the object is the periphery because the object can have a periphery of its own cover, and this has to be discovered. Who can stop the SUN'S penetrating rays?

The strength and power of the penetrator can decide, so who can be the penetrator, the reflected rays or the generated one?

Is the light created by the SUN or the moon, or by a torch, the streets, houses and places: is it generated by the same or similar one or by a different one?

Movement is one constant from the SUN'S point of view; the Sun, being the constant (permanent) ultimate cause for different movement, change of movement is because of the change in pressure (more or less, high or low), and this becomes the cause of the movement: positive or negative etc., are expressions for concern or related fields.

The remaining two are affected by that movement. Even their existence is because of that out going movement! Although this movement is one-sided from the SUN'S point of view, from that side and centre it is out-going, expulsion, to bring out, to throw out, to vomit out, to move away, to move out of the centre, to get out, to extend, extension, to expand, to move towards the periphery. This all happens because of the constant heat, increase in temperature, increase in demand, increase in consumption, increase in pressure, constant interaction and reaction, increase of burning and bursting, constant pushing of the waves of the tides, of the rays, from one side to the other side.

Who just gives and gives and doesn't care to get anything back (either more or less or the same)? That giver is HAPPY, while others become HAPPY and unhappy.

The remaining two try to be the same as the SUN! They started and became very happy, and are proud, have pride of that giving movement. Happiness appears and as it appears so it disappears. This is also a part of the movement of that ENERGY.

Who plays the role of the giver? For how long and how much? Not for a long time, and not without any limit. This means that the time factor and continuity, the flow, of the movement is a ONE CONSTANT MOVEMENT. It is not possible to be two because of its own cover, generating capacity and ability, it becomes the cause of break-up, separation, dis-continuation, the on-going movement, action and interaction.

How long, and how much? As long as enthusiasm, endurance and stamina is there, for that much time it can continue, then the return journey, reverse order, withdrawing, shrinking, contracting, coming back, going back to the normal, natural position (state), and this two-way movement is accepted, and appreciated. This has done the testing and tasting; this has established the record and has also broken the established record! To establish a new record, the old is broken, is given up, thrown away, put out on the street, and because the new has to establish itself, it needs a place, so space should be made available to the new one, either by throwing out and removing or restoring and changing part by part.

When to do what? To movement from movement, and with movement by movement, for MOVEMENT, ENERGY is a constant moving principle. Accident is the meeting-point of two types of Energy.

Who has done the preparation for that happening? Was it was well planned, or was the plan and programme made by the other Energy as a revenge or punishment, or to teach a lesson? The arrangement, management and organisation and all the set-up is made (created) as if it is natural and it is not natural! To cross the movement or to move in parallel is an option or choice the result is according to the nature or type of movement – to oppose, to go move against, is also a variety. To jump out of line, to go away from the point, to run away, to throw out, etc., needs specific purpose and movement to achieve the decided goal or target. Success and failure, happiness and unhappiness, is the result from the result of the result! Two occur at the same time from one event, one happening!

What can one expect? What can one avoid and prevent? What is not connected and related to expectation and can be avoided and prevented?

Water is given to the plant by the gardener as a duty or right or hobby? To give the response to the given water by the gardener to the plant, is it optional or compulsory? How much and in which way? Can the plant decide, or can the gardener suggest, request, order, or dictate? Ultimately, who is the GARDENER? And where is that Garden? Which type of plants are in the garden?

Plants belong to the garden! Garden belongs to the GARDENER! Although all are trees and plants, altogether they are not considered as a forest of trees! So, they are the trees and they are not the trees; they are the TREES of the garden and they are not the trees of the forest!

How can an apple say whether it is sweet or sour? Why is this needed to be known when it is not told or taught? Why do that which is forbidden or restricted? It's natural not to accept and not to agree on one side, and side-by-side to listen to the other, to have a second opinion, to be safe and secure, to please others, to satisfy others and (as a listener) why not listen along with the many other sounds to a specific sound.

Listening is an action done by a listener without knowing, thinking or imagining the result of that action of listening. That's why there are the expressions of ear-poisoning, brain-washing, etc., because the listener was clever but later on becomes an idiot through the act of listening! This means that one doesn't know when to listen, what to listen to, and to whom to listen!

There is movement in that action, and there is not a movement of that action for that action! That is why the result is that one is happy while the other one becomes angry. Two results of and from one movement, after another movement! One becomes the cause, and the other the effect or the result! So, it is a movement of one and it is not a movement of the other one!

How can Energy be without movement? How can two be free from movement? Which movement needs to be done? How can Energy change its own state of being or status? How can it be SPACE? Who are there, two?

Two are different, different. Here, the remaining two are single, alone, one, mono, individual, a living being, and the other one is the Earth. Two are single, alone, one, mono living being having flame and fire within, with a cover having layers and levels within, up to the flame or fire!

An individual as a living being exists and survives for a certain time duration (measure) known as age and that period is known as the lifetime of that living being. This time period for both is the same, except that one is doing the measuring work for or of the other!

Earth, as a living being, doesn't bother about the measurement of time, it has its own standard constant movement which is measured by the other one, who is also a living being and single, alone, one and mono. Today, that mono is living like a monk living a mundane life (single and alone) with many others living similarly: similar to and also different and also opposite to each other. There are many, many living alone, one, mono, on one side and, on the other side, one Earth with its one moon, along with the other planets and their moons, in SPACE.

In this way, two are two different connecting points to the SUN, which is ONE. Both have a living body, the difference between the two living bodies is their size, time duration and movement. An individual's living body is known as Earth, while Earth is a LIVING BODY. The individual has a flame within, while Earth has a fire within.

An individual's living body is made up from many, many living cells. How many living cells are included in all different forms of the Earth as a living body? The life of a single cell is not the life of a living body. Cells change many times, new ones come and old ones go, and in this cycle life is sustained and maintained or transformed, growth and other developments take place and the experience of health is also a part of this transformation process.

As the movement of Earth affects the life of an individual, similarly the lifestyle of the individual is affecting the Earth. One individual can become more and more aware of the surroundings and space and show superiority among other individuals. It is possible and it is not possible, because how can an individual show superiority to THAT SUPERIOR?

In this context, it is not possible; what is possible that much is done, what is done, that has given the result. Achievements are the best, and the best has the other side, that is the worst! The best is happiness and the worst is unhappiness! How can this be avoided and prevented? The good has bad, and from the good comes better and best; this constant progress (movement) has brought that position of the best. Automatically, bad becomes the worst as the other side – because of relativity this happens.

Earth is loyal and dedicated with full devotion without bothering to take care of unnecessary points. It keeps moving on its axis as well as moving around the SUN while all the time maintaining relation and relativity; it is an example for the living being (the single individual) of how to be and how to move?

How is the individual moving and living? What is at the centre in the life of an individual? What is at the centre in the life of Earth? How are both living and moving around the centre? Who is taking care of whom?

Earth has seen many changes; it is a seer, a witness and an observer of living beings, of life and interpersonal relations and bindings and many other movements, while the individual has history and geography! How old is it?

The Space around the individual is polluted but it was not polluted in the past. All is done for a better future! From the viewpoint of the past, the today time period is future and at that time the past was present! So, where is that better future?

Inventions, investigations and research start from a strong base, and although they believe and accept relativity, they neglect and ignore to consider the other side – that's why the expression remains throughout all time: a better future, which is yet to come! This means that what is yet to come and not yet come is future! Is it not a carrot without a stick, or later on it will be! No, it is only in the present where more can be done, more can be run and more can be had. More use of a stick is here so that the individual constantly moves towards the carrot, which always (all the time) appears fresh, attractive and easy to catch, to reach, just nearby, not very far away.

As Earth is moving in one direction, the individual is moving like the Earth in a better way in many directions and gets lost and confused! When and where to go and what to do? Who can tell? And that one (the inner one) who says to act belongs to whom? Intellect is the property of ENERGY. Who is the listener?

Energy's role is a doer; ready to do and get more is the plan of the doer. Each doer is busily engaged in obtaining the maximum, to earn and to save the maximum, so how do they do their transactions, exchanges: very tactfully, skilfully, giving on one side while taking more on the other side at the same time. Both sides are busy; the candle is burning at both ends and burns out quickly. In the same way, Energy is entangled with each other in such a way that it has to wait and watch for the receiver, to search for the receiver, to wait for the client, to wait for the student, and to wait for the patient. So, why not create more, produce more, transfer more, convert more, to that type of individual who can play multiple roles, one after the other: will the last one be the patient role? Healthy is transformed into unhealthy in a very healthy conversion-visioning way because taker becomes a recognized term, rather than receiver! Taken is allowed and permitted and, for that to occur, rules and regulations, do's and don'ts, discipline, conduct and manners, morals and ethics, and so forth, came into existence.

Taken becomes more and more polished and refined day-by-day in terms of how to take and how not to take and avoid. Now, taker appears and looks like a receiver, an honest receiver who is receiving without any effort, and is obliging the giver. What is given is received by that receiver who was originally the taker, who has changed the original status from receiver to taker, and afterwards using own skill and efficiency, again becomes the receiver. So this receiver and that receiver means that the receiver is a receiver and is not a receiver because the not-receiver is a taker who knows how to take and is not ready to receive!

Why this change?

Energy prefers to take as it's easier to take than to receive because to receive, Energy has to wait, to have patience, to accept that it can be (may be) given or not, more or less or the exact amount by the giver who is also Energy. Energy knows how the play of Energy works and how to be energetic or dull while the Energies are playing with each other. Either playing any game or fighting an opponent is a must, it's needed or required. Two opponents blocking and smashing each other, then there is winning and defeat, success and failure, finally the result of the result: one is happy and the other one is unhappy.

Why does this happen? It's because of the two! Where are they, in or out or at both places? While two Energies role-play and entangle with each other with their fixed motives and purpose to fulfil, both are ready to compromise, to adjust, to give up, and to say let go about any dispute or non-agreeable point. Both know they depend on each other even though they both try to show (demonstrate) that they can live without each other: "I can live without you"! "I can be without you"! "If you leave I don't mind", "I don't care".

Threats in a mild, moderate or intense way are made by Energy to Energy. A threat is perceived by Energy of and from Energy. Energy knows how to give punishment and take revenge! Why to give and why to take is very clear to Energy, to the 'I', to the ego! There is a progression in the movement from taking: it can be snatching, grabbing or catching, which shows variety in the movement, the purpose or intention behind it, the use of power and strength through aggression along with its motor, anger, helping it to move towards the object.

A simple game to play, two have decided to give and not to receive, then how can they both give to each other? Both are extending an arm to give and to take the object in question, then what happens? What will happen? What is possible to happen?

First, a question related to the present time period: without playing in that particular way, it is difficult to know what happened! It has to be experienced by the two, by both of them. Next, what will happen, and what is possible to happen? These two questions are related to the future and either can be answered with the help of thinking or imagination! Happening is going to happen. What has to happen, that will happen, and what will not happen, that will not happen! Here comes the pre-decided decision. The computer operator has the answer or result, or the programmer has the answer or result already inside the programme! From the operator's point of view, the operator has got the answer or result but from the programmer's point of view, the Operator's effort has not got the answer or result because it was already inside, kept there by the other ONE! Even after that, the credit goes to the operator of the programme because payment was made for that, or even was paid in advance!

So, from the giver and job-giver point of view, the ultimate giver is ONE, the others are related. This related one changed the status of being and for that there is no difficulty. The difficulty and problem at the time occurs when two similar ones are meeting and are trying to complete an exchange (transaction), and as they know each other's way of being and working from their own reference points, both are able to check and evaluate each other's policy and strategy to avoid an open clash. This avoiding (preventing) technique or method for an open clash has developed the closed and cold clash or meeting so as to achieve the object in a more skilful way, with friendly gestures and appearance to fulfil that specific motive. So, moving further both at the same time to give and take gives rise to an open clash! To avoid this, delaying the decision and movement can or cannot be a solution?

Examine the position of the hand in both of them. What is the position of both hands during giving and taking? The extended arms are not going to meet each other; the total of four arms, two from each side are in which position? Both (two) are ready to give and take, is it possible for them? What happens? Who will withdraw? Who will change their role? Who will prefer to be the receiver first and then the giver? Who will be ready to have the obligation first, then the chance to oblige? Who is ready for binding first or? These are subtle questions, the balance of the plus and minus and the consequential effects and results. Is it not a game of chess which the two are playing all the time in all places, these two ENERGIES, meaning that the two belong to ONE ENERGY.

Here, the MOTHER PLAYS A ROLE of INDIFFERENCE, because each child is ready to prove that their own standpoint is right and correct, and not the other one! Each has their own standpoint; they are not standing at one point as their position is different, their place is different. This different is because of the difference in their position of standing, so naturally their perception is different although the object is one and the same, common for all of them! Here, fear is the controlling factor: the ego, the 'I', is ready to give the understanding rather than to get the understanding. It is not ready to change its own position due to the fear of losing its own existence, like a shadow has fear that the light will go off! So, emergency lighting is there all the time, kept ready, to think very easily, practically, "You do it, it's your duty and responsibility, I am busy"!

Knowing that to maintain, to sustain, means to enrol the name as a candidate in the race of life (marathon)! It's already done from birth onwards; those who know, they don't want to reach the finishing line because their position is in a natural way, an opposite position such as East and West, North and South. Different places on the Earth have a big time and temperature difference. Sunrise is sunrise, and sunset is sunset for all of them. There is a time difference because the places are different and the viewpoint is different, the sun is on the other side and the positions of the individuals who perceive, experience and communicate to each other are different. The sun is a common point of observation for all, and they report their observations of sunrise and sunset to others who are at different places.

Is it possible to imagine, to think, to visualize, what the other one has experienced and communicated? In-between their viewpoints there are forests, mountains, deserts, oceans, big buildings of a metro city! How big is the sky? How big is the space around the observer? Won't it create doubt, lack of trust? Won't it work with one's own belief and faith system? When the SUN is common for all and no one has to pay a bill or a tax for sunlight, everyone has equal right, or will everyone have more or less right and responsibility? Duty and right are two, are dual sides of one coin (service). How is it possible that one has more duty so the other one has more right, or on the contrary, one has more right so the other one has more duty?

For as long as Energy is considered as two separate Energies, the problem of polarization remains because being two separate entities means either me and you, or you and me, not ours and theirs? We is the plural of 'I', and the collection of all single ones, alone, mono, uno, 'I', all together gives formation to the we, and now the we is mobilized! A group is formed with a small thin dividing line! Later on, for the break-up, a hairline crack becomes responsible, not the thin dividing line! Where does that we exist? They exist? It's an established fact that we and they exist! Is it a TRUTH? It is true and not a TRUTH? This is the basis of our belief system, taking it for granted!

The collection of all the 'I's' says we are one. So one, single, mono, uno, and the plural of one is we! Now, instead of me, my and mine, it becomes ours. In this transformation, 'I' becomes we, one becomes one again, and mine becomes ours. Also, alone becomes together and expresses "we are together and one". Later on, in that one and oneness, that single identity (individuality) becomes separate from the unity and one-ness, developing alone and loneliness. Inside that we as a one and all together having one-ness inside, that happening has happened – why?

From the split the seed has sprouted; a gap appears and then the distance increases with the difference and becomes separate and different from that formation of we! As one has formed another one, a bigger one, the bigger one all together has formed the biggest one. According to them, it is the biggest one. In this way, the formation of Energy's form, functions, systems, and structures, and their results and effects start appearing and coming into existence one by one. This is with different terminology to make it easier to communicate on one side, but on the other side that easy becomes difficult and creates confusion rather than clarity!

Because simple is kept for the simpleton and complex becomes available to the clever one who adopts the complex style through creating a big complex out and in, the outer one is cleaner and clearer than the inner one has to be. This is because what has to be developed and cultivated inside is developed and cultivated outside. As a law of action (movement), one is gone, shifted outside and the outer one who has to be outside, enters automatically inside: as the peddle of a bicycle, one side going up and the other side coming down at the same time and speed. The more it's pushed down to move further, the other comes up to go down, to push down. This becomes a normal, natural and instinctive action to achieve speed in the movement, to be ahead, early, to reach before the other and grab the opportunity, to achieve that which makes it superior and the best, better than the others.

For this, very cleverly, one remains inside and does the formation of the other one, the bigger one! A piece of cake is always smaller than the open mouth, or the big fish eats the small fish. In this way, two are co-related and together to have more and more benefit and advantage.

As per need and necessity, the form changes formation. It looks like destruction and demolition of the old structure and systems but, side-by-side, a new structure and systems start appearing and functioning. This also creates the division of two, the old and the new. Either a connection with the old or the new will take place and, accordingly, the result will be available.

Invention and new terms on the basis of the old terms is taken for granted as the base-line to start, and from generation to generation this base-line is shifting: just as snow melts and glaciers change their shape and move because of global arming. Heat was necessary for survival in cold countries, and to remain cool in warmer countries the heat is reduced inside and expelled outside. Systems start working and functioning to have more, create more, use more, consume more, more and more, until finally what has to happen happens: it started from big, then bigger and biggest, largest, scale measuring started. At the global level, world level, universal level, international level, multinational level, this means that thinking started, actions and programmes were prepared by that single, one, alone, uno, mono, individual, who had a limited time and energy to do, to carry on the activity.

Everyone has freedom to choose, to select a path; at the same time, expectations and norms, conditions and structures are to be kept, prepared and arranged in such a way that it can be managed with freedom. This means related freedom, so it is a freedom and it is not a freedom. First, to accept the object as it is, as what appears without any connection and relation in trying to know that object as it is, from the object point of view. Next, the viewpoint is changed, which in turn changes the total picture (perception) of the object. The two points of view, then a middle point, a point in-between, a position to remain indifferent, and then to move further; that is the job, work, task, of ENERGY. To be on the extreme side is basic nature, and easy; the job, the task, is more difficult. The connection, the union, the joining, the combining, once it is carried out, the OK signal is given, then control goes to the connection, union, joint, or combination.

The one who has done so, the doer, is not important because the doer has given the OK signal, handed it over to the other side and became free to contemplate, ponder and to meditate, to establish the oneness, in ONE! Or is it two, or is it the other side of the One! Hand it over and become free to grab, snatch, to take the next object of achievement! The doer becomes in charge of the process or function or any activity, then that is handed over to another doer, so then there is the expression: charge is handed over and charge is received or taken. This is the same in a relay race where the runner runs the fixed pre-decided distance; how that distance is to be covered and the time taken is also important to compare with the others, then start and finish, and again start and finish by the other one. That's why work in the workplace remains the same, while the worker comes and goes, and changes duty as the shift is finished. In the case of the single, independent, free and alone doer (worker), the decision is made about how much time to give to work!

Is it enough? If more is needed, then what is the purpose, less than what, a moderate time period, how can it be decided? The result of the result is because of the action; the action is because of the decision by the doer, by the worker. The doer (worker) is not happy, and is happy: two states of being of the one doer because of that decision, so it was the decision and it was not the decision from the correct and right, and wrong point of view. It was not the right or correct decision by the doer, by the worker.

Why has this happened? How has this happened? The doer has no time to analyse, done is done and gone is gone. Then, how can one learn from the past? Looking forward towards the next achievement is necessary in order to move further, so the motor cannot be dull or idle; the active becomes over-active or hyper-active because when the speed is increased, slowly and gradually, acclimatization takes place. This is similar to mountaineers who stay at base camp to prepare for the next hard and rough climb. Here it is a mountaineer, there it is a worker, doer, the 'I', the ego – the Energy is the same!

On one side is alone, single and free; on the other side, that alone is together! How? Single is double! How? Free is bound! How? Because the three are not ABSOLUTE, they are related, they have relativity and relation. Freedom is on one side, on the other side having an insisting nature, having compulsiveness, having compulsive obsessiveness. Is it not binding?

It is the nature of ENERGY to be free to move in any place or space at any time: this is a strong demand on

Energy. No restriction, no doubt, no questions and queries, no inquiry. Energy as a whole is working in all its own parts as forms, functions, structures and systems. Energy is demanding, and the supplier is Energy! To have it, posses it, and to be the owner and author, proprietor is the goal or aim of Energy.

How can ENERGY be happy with THE ONE and search for the other one, and another one, and one more, again and again? That is the nature of ENERGY. Being in ONE SPACE, moving in ONE SPACE, TOGETHER all the time with SPACE, Energy tries to imitate and copy and becomes quasi-steady because it is Energy not SPACE!

Although ENERGY'S role and form prefers to be alone, it somehow wants to achieve that state of being while at the same time has a fear of decision-making, or not knowing how to decide, or how to be together for a long time without breaking-up and separation; all this is difficult work! Being independent has the same problem, because everything is difficult to produce, to create, to have and so to be dependent becomes necessary, even becoming interdependent rather than independent! In the same way, free has chaos to face and has to select properly to be at peace instead of peace having pieces of peace at each interval or pause between two hectic events; free has a tendency to insist, to make something compulsory: there is too much discipline to achieve not only one goal, but one after the other and many more, much more! Then how is it free?

Free means no one should object, prevent, ask, have doubt, restrict, control, bind, etc., etc. The decision to do, to move, to act, to achieve must be made unconditionally!

To play all the different roles, Energy has to be more active than passive. The passive side is the other side of active, just as minus is the other side of plus, and the receiver is the other side of the giver. ENERGY has two sides: ready to leave, and ready to reach the other place! It has to move without fear concerning the place it is leaving, while it must confront fear, worry and anxiety before leaving that place or position. That's why (or therefore?) Energy tries to be sure at each move, each step, each action, and that develops doubt and checking, which later on crosses the limit and starts appearing as too much precaution, too many doubts checking the move to be 100% fool-proof. Is it possible?

To maintain what is acquired because it is not inborn needs more effort, more strength and power, skill and efficiency. Naturally, to receive as a passive receiver and be at the mercy of the other ENERGY'S role, to have obligation again, is not good. It's better to give; giver is higher and upper while receiver is lower, and again to have double profit, that single having a double, or dual policy, for one! So, the receiver becomes the taker and taker prefers to grab, to snatch, to catch, to grasp, and to take rather than receive! It is for the other that they should be passive, that they should have patience, that they should learn to accept and appreciate and recognize me! These are unspoken, unwritten, unmentioned conditions, it's a language of the deaf and dumb and, for that, the other should be blind! Being in that state, it is expected to know, evaluate and conclude what is in-front at that time and at that place from all different viewpoints, to summarise, to abstract, and to hand it over to the next to carry on, continue, with that provided work or task, to be 'A live', HAPPILY and BLISSFULLY!

In which way is it possible:

1. As SPACE?
2. As an ENERGY?
3. As Both?

From the point of view of family terms, the relation and relativity of that Energy and Space, why not start with a question – Who are you, and, where are you?

Are you alone or together?
Are you single or double?
Are you free or bound?
Which position are you in?

See, it's easy to ask the question – Why? Three letters in that one word, which takes very little time to pronounce but how effective it is! In avoidance, it's better to ask why, and then the other has to explain, and again at the end ask why, again explanation and classification, then much more time is spent and finally, in exasperation, it is given up, so it is avoided with the best tool, the question Why. Honestly, simply, truthfully ask who is ready and eager to do, to act, to work; the condition is without knowing in detail how I can do, act or work? Is it not the best avoiding mechanism, those who are not ready, never eager, to know how to do, to act, to work because no interest is given, yet having an interest to pick up according to their plan and programme from here and there, and in that movement or moment need to ask 'why' rather than 'how'.

Once 'how' is asked, then responsibility comes, there is expectation to face, success and failure will be there, and pain and pleasure, happiness or unhappiness will come. Now it's not the time to do, to act, to work, it's not for me and my future or to the related one, why should 'I' spend my time and energy on the other. So it started with 'why', rather than 'how'!

How powerful and effective this small three letter word 'why' is. To find out, just play a game for half a day or a few hours saying or asking 'why' and speaking nothing other than this word 'why'. In each response and reaction, just utter "why?" and see what happens. Is it possible or not? Play the game as a test, to examine the effect of 'why': say, "why don't we play"! Energy is a player, it says, "either you play with me or I will play with you!" Further it says, "either you eat me or I will eat you"!

The challenge is given and accepted by Energy to Energy. Exchange is a transaction, market is a known and familiar term where two are together, profit is expected and loss is happening. Honesty is the appearance and cheating is taken for granted! Both ends of Energy are plus, it's where no minus exists! Never and nowhere does the minus appear. One negative, the passive, is not possible to be below the zero line, therefore it's better to draw a zero line down below 'me', so all the time "I am" is above the zero line, in plus, in positive and active or inactive!

"Who is you?" is the wrong question to ask. The question needs to be "Who are you?" The meaning is changed, 'you' is treated and considered as a single 'I', so who is 'I' or who is you! A mistake it is and a mistake it is not because 'you' never exists, it's the existence of 'I' in the form of 'you'! That's why 'you' is singular and it's plural, is also 'you'! 'You is you', not 'I', 'me, 'my' and 'mine', it is you and yours! It's not my problem, it's your problem! Why should 'I' interfere in your private personal problem! It's yours! Do you need help? Don't hesitate to ask! OK, "I am ready, I will wait", and both are waiting and waiting with patience, certain that help will come! Too much patience is a test for the other side; the other side justifying, "let me see and check how much tolerance there is along with patience for my negligence and for ignoring them, and not for taking care whether there is acceptance of it all or not. Let me see and check!" Then, the other who waits and awaits becomes impatient and, seeing the possibility of very soon becoming a patient says, "I had better decide and act so that I can see if my act is appreciated by the other one or not!"

Out of many different possibilities is it possible to say, to imagine, to think about one possibility? By this is meant that one has many possible connections, responses, reactions; one-to-one is alright, but do you know from which one it will be one-to-one? How will the other remaining other one be? Will they keep quiet, or will they ask for pay, to give a little share, to keep quiet, and not to be the cause of noise pollution! To settle quietly, to accept, becomes compulsory when and where the options are many!

Then, who can manage freely and independently? Was it given or was it taken by the receiver? The receiver has taken that which the giver has given in order to co-operate, to remain quiet. It was for the one-to-one to become one, to establish oneness that all the effort was made by the one-to-one', and that happening was observed as one by many observers, witnessed by many, seen by the seers!

Nature starts blooming as spring comes! This means changes take place because of the movement of Earth as a living body and also the living body as Earth moved; what was already in the ground, came out and starts blooming! Now a time comes to give a name, to know by a specific term for communication, to that manifestation which was unmanifest from one point of view while, from the other point of view, even that unmanifest was manifest before! So both views exist together: it is and it is not, or it was and it was not unmanifest!

To answer that question, Who are you? The answer will be 'I am', or 'I am this or that'. 'I am' will be an incomplete answer, although it is complete, it is incomplete in providing further information. So, to complete that answer one has to express "I am this or that" in relation to the expression, 'this or that' by that you as an 'I'!

So, where does 'you' exist? It's easy to become this or that identity for the 'I' through showing one's own relation, or connection, with this or that. How many times a day does one become this or that? As and when the relativity changes, or connectivity changes, relation and connection change; in that much time the change takes place automatically in the expression of that 'I' or 'you'. This expression is kept on auto-system; it has no option for manual change because to err is human! It is taken for granted that the expression of 'I' or you (as I am this or that) must be in that particular relation or connection, fitting to it, not here and there, but 'somehow I am this or that'.

The next simple question is, where are you? "I am here, I am here at this place!" Will you be there or move? "No, I will move from here." With confidence that 'I' says, "I will move from here", then only I can come back here again, or move from here again, not to come back again. Two ways to move away; it is the nature of Energy to move with or without any reason or opportunity. So, that 'I' as a representative of Energy and also of Space, half and half, becomes confused to decide when to do what.

"I am here", means where? Total address, position on the map, along with a full description of locality and surroundings, in an exact way, is so that the other one can reach there and meet. A detailed description, map drawing, everything is given to meet outside, not inside! These two have tried many times to meet here and there, in and out, with this and that reason, either up or down, in front or behind, from left or right side, with all variations, these two have tried to become one, without giving up their own identity: it is mine, through this they know me, how can 'I' give up my identity?

The highly insignificant point zero one percent (0.01%) becomes highly significant for the separation. Because from that hairline crack, the break-up starts, the gap increases, distance increases, and every moment becomes contrary and opposite. Now, who are they? They are not mine, I don't belong to them, I don't know who they are, maybe we must have met somewhere on this planet! Relation and relativity changed becoming free from it because what to forget is remembered very often: Energy is that principle which occupies Space! It is very difficult for Space to get rid of it. Acceptance, patience and tolerance are the best solutions for that!

So, Space allows and permits Energy to move, and it moves away by its own movement! It can't possess and be there without moving, it's not possible. Ask the earth how to apply the break! The path is Space, on that path Earth as a body has difficulty in stopping, while the body as an Earth has no difficulty in stopping on the path, while moving on the path, on the Earth. That's why there is the question: who are you? When asked to show your identity, immediately the identity card is shown, a plastic card. "Where are you?" "I am here on this card, in the photo, it is me!"

This means that there are two backgrounds, one inside the photo, and the other for the photo itself, the plastic card! And everyone believes that because it is a common and an established fact that you are a plastic card! A photo on the card! a well-certified photo and card, that you are? They first look at the photo then at you! Both should match. If it is not a match it is not allowed and there is no permission to move further from here, so go back, the return journey becomes necessary because the photo does not match.

How is it possible to give proof that 'I am that' and 'I am not this and that'? Where is the evidence?

Show it and go move further or back to the starting point. To avoid (prevent) this return journey, what to do? How to make that matrix match? Even the matchmaker and fixer has difficulty here, not there, because here it is different from there! Energy prefers to be here and is not ready to go there, and later on it finds itself there, not here, from here it has gone! It has moved! It is a moving principle, which has a wish and desire to stop! Many times it expresses and demonstrates like a magician that it has stopped, that it looks like it's stopped. It is free from stop! Stop is death; when there is no stopping, there is no death!

Then who dies very often?

SPACE?

How is it possible?

So, think about death, who dies and who remains?

Relatives remain!

Relation remembered!

Relativity renewed!

Now, here it is not, there it is gone!

Meaning it has come from there, so gone back?

Why live?

First ask why leave?

Ask again?

Live to leave is the answer?

Live to leave can be the answer. It means learning and knowing the importance of giving up (renouncing) and living without ownership, to lose or give up all claims on possessions, not to be the proprietor, and to live without any relation with relatives. The close relative (relation) is of or between children and parents, father and mother, between husband and wife. Inside the family itself its members say that the blood relation is thicker than water; blue blood classifies a regal state (standard) of living by that particular being.

All relations are based on the relation of child and mother and father. Before that, the mother and father have lived as husband and wife or without that status! Before that, both of them belonged to a family, belonged to their mother and father and lived as a child of them. To travel back, to go back to before, then to say previous, then long ago, and then to say a number of years as a time period from one present back to the start from that ENERGY is a reverse journey, the gear has to be changed, to stop and to accept that one as an Ultimate Cause. Otherwise it becomes non-stop search of the cause of the cause!

So the SUN is accepted as Ultimate cause for the time being. There may be a cause of the cause, to be proved, established and accepted and to be equally familiar as the SUN to make the place an altar. The cause and source of the living body as the Earth and Earth as a living body is the SUN. These two, who belong to different families as a child of their mother and father, after growing up and in due course of time separate into a single, uno, one, 'I'. Then, to overcome that aloneness, each decide to join together (to be together) to become one and experience again the oneness, the goal. After the goal, how many times does the football player change the ball, the shoes, the ground, and the team uniform?

Now, the status has changed. Before that 'I' belonged to the family as a child, and now have a child and family belonging to both of them, proud to become a father and mother! Now that child belongs to them, as they belonged to their father and mother! Memories from the past suddenly become active from the sleeping state, and each starts giving guidance for do's and don'ts. Possession of the child through childhood is not possible after it becomes an adult. As a husband and wife (two) know that one is their child, they become happy; there is no need to introduce them to their child because they knew about the child since the date and time of its birth, that is its manifestation, first appearance in the external world. In that relation, context, that manifestation is from the state of the unmanifest in relation to the external world, and what is appearing will disappear also! The mother and father both know they are husband and wife, they are not the father and mother for each other, there is not that relationship connection between them. So, the two are together as a father and mother because they are husband and wife (or in another state of relationship)!

Through the eyes of the child, one is mother and the other is father because mother has introduced the father as father to the child and, from that time onward, the innocent child has accepted that one as father, and starts calling him papa (daddy)! Before this sound of papa, ma and mama was there and the child knew the mama (mummy) before birth when they were together as one! That's why it is said that 'life is a journey from the womb to the tomb'. Being in the womb of the mother and then after the birth, to that child that one is a mama, a mother and not a mother! After giving birth, that one becomes a mother; later on the father introduces another one as a stepmother, and in the new family photo, the child introduces her as wife of the father (or father's wife) just preferring to avoid saying stepmother!

Again, while moving and travelling, that child has to meet the mother of a specific group activity, a Mother's Group and through that, all are recognized as a 'mother' and start to be called mother! The child knows only the biological mama (mother), but then comes across the terms Mother Nature and Mother Earth and further, as an object of worship, the Divine Mother! Now ask to that child, how many mothers do you have? Biological one, and the others are and are not!

Biologically, to become a mother or father is one, and to develop motherhood and to develop fatherhood in one is a more difficult task. A father can take care of a child like a mother, utilizing his own motherhood quality from within; in the same way, a mother can play the role of a father, utilizing her fatherhood quality from within.

All the details along with a photo and bio-matrix are called an identity card, which is certified and verified by the other authority. There, all personal information is given, even the names of the father and mother or guardian. So, one has two connections (relations), a two-way approach, two sides are working as one, becoming one, to give one result; while that one has a choice (option) to use, to utilise the two together or one by one. And that one has no choice, no option, to utilize one by one because the two are working together and impossible to separate! They have to work together as one. Any one of the two not working, not functioning well (properly) in the right way, harms the totality!

This totality is inside as well as outside from many different points of view. Being with two, two different types show they are two, and they are not two because they can't work separately, they are one, which appears as two.

What are you? What are you to become? Two separate entities, or two as a one? One pair is the ideal for the other, or are both the pair and that one separate? This means double dual-ness, or duality, or a variation in becoming a pair! Are their combinations and connections pre-decided or decided by the doer? The doer is a child, and the child adult (kidult) is a mixture of the two in one, so one knows when to use what? What is right and proper according to the other (opposite one) the two similar ones agree and the two opposite ones disagree! Now these two are similar, so they agree on certain points, and they are opposite, so they disagree also on certain points. This is a mixture of the two in one, a combination of two together as one.

Even though the two opposites disagree on one side, on the other side they agree to connect, just as the enemy of the enemy becomes a friend to fight with the other. This shows a two-way development, two-way progress or growth, because of the connection of the two opposites on one side, on the other side they are similar, so both are ready to go together for development and progress, growth on the positive side, which is same as the negative side. Which one is more, or will be more, is difficult to predict, judge or to say because of the good and evil forces behind the formation of the different forms. To increase strength and the power to dominate, to rule, and to control, for that, exchange and transactions at various levels are constantly going on between these two sides: changing, transforming and converting, is going on by the two opposite ENDS of ENERGY! It keeps busy and excited, it even creates the problem and solves it too, it becomes the cause of death and birth, sorrow and joy.

They say, 'think before you act'. What about reflex action? It is that reflex action which doesn't require thinking! In day-to-day life, responses are given as reflex actions without thinking, spontaneously! It is because of auto-control over the responses, disconnection of thinking, where the 'I' is absent, busy with another interesting item! So, it is attended to and listened to, and it is not. ENERGY on one side, Energy on the other side, and Energy is caught (or become a place) in-between. Three are the Energy, it is a one-in-three and the three are one, the communication term and their effect (result) enables the choice of selection and preference.

As a principle, ENERGY is ONE in all: as a child, child-adult, adult, older and elder, then sick and ill, then birth and death, then the observer-seer-witness in all these stages of life and what is happening in it. Is it necessary to go through all the stages and phases of life to know about life? Be the observer-seer-witness and collect all the vital points from each different form, each different form of ENERGY. Then decide when to do what? How much and in which way?

Are you ready to give the benefit of your action to others? If not, why not? It can be best. One can start to give before getting! To push the 'no' onto the other side is the art, to give 'no' is the art, what is the science behind that art?

Both are on each side as together, yet they appear separate to prove their own utility in the area of the other. As an Energy, sneaking and infiltrating, they do to get the place, to occupy the place, to capture and acquire the place that is SPACE, also in the opposite term. That's why place in the Space and Space as a place inside appear different from each other. Who exists on that place or Space? SUN, EARTH, other planets and stars, known and unknown or yet to know, all are existing on, in or at that place as a SPACE.

SPACE is totally different and opposite without opposing and without opposition to ENERGY. Both are together, one without the other is not possible, although it is accepted that one without a second is the ABSOLUTE, the ULTIMATE, and then, to give the answer to this creation and existence, that ABSOLUTE ONE becomes a related ONE, a connected ONE. When it becomes one, it means it gets the form and principle form, then the two unite together and become one at the level of the PRINCIPLE, known by a popular, colloquial term. Two principles start (begin) from the zero, on one side is plus and on the other side minus. They both come outside and zero appears, becomes zero, now plus and minus, or minus and plus together help to achieve the zero, also said as zero-plus or zero-minus and zero-as-zero: three types of zero! The balance of the balance sheet shows as plus or minus. That has acquired zero identity! Either in plus or in minus!

This acquired identity is on one side, on the other side it is provided identity! Identity is Identity and once it is recognized and gets acceptance and appreciation, then communication between the two starts on the basis of that identified identity. The limit, the boundary, the boarder line is taken for granted and the two talk freely, both enjoying their freedom to talk, to discuss. It becomes a very open discussion between them, which remains very closed at the same time!

In a limited way, considering it to be maximum freedom, construction is carried out by that architect of life known as 'I', the ego. Energy is made to look, to appear unique, exclusive, higher, and superior to the others! Either one, single, alone or more than one, single, alone are busily engaged (involved) in these types of constructions for their concerned related body. This body and that body both are different from each other. Although both have a common term to know, to express, to say, to communicate, what is meant by the body is taken for granted, even they (two or one) says, “I know the meaning of the body”, “I know what is the body”, and also, “I know I am not the body”!

That’s why the question: Who are you? Are you with the body, or are you without the body? If you are not the body then these questions arise:

Why do you have to be with the body?
Why is the body provided to you?
Or have you selected the body?
Or have you selected the parents?
Or have you selected the time, date and place of birth, and death?
Or do know how it will end, what time, date and place, and in which way?
Or are you comfortable inside the body?
Or have you torture in the body?
Or have you treated the body for your pleasure and fun as an instrument, a tool?
Or are you looking outside from your body, or are you looking at your body from the outside?
Or where is your position inside the body? Your address?
Or are you receiving from the body? Are you giving to the body?
Or who is controlling and listening to whom?
Or how are you not the body? In which way are you not the body? Can you explain?
Or what you are not, is all that body? Then what remains?
Or when the body has gone to the cemetery, funeral, then where are you? In which form?
Or are you not in any form, is it not a formless form?
Or who has identified with the other: have you with the body, or has the body with you?
Or is it not a oneness on the identity card where both of you exist on that plastic card?
Or is it possible for the eyes to see the eyes? Or to see and recognize the other?

Or have you recognized the body?
Or how? Through contact or without contact? In which way have you recognized the body?
Or because it is through being told and by listening that you have believed the gossip is the truth?
Or first you or your body?
Or it is not gossip? How? How are you, or are you not the body?
Or at last you are your body?
Or are you belonging to the body?
Or does the body belong to you?
Or what belongs to the body belongs to you? Is yours?

Or when you are not the body, when you are not belonging to the body, when the body is with you and you are not without the body:

- Then, what is produced and created by the body, through the body, is it for the body? Or for you?
- And, is it yours?
- And, is it your property?
- And, are you are the owner of it? So, you can decide to whom you will give the body or not give the body?
- How is the transaction?
- ONE who is not, why to do?

OR

- Is it not one way or the other that the body is taking care of the body?
- Gives us the body, taker is the Body, receiver is the body?

It grows, increases and decreases, expands and contracts, gives pain and pleasure, it gives identity, it gets recognition, it appears and disappears, it is composed and it decomposes, it is smallest and biggest, it has a body within, and it is inside the body!

It is not the object of worship. It is not the goal to achieve. It is a cover to the flame which has to burn and give light and warmth without shaking! It is not the cover to discover how to use properly. Cover is not clean, light is not clear outside, clarity is not there, so mistake! Fuel to the flame is not in a good quality, so it has fumes and smoke, and is harmful and unhygienic as it burns!

Notions are protected. Before that, notions were cultivated and nurtured, either raw or ripe, delivered as projected, and that projection is accepted as if it is 'mine', that mine is perceived and now rejected as it is not mine!

- Whatever is with you, is it yours?
- Does it belong to you?

It is a co-existence; to be with a science of co-existence is ecology: 'e' for existence, 'co' together, existence together, 'eco' together as friendly, not as an enemy, so eco-friendly.

- Is it only for external nature or for internal nature also?
- Is it that flow of Energy which flows and is known as a cult and becomes the culture of one and of the other?

ENERGY flows continuously, it is a one flow, with many cults and cultures coming out of it. It is nature and has Energy within; before it was forest, now it is park, garden and wildlife society! As it was a forest, so the animals have different movement cycles of wake up and sleep times.

1. Day to wake up and move,
2. Day to sleep and night to move and wake up.

In the beginning, all were considered as animal and then there was civilization: does it have civilized animals within? From the body, form and cover point of view, you are not the body, form, or cover; then you are totally, fully different.

The choice is to associate and identify or not, to connect and allow the connection to become the governor of all and to hand over (surrender) that connection for all the next happenings; this entails making a driver of the car be the owner and as an owner to sit on the back seat. The driver knows how to drive the car, while the owner knows what to use the car for? Those who know about cars are different.

The object of knowledge is the car, which is the same for the two who know; for them the known is the car, a vehicle, a body! The knowledge is different because of the difference in the position of the two who are inside the car, which is one! As a driver and as an owner, the two co-exist in it! It is very clear that the owner, and even the driver, can both say (express), "I am not the car, the body"! Both are different to the car, the vehicle, the body! The driver, one, is in relation (connection) to the car, and is known by another term, 'doer'; the driver has the freedom to drive and the owner has to decide the destination; then, according to the destination, the driver has freedom to select (choose) the direction after looking at the condition of the road.

Starting and stopping on the road is different to stopping at the final destination! It is a stop and it is not a stop, because the final destination is not yet arrived at, the car and driver have not arrived!

How big and long is the road?

How far is the destination?

Where are you on the MAP of life?

The MAP of life has one single path with many possible paths to move along! The difference between the two paths is that one is chosen first, then the movement on it starts (begins); the other one appears as a path as the vehicle moves, or the movement is done! Those who are looking for the path, for them it is difficult to move because there is no specific path on which to move: on one side, on the other side, how can freedom be used to move on this ground (area) where there is no specific path or rules and signals to move? Fear of the unknown, fear of mistakes, fear to survive and phobias, etc., arise from within, for example the car can move when the driver is not ready to move or drive!

What can the owner do? The owner is not the doer, the driver is the doer, and the car is the cover for both of them! The driver is in the state of in-between the two sides: car as the body on one side, and on the other side, the owner. The driver can stop the car. The owner can ask or order the driver to stop the car. The car can decide to stop. The three are able to stop. It's better that the driver stops. In the middle is the driver, the doer, in-between the two. It is better for the driver to know the decision and to stop as if it his own decision to stop, to make the others happy because movement has stopped for the time being! That's why it is known as a bus stop, where the passengers have to enter and get off or to wait to enter the bus! A place to wait to enter is a 'stop' for that one who moves. Energy moves constantly, it has many stops!

Energy collects, receives, takes, grabs, grasps and snatches, to give, to distribute, Energy to Energy! Stop and start or start and stop, these two opposites exist all the time that Energy exists. It's possible to prepare and create a long list of the two opposites. The opposites are made for each other to be complete and complementary; so they are opposite and they are not opposite because of their complimentary nature, quality or aspect; they are also contradictory and opposite because of their form, function and status, etc. ENERGY in this way appears as two opposite principles: plus and minus, positive and negative.

The formation and deformation and further formation with transformation of these two principles are within this process of change, development, progress, or growth. There are two principles of Energy known by different, different technical terms; the final cover, shape, layout and appearance has received the name according to the form, shape, size, and function, etc. This final cover is the outer point of view and becomes the object of perception and knowledge. It has a specific size and shape, details are available of this final cover: it is gross, solid and hard to measure, to check or verify by any tool or instrument; it is known as a body, cover, vehicle, even temple and house! It has a name that it is given by the other to know who is who, with the time, date and place of birth detail to differentiate the difference between the two; for identification and proper communication, each one has either a name or a digital number! It is finally known as (by) a character that requires a space or a place when it is written on a piece of paper or when it appears on a screen.

That Energy, as a principle, exists even now in each single, smallest unit and becomes responsible for changes within. The outer appearance has its own freedom, while the inner principles become the cause of support and binding, restriction and encouragement. A single cell or atom is behind the biggest form and shape. The form has a fixed shape and it has not a fixed shape because it changes from time to time.

Although it is made out of cells and atoms, the gross formation is different from the cells and atoms; it has its own identity and identification marks and terms. From this point of view, each one is different (opposite and similar) and has the same Energy and its principle within. According to the purpose, doing analysis and synthesis, collection and segregation, anabolism and catabolism, conclusion, stock and metabolism, will be a part of the happening which has one more term. Manifestation of the gross living formation is because of the cells, living cells and the Energy which is responsible for this formation.

Who becomes the mother of that child? That ENERGY. Who gets the credit of becoming a mother? The one who carried the child before its birth, who took care of it until the time of delivery, then labour pains, hard work, a time to separate, to dis-connect on one side, and to connect on the other side. First the pain then the pleasure, or first the pleasure then the pain!

Cell and atom is a creation, and creation becomes a creator of further creation. A living cell has a shape and not a fixed shape, it has an intelligence which differentiates between body intelligence and the intellect of the individual as an 'I', ego. That 'I' can express as "I am an Intellectual" and "I am Intelligent". To identify with the intellect is one thing, and to have intelligence which is related to the body and indicates "I have body intelligence" is another. Is it an animal instinct?

On one side, that 'I' has to use the intellect to do the work, while on the other side, that 'I' has to allow body intelligence to work for health, peace and happiness within! For that, the 'I' has to withdraw and move away so that the other can work smoothly. To remove the pressure of the presence of 'I', the ego', pressure technique (methods) can work outside, but it does not mean what can work outside can work inside! Intellect is the property of Energy, while the intelligence of a cell within a body is also related to Energy. One is stronger outside and the other one is stronger inside.

Today, the function of the intellect is becoming much more important than the function of intelligence because the intellect has invented artificial intelligence outside and become the controller, creator and manipulator of that artificial intelligence. Here, non-acceptance of the manifestation of inner body intelligence, and being subordinate to it, is not accepted by the 'I', ego: instead of working for inner intelligence, we have managed to have an artificial intelligence worker. In this way, the worker has to find a worker for its own work and then becomes a work giver: from the old expression: 'the servant becomes the master'!

Now the intellect has to work as a servant and not become a master. It is contrary and more in connection (relation) to the external or outside, or outer appearance or performance. This is done so accurately, in such a perfect way, that the photocopy becomes an original and is treated (accepted) as if it was the original, but the photocopy is many while the original is one only! That ORIGINAL ONE, as well as the copy are both kept together in one file; that file has many compartments, parts and subparts or divisions and sub-divisions. Body is a file. One side of the paper, of 'I', is the ORIGINAL printout and on the same paper is a copy of it, of that 'I's printout. Normally, there are two separate papers, the original and the copy, two papers in the external file. The internal file has economy and an economist, and is the 'I' that is ready to save and use the minimum. It is thus ready to play the role of more than ONE ORIGINAL, because it says, "I can do this and that" and "I can be here and there"; without considering the provided limit the 'I' becomes more aware about the possibility of freedom and starts planning, programming and making the policy to execute and get the expected, calculated result.

This is the most interesting process and work: doing for that doer as 'I', the ego. Many roles are attractive and interesting to play, all have a new challenge and change with exciting possibilities, etc., while the role of the ONE ORIGINAL is constantly the same without change, challenge and excitement: it's boring, monotonous, creates fatigue, becomes exhausting, gives suffocation, appears to be binding and like a prison, has no life, just to be, relatively.

How is it possible for ENERGY to be in that particular specific ROLE? It is ready and able to play one of the many roles for a while to impress the other, to give the impression 'that I am', to play that role with interest is important for that 'I'. This 'I' knows that the particular role is a role which has to be played occasionally; behind this play is the planner's plan and that 'I' has played the role of a planner and scanner.

That is Energy as 'I'; it stands in-between the two, Intellect and Intelligence. These two belong to the body as a whole. Intellect is a part, emotion is another part, two parts making one! Two are hemispheres! Two are science and art! Two are related to each other. Two are governor and monitor. Two are different to body intelligence!

Intuition is inside and that 'I' can have it: "I have intuition". Where did it come from? Intelligence can be intuitive intelligence and it is different from artificial intelligence. That 'I' connects with the intellect and becomes intellectual; when it connects with the emotions it becomes emotional; the 'I' is not the intellect or the emotion, it becomes intellectual and/or emotional but not both at the same time. Access to intelligence is all the time. Intelligence is all pervading inside up to the outer surface. Living cells are everywhere in the living body with their own intelligence that makes and keeps the body alive.

How does that 'I' decide to connect with (join) the intellect, emotion or intelligence? How much and for how long? With the help of intelligence, that 'I' expresses "that I am", but how can that 'I' express with the help of either the intellect or the emotion which are part and parcel of the body on one side and, on the other side, they provide help and support to that 'I' to express or say, "I am not the body"? Being indifferent to both, that is intelligence on one side and on the other side, the two (intellect and emotion), there is a state of in-between indifference with proper difference maintaining that 'I' can say (express), "I am not this and that" and "I am not the body".

Again a question comes (a reflection or an original): where are you? Where is your position? On which ground are you? Two can be a ground for one, whereas one cannot be on two grounds. One has to select the ground. While the ground is already provided to one, that 'I'-provided ground is a ground in-between the two: on one side, that one, 'I', single, on the other side of the ground is space – it is a GROUND of the Ground! So, it is a ground and it is not a ground to stand, to live, for that one, 'I', single.

So a question –

Where are you?
On which ground?
On Energy as a Ground?
Or SPACE as a GROUND?

Energy is a constant moving principle. It is the mother of duality and relativity, the cause of all relation, relationship and relatives, and becomes the final Ground for that one, 'I', to stand, to run a race, to achieve the fixed goal, that is also an Energy, as the runner who keeps running is also an Energy! That's why: who are you?

Are you a ground to reach?
Are you a goal to achieve?
Are you a point to start?
Are you a runner to run?
Are you a jury to judge?
Are you a spectator, the audience?

Are you a wall of the ground?
Are you a guard of the ground?
Are you the Energy to run?
Where is your position?
According to that, who are you?
How are you?

It's important to know which state you are in because of pain and pleasure, joy and sorrow. Neither/nor is one or either/or is another choice to give for the answer of the question, how are you?

As an artist, can you demonstrate anger, smiling and crying all at the same time? Have you been to that point before connecting with any one of them? Can you stop, look and move further from that point under your own steam and connect with the necessary exit to bring out the Energy flow from within; or have you missed that opportunity provided by the other; or have you just used the easy exit to bring out your Energy flow to get rid of it and be at ease and at peace? Have you achieved what you expected, or has it increased more, rather than decreased and subsided? In that case again, how are you at the end of the game, drama, show, and work?

The next question to that is: Why are you in that state, in that position of being?

It's like a pendulum all the time going tick-tock tick-tock to show the time through the position of the three hands of a watch (second, minute and hour). For a moment the three become one, the next chance is always there for the one who missed the chance (opportunity), it comes all the time that it indicates. One should not turn to look on the other side at that time, then it's possible to notice the three are one 24 times.

From out of all 24 times, how many times is it possible to notice?

Imagination, thinking and decision on one side, result on the other side, shows how the performance was! From that, it is possible to know how the decision was taken.

In which situation, circumstances, was the decision taken, and which forces and factors influenced the decision?

Who has taken the decision? Is it 'I', me and "it's my decision", or your, or our, or their decision? How many decisions and how many are the decision makers? From the Energy point of view it's ONE, and it becomes many to make (take) a decision, and each one is related, connected with the action and result, and its result! One is the out-going trend or flow of Energy, and the other is the incoming or returning flow. The result and its result is the returning or incoming flow of Energy to Energy by and through Energy. This is generally and popularly known as cycle and recycle, production and reproduction, birth and rebirth, action and reaction, and so forth.

This is a complete circle where two sides are meeting and matching. Once the circle (the round) is created and finished (completed), the space is caught in-between, or the space is also encircled and now known as outer space and inner space, with the help of that circle as the limit and boundary! Periphery is another term for it, and the centre appears, comes into existence, inside the circle known as 'I', me, my and mine and ego – ego centred inside the circle, known as egocentric, ego centred.

Who makes, takes or took the decision? This centre of the circle, what is its size, shape and known terms? Is it one or many?

It is one and many, both in different ways: one is inside the many and many are inside the One! The reference point (standpoint) makes a big difference and it becomes different for each expression. This is the ground from one point of view for Energy to evaluate from the other side, or the other way, through dereliction of one's own duty, to sustain, to maintain, what was produced, created or born. That's why negligence, avoiding and neglecting, and not taking care etc., is important to transform, to destroy or to change totally, completely from good to bad, living to dead.

This is going on in the eyes of a third person and a third person is an observer, seer or witness, and later on becomes an informer and reporter etc., who vomits the knowledge and expects others to treat and accept it as food! 'Vomit' means to bring out what was eaten before, when it becomes difficult to digest and hold or keep inside. The body intelligence decides to keep and hold it inside or to bring it outside; when it comes outside, it is 'thrown' outside, it has specific communicative terms, 'vomiting' is one of them. It is a function of ENERGY.

That 'I' has decided to know, to become curious, develop interest, finding it difficult to resist the impulses, to check, to investigate, to search, to know what it is! Then, using or taking the help of either the intellect or emotion or both, tries to find out what it actually is. Once this is known, the doer has finished the search and that 'I' becomes the knower of the Truth – it is nectar on one side, poison on the other, as one side is PERMANANT, the other side is IMPERMANANT!

When indigestible food is eaten by that 'I', the body is not ready or able to hold and keep it within. It is considered as food poisoning: to whom, on which level, in which way?

That 'I', single, one in-between the two sides has all possibilities to utilize for its own achievement as tools or instruments: the intellect and emotion on one side, and the inner body intelligence on the other side, connecting one at a time, the ground that is body intelligence, is taken for granted. Just to be indifferent, disconnected from the connection, without having any relation and relatives, then the 'I' develops freedom from relativity through lifting, detaching, separating and levitating just a little, to make it free to move away, to slip out, to fall out, to go away, to pull out, etc.

All this has to come on its own by itself without any effort, without force and pressure, just waiting and watching the smooth movement and co-operating with that function to move, without being an obstacle or creating or developing any objection to the ongoing movement of expulsion. Being ready and able to lose, not to claim it 'as mine' and to hold it back, or to give, to lose partially and not completely only part by part in instalments, one at a time, to keep others waiting and expecting the next bit.

So, my own importance is created by my own skill as if they provided it to me, 'I' am not taking it! It is and it is not true!

Is it possible for Energy to decide not to participate in activity?

One way or the other it has to participate. From a qualitative point of view it makes a difference, that difference further creates the different, different standpoints where to exchange either one's own views or material is possible. There is a big network or (knitting work) of Energy to catch the Energy, because SPACE is caught by Energy and also remains outside. The problem and difficulty is for Energy: what it has caught it cannot to lose. How? By the struggle and stress in not losing, it has to increase the grip, the space in-between goes as two parts of Energy become One; and then again it appears as two, becomes separate, with a distance.

How much should the distance be between the two points? Who can decide? Is it possible to standardize and fix? Point is one, therefore there is no question to decide about the distance. Points or more than one are different in variety at different levels; point or bubble exists. Point to connect or bubble to burst, it's a two-way development of one Energy. The mixture in two ways gives the appearance of a third one, creates a third one; two have their own identity (quality) mixed with each other. The identity and quality which comes out of the mixture is the third one, is different from the two. To illustrate this, it can also be described as green is a mixture of blue and yellow. When it is green, then it is not blue and yellow, and when it is blue and yellow, then it is not green! The two united become green (lively and fresh); then separation starts, green doesn't remain as green! It is a message from nature!

Water is a liquid and juice is a liquid. Easily available to all living beings is water; thirst shows dryness and due to increase of heat there is a shortage of water; water is provided and the thirst is quenched. Water has three states: liquid, solid, and vapour. Gaseous water is used for different purposes. Many chemical compositions are made by mixing two substances, often one of those is water! Inside and outside water is everywhere and recycling takes place with the help of the SUN. In one form of vapour (gaseous), it goes up vertically and becomes clouds; these formations move higher and horizontally, thus there is transportation of water. Then back to the land (Earth) it falls as rain and snow, then the collection of each drop and finally it becomes a river flowing from higher to lower towards the ocean. The taste is different, one is salty the other is sweet, both are water having fish in them as a habitant. Change or empty the water and the fish will die. The fish's habit is to survive in that particular condition of water and to swim; the water is important, the quality they don't care about.

In just the same manner of a fish there is a pig: they are what they eat as food and they become the food. What does this mean? Who is eating whom? Energy is consuming Energy. How can SPACE consume SPACE?

SPACE as a place is the provider of all, and Energy – as a consumer, eater and user – uses its own Energy form, function, system and structure to have the result and effect that is Energy. As a mixture of the two (union and combination) it gives rise to a third, which is different from the two and gets a new term for communication. In the same way, instead of repeating the same term with or without another it's better to use (give, repeat) a new fresh term for expression and communication to avoid confusion. For example, 'dark' = absence of light, 'cold' = absence of heat – because the presence is stronger and prominent (dominant) for a certain time period and the source also exists permanently then, first is heat, then cold as an absence of heat. With regards to light, it is known as moonlight from the opposite point of view, the new term (second term) is the same as presence and absence of the two separate sets of terms, for the opposites and opposite of the opposite. This means that black as the opposite and white is the opposite of the opposite, two opposite (contradictory and complementary) sets or pairs of terms, such as hot and cold, black and white, male and female, man and woman, Adam and Eve, plus and minus, positive and negative. Like this there are many terms to indicate (highlight and show) opposite forms, functions, structures, locations and sides, etc. Each other has increased the number of specific technical and non-technical terms for communication.

Again the need to clarify the neutral, middle, centre, zero and moderate from their concerned and related fields although their meaning is different on one side and they are different on the other side. From the utility point of view, new terms are coined from research and new inventions to inform others that a new term, not an existing one, is used. This shows there is a repetition and there is not a repetition of the term for the object, while for certain objects it is permitted and allowed in order to show respect, regard and honour, so the name is given to that object which is acceptable by all.

In this way, objects and their related terms are established. The object is destroyed, demolished and no longer remaining in the present, yet the given term remains. So, the term becomes immortal, while the object is mortal. The image is carried forward by the term, its message and meaning is conveyed by the term, yet it is with or without specific purpose that the term is used.

How can the proper meaning, connection, and a reference to context for that used term be found? This shows that one term may have many possible meanings. One term or word with only one meaning, without giving more possible meanings, is not possible for the dictionary. This means that ONE has many possible ways, means and paths to find out about it!

To know the ONE means that deduction, minus, elimination is to be done and what remains is that ONE. The cutter is cutting the object to cut, to break, to divide, to separate, etc. The process of cutting, breaking, dividing, separating, etc., is going on continuously to all available objects. Cutt'er', break'er', divid'er', separat'er', etc., – 'er' remains from the outside, external point of view, while there are many inner, internal points of view. Many are in ONE, and ONE has played many roles.

Energy is the cutter, in an energetic way the cutting is done, Energy's form is the object to cut. First, the object is cut. Next, the cutting is stopped. Next, the cutter Remains! So, who has cut what? How? How long? Why? Is it possible for SPACE:

- To cut SPACE? As an object to cut?
- Next cutting is stopped, in which way?
- Next cutter and SPACE remain.

Remains! How is this possible? SPACE is a PLACE to cut, the object to cut, by the cutter, ENERGY. That's why the questions: Who are you, where are you, and on which ground are you?

There are many terms coined by countless experts, scientists and technicians, academics and educationalists, each having their own terminology to differentiate subtle differences so that they become different from each other. The terms are maintained and sustained on one side and, on the other side, they try to become one by piling up one by one, the many become one after joining and uniting with each other. Luckily individuals have many bones and not just one, which are joined by joints and so are free to work apart, or together.

How much is the distance between the two bones? Do they use their freedom to control and regulate? Does it mean that the brain is the controller (regulator) partially or centrally? How many parts and centres are there for management? There are many centres, not only one can do the management. Why are co-ordination and co-operation needed? How is it externally?

Many are working uniformly; uniformity of many creates the image as if it is one, then investigation makes it clear that one is made by many. This is on one side, and on the other side, the other ONE without a second, or any one more as an OPPOSITE of the OPPOSITE – SPACE, and ENERGY is opposite to SPACE.

To change they try, from the result they know it is not a change, it's a repetition of the same!

To transcend they try, due to fear they stop transformation!

To levitate they try, as energy leaves the matter or mass!

To separate they try, unable to remain alone, together they become again.

To become SPACE, ENERGY has to try, unavailability of a converter, Energy has done the conversion, so Energy looks like space! Is considered as a quasi-steady state!

To become a FATHER, ENERGY has tried! MOTHER is ENERGY, fatherhood is developed within.

To become the ABSOLUTE ONE, MANY have tried! As a result they become one or remain one! The process is different to become one and to remain one!

To fill up the whole space, Energy has tried becoming bigger and smaller, Energy has tried!

Whole having a hole within where many bigger and smaller are moving inside. The child has to try to know more about the FATHER. Mother Energy has given a clue through light and sound that the child has a father. The child is searching for a FATHER. One is related, the other ONE IS ABSOLUTE! The related one (father) belongs to Energy. The ABSOLUTE ONE (FATHER) is opposite to Energy, is SPACE! The related one (father) is a form of energy and principle also as a plus.

ABSOLUTE ONE (FATHER) has a PLACE that is SPACE. This is an opposite term of Energy Mother, which is a related one.

Mother is an Energy and child is a creation, an individual among others, is one of them.

SUN is a LUMINOUS mass, Mother and Father of the many children (planets), Earth is one of the children among the other children.

Father and mother are two separate individuals through the eyes of a child. The two have their own mother and father as separate individuals with their own family set-up and structure, each one separately connected (related to) the SUN, a luminous mass. How many rays has the SUN? How many peaks do the flames have?

Who can shift that bright SPOT on a Dark Black Back Ground! Is it possible to be without a back or background? It is taken for granted. No need to elaborate and discuss and talk about it. 'I', we, you, they, all know about it.

That back and background are also related and Absolute. Related is opposite to the Absolute and, in the same way, Absolute is opposite to the related. Absolute is opposite and related is opposite of the opposite!

Now, the related one (made by many) is the opposite one, like an image reflection or a shadow; this opposite one is the other side, that is the ABSOLUTE ONE. That is the EXTREME POINT, ONLY is that, only is opposite also! Mixing up the terms, using the terms in a loose way to convey the message, the loose way gives possibilities to connect to the other way or side, and the message is changed because of the change in context within. The terms which are used for the ABSOLUTE, when used for other than the ABSOLUTE, that is related thus it changes the status and no longer remains the Absolute. Later on this creates confusion, disappointment or becomes the cause of dispute and quarrel because of the insistence on using the wrong use to prove it is the proper and right use.

How is it possible that one side of the related is Absolute and the other side of it is not Absolute?

It means that what is considered and taken for granted as Absolute becomes related with developing connectivity and relativity with others.

Then, how can it be ABSOLUTE? Or it is related having relativity, relation and relatives! The background is opposite and should be in contrast so that the contrast can help to find out, distinguish, further select and pick up so the choice becomes easy. How can white ink written on white paper be read?

Similar goes with similar, matching becomes one and appears as one giving the possibility of writing again over those white letters with a contrasting colour; the existing ground, the background, now becomes two backgrounds. It's a printing technology! Without paper it is not possible to write. Transparent paper and transparent ink creates invisible writing on visible paper! The writer is different from the paper, then the paper is destroyed and writer has gone away and written remains inside the memory. This memory of the other continues the writing of the Human Script, again and again, and it is re-written until the EDITOR gives the OK! We, as editors take care of the readers and, from their point of view, ask the writer (author) to rewrite until it is approved by the Editor! Who cares for THAT EDITOR? The writer knows how to avoid the One and to go to the other one, the related one! To publish the writing is important for the writer because it increases the list of titles; although it is ONE, many titles are needed to explain, to clarify, and to know that ONE!

Who can provide a photograph without a background? The picture is more attractive because of the contrast inside! Knowledge about the contrast is important to create a beautiful picture! The shadow is a contrast to the light, and the light is a background to see, to look, to know the shadow.

What can you do to fix your shadow and for how long? So long as light is there the shadow will also be there, so is it possible to be free from the shadow? Dark is the shadow and its density is different from light. Although it is a light it's a different light because it is not SUN Light!

How far is it possible to have equality of light? To find an object in darkness a light is used and the other use of light is to remove darkness so that to find out becomes easy, to distinguish becomes easy. Ignorance is the obstacle on the path of the inner light!

Use of a colourful light reflector by the projector to focus on various objects is the first action, then the rejection and non-acceptance of that colourful object as it is projected by and through the projector. First it was two colours (black and white), now many colours have brought the life inside. Two becomes boring, while many are attractive and contrast is the cause. To illuminate the colourful light a reflector is used and the object becomes colourful and attractive in that light; attraction to that object, and temptation from within, ignores the fact that there is a change in the colour of the light. Avoiding this and starting to appreciate the beauty of the colourful object as if it is recognized as original and natural, there is readiness to accept the next step to that object. Up to this point, for acceptance, preparation was completed, then a sudden change in the flow has brought rejection (non-acceptance) to that which has to be accepted because it is considered an offer to that which is provided to be with, that is a body! Is it not necessary to know what is necessary, and to consider what is not to be considered? Illusion is the result of this colourful illumination.

The source of life is the intake or output or putout? Is it two simultaneously, or only one? Today, output is becoming more important; to prove one has to do more, output is the result, which gives the recognition, and for that, input is taken for granted! More and more stress, emphasis and insistence for a specific output has disturbed the other cyclical flow. Later on, this disturbance is converted into dis-ease, or the disturbance becomes the converter of the ease into disease! After converting the ease into disease, the conversion process remains and continues until the living body is converted into a dead body! Thus, the converted ease into dis-ease becomes the converter again to do the conversion to carry on that act, that process, that work endlessly! Because of relativity and duality, it is possible to change the role to a different field with reason behind the move.

The living body becomes the dead-body. What happened to that 'I' who was living inside? The absence is recognized as death! The last is out and the first is in. In-between the first and last, in and out, many ins and outs or outs and ins, a fearless confidence develops and there is certainty to be back again, to return and to be in a gain, to get out! The living place becomes familiar and well known, well acquainted and comfortable to be inside that place as a body, which is actually living in SPACE as a PLACE and considering place as a space in a contrary way.

That's why there is the expression: how can I share my space? That one has occupied my space! That one is taking away my space! Energy is complaining. Energy is responding. SPACE utters, it is your problem, it's not my problem! The echo is picked up by Energy, to repeat again! Energy is the speaker and the listener is Energy! Speakers are two, while the listener is one and has to do accordingly. Two voices, two opposite guidance, which one is correct?

Doubt occurs frequently, doubt on the doubt is very rare! Energy has two sides: plus and minus, positive and negative, good and evil. Representatives of both sides are different, are opposite to each other; although they are not the same they try to be similar, try to look as if they are the same – that is also done by Energy! Cheater is Energy, cheating is done in an energetic way, and cheated by Energy is also Energy because Energy is ultimate, and ultimately Energy is either in parts or as a whole ENERGY! It is not SPACE! It is different, opposite to ENERGY. As MOTHER ENERGY can play a role of a Mother and Father at one level, at another level Motherhood and Fatherhood together are of and from that Energy. Beyond that, to transcend and not transform any further, a point comes and from that point to transcend needs the ability to jump, to cross the limit and get lost, merge, lose identity and identification, separation, death, so to speak.

FATHER is the opposite term of MOTHER; SPACE is the opposite Term of ENERGY. MOTHER ENERGY AND FATHER SPACE! This FATHER SPACE can also play the role of MOTHER and on that level can show Motherhood or MOTHER HOOD.

On one side is SPACE without particles, the DARK BLACK BACKGROUND; on the other side is SPACE with particles. From the SPACE point of view it is two, although it is ONE without the second SPACE! There is no other SPACE beyond or transcending.

The conclusion is that the ULIMATE IS SPACE, ULTIMATELY IT IS SPACE. This is taken for granted for to go beyond (out of it) is not possible. This conclusion gives the freedom to move and also the possibilities to increase or decrease mobility. To stop is an illusion; it's a relative term, which looks as if it's a steady state, a quasi-steady state, because the constant moving principle is ENERGY. To be without movement (stopped) is a paradox, it's cheating and only looks like (seems to be). From the relativity point of view, it is possible to express that it seems to have stopped, it looks like it's stopped and that there is no movement. Continuing ENERGY means no death. As a STOP on that level, death is separation, going away, transcending, jumping out, etc.

As an opposite term to distinguish (specify) the OPPOSITE ONE, the use of the term FATHER for SPACE is given by scholars, learned wise persons, or individuals. The pair of two opposite terms is popular and accepted by all. Similarly, opposite of daughter is son! Daughter is a smaller unit in relation to the mother, while son is a smaller unit in relation to the father. On one side is FATHER and SON while, on the other side, MOTHER and daughter. SON is more specific, different and is also opposite to the normal day-to-day son. From the family term, it is well established and popular, accepted and known by all, and it is taken for granted that they know very well what it means by son!

On one side similar, on the other side different; similar from the term point of view, while different from the freedom to select, to choose point of view. All concerned are related means to fulfil the purpose in the best way, that it looks as if similar, as one of them and one among them, so that they have a chance (opportunity) to observe, to be a witness and to test, also to verify, to check, to re-establish own faith, belief and trust in another way, that is on the basis of their own personal observation and experiences, which differs from each other. This one is popular as an Incarnation, SON, who is different from normal individuals. They are also son and daughter who are going to be a father and mother; the change of role is from being a son and daughter to being a mother and father, having their own son and daughter. So, it means becoming a father and mother from the state of being a son and daughter. So, two are son, similar and different. These are the best use of popular and colloquial terms to communicate that ABSOLUTE PRINCIPLE. It is clear and it is not clear from the other point of view, and this unclear becomes the cause of argument and justification, explanation and dialogue and negotiations!

FATHER IS FATHER and SON is SON, then where is the question about one's self (Who am I?) because the individual is neither FATHER NOR SON and yet is a father and son! Two together! This state of being is also explained by using the term opposite of unholy, that is 'holy', and by the opposite of the living body, that is a dead body. That PRINCIPLE which is responsible for keeping the body alive, that PRINCIPLE of Existence is now absent, gone, expelled and the living body becomes a dead body, not that one who lives inside the body!

When there is a separation, divorce or break up, the two are with a distance, and the oneness which was established is finished. The cause behind this event is desire, expectations and ego! To hold together and not to give up until it breaks is the plan (idea) because it is necessary to do this, to achieve that! There is a very clear intention (purpose) for both parties, so they both agree to break that knot and to be separate, single and alone, again!

In the same way, this related connection is to the existential principle. Holy and sacred go together as does obsession with the idea of hygiene and a hygienic approach to maintain and to sustain health, which is the other side of happiness. Health and happiness go together; then a question: is healthy happy? Happy can be or may be healthy, but desire, expectation and ambition to become more and more happy is the cause of becoming unhealthy on the other side. Even after that, desire, expectation and ambition remains stronger on one side, the other side is weaker and unhealthy. That 'I', ego, keeps the flame of desire, expectation and ambition burning without accepting the condition of the living body, rejecting and refusing even to recognize the state of that living body; there are no negatives, only positives, toward that desire, expectation and ambition.

How is it possible?

Now a choice (option): before leaving finally and going away from the body, is that bunch of desires, expectations and ambitions left with the body, or is that bunch which belongs to me, my and mine carried forward?

Not ready to be given up.

Not able to forgive, so to forget also becomes difficult.

This bunch, is it holy and sacred? Is it possible and good to say that desire, expectations and ambitions are holy, or that 'I', ego is holy, or that the living or dead body is holy? HOLY and HOLINESS belong to that Absolute ONE.

SPACE became for ENERGY and the term 'Divine Mother' has been used, or a related term 'good and evil' Energy! First the guest appearance, then the guest becomes the host developing possession and becoming the owner, thus changing the status of being that guest in this world. It came from outside as an astral light, and instead of remaining as a guest, this guest became the host and invited others!

Does the world really belong to this single individual? Through a conversion mechanism, the guest has converted its own status and become the host, a surrogate mother! That individual one – basically originally a GUEST, which is the opposite term of host (HOST) – is related and the other one is Absolute.

The womb is a space and a place, the cover is the body; when that cover is discovered, then SPACE appears as BODY AND WOMB together, and from there the process of delivery starts. Contractions are the cause of movement until delivery is over, finished, completed. Relatively it is and it is not complete, finished and over because it is endless. How can 'something' endless and infinite be complete, finished and over?

It is possible to use these terms in connection and relation: so it is, and it is not! Because of the WOMB EFFECT and then growth and delivery from it, this functional aspect of SPACE has the opposite of the FATHER term 'MOTHER', that is from the functional point of view.

SPACE is SPACE,
SPACE IS FATHER,
SPACE IS MOTHER.

Changing the viewpoint produces two opposite TERMS to ONE! That's why life is said to be 'a journey from the womb to the tomb'! This is a journey which begins from the womb: an individual has arrived there as a GUEST and later on becomes a host.

Is that individual really a host?
Then why has the host gone?
Why has the host had to leave to go away?

It's an Energy. It is a different, different role of Energy. It came as an astral light from space that is Astral, and that is a holy place, Space. Now, the guest becomes the host and afterwards the GHOST. The first letter of the word guest 'g' and host come together, two statuses. The possessiveness of desire, expectation and ambition remains even after leaving the living body, and as soon as it leaves, it becomes dead: it's a happening, a result of separation. Death and Dead are the terms given to that end as The End: The host becomes the ghost! A body as a place and space to be inside is not there anymore, the one which was composed has now started the process to become decomposed. This process started in the absence of that existential principle, or the absence of that guest who had to be inside for a time being with a specific task, or a purpose. That's why this type of question arises and is asked, "Why am I here?"

Even the arrogant ask their parents, "Why have you called me here? You are not taking care of me, not paying attention to me", and that one becomes an attention-seeker ready to enter into the trap of that one who pays attention more and more! On one side, that one is not ready to pay attention and, on the other side, becomes ready to pay. What is the need behind this?

The seeker inside starts seeking attention and becomes fixed like a fish which caught the hook, and credit goes to the fisherman: that fisherman caught the fish. Yes, it is and it is not caught by the fisherman; because of the wrong use of its own freedom, it becomes the cause of the mistake, and that mistake again becomes the cause of the credit! Negativity turned into the positive! Unhappy on one side, other side happy (fish and fisherman), and because of the fish that man becomes a fisherman. Professional terms came into existence and use, becoming very common and general, taken for granted. As the word 'fisherman' is pronounced a total picture appears and there is no need to explain what 'fisherman' means: to avoid unnecessary explanation, to save time and to be to the point, taking something for granted becomes necessary.

Similarly, ghost is without a body. That individual with name and form living inside the body now it is without the body! The phases of development: first the guest as a being, then becomes the host, then without the body to become a ghost. Between the two terms, guest and ghost, comes the living body and afterwards there comes a dead body, and death is declared as birth was declared!

Normally (generally) the use of a filter is to purify, it's known as a purifier and purification is the process. Peace and happiness is the result of the result. The living body is just like a two-way filter, so it should be clean and clear from two ways, out to in and from in to out. Ultimately, it is a final out from in because 'It' came from OUT. OUT is SPACE, and from there 'It' came as an astral light, or Holy Breath, which started the function, activated the system and took care of the structure to maintain the form and appearance, to get the result and its results, just as each vehicle has its own driver, each house has its own owner, each temple has its own deity. This means that many separate ones with a distinct difference came into existence, and it is possible to distinguish, compare and evaluate them.

This is done by ENERGY in SPACE. It is done from the ultimate point of view and from the relativity point of view: each one has their own standpoint. The many have to stand separate, their viewpoint becomes separate and, at one time, opposite and complimentary also! This is because they are many and separate yet having the same outer breath inside each one. PURE it was, impure it becomes, as that breath goes out to come back again! One breath is not life, or enough for life, which is a long time period; that's why again and again there is respiration, inhaling and exhaling to keep the body alive. The inner one who came inside is responsible for taking care and to continue the respiration that is very simple but difficult sometimes!

That inner one is the guest appearance in that body, taking charge later on and becomes in charge of that body! Utilizing its own strength and power, it increases the list of achievements, improves the standard of living and projects a better image to impress the other; all is done on an external level in a beautiful way, arrangement and management was completed successfully. There can be a failure on the other side to continue respiration: oxygen is in the air but not able to be taken inside (brought inside) with the act of inhalation.

That inner one lived independently without allowing the other to do on one side, so that inner one has not been in the role of receiver and the binding of obligation couldn't bind because the receiver was the taker and knew very well how to take and not to receive unnecessarily! That inner one is now not able to take oxygen from the air, which before was very easily taken and taken for granted that there would not be any difficulty to take oxygen in and to bring out carbon dioxide. On the basis of this, the most necessary movements, which are directly related to breathing and respiration, were neglected and ignored. By ignoring and neglecting this most necessary movement, it is not possible to take care of the many external out-going movements which were most important to enable achievements. That's why it was taken for granted that the respiration movement is not my responsibility, not my job, work or task, as this task belongs to my body and my body knows how to inhale and exhale!

To know and to do accordingly, both are two sides of one coin. To do accordingly requires strength, it needs effort including awareness, attention and alertness for the movements, because there are a number of movements one after the other along with breathing and respiration that are used for other purposes and their fulfilment, and these movements are continuously going on. Naturally, the co-ordinator, the 'I', the ego, gives increasingly greater importance and emphasis to external achievements, the outer level development, so that co-ordinator, 'I', ego just allows the body to do the movement for inhalation and exhalation, thinking: "you do your work and 'I' will do mine"! The ego, 'I', co-ordinator of all the different movements is the manager also, and knows that without demand there is no supply. To increase own importance, demand is increased and supply reduced, even creating shortage and scarcity. The mother manager frequently makes the child cry, giving the reason and justification that the crying increases and strengthens lung function and capacity, which was why attention was not paid and care not taken.

The correct and right from one side is wrong and incorrect on the other side. In the case of a child or a worker, anger, agitation, irritation and revolt appear slowly as mild, moderate to intense; in the same way, the child or worker is the body and by getting this typical treatment then, similarly, the same type of symptoms start appearing, manifesting from the state of the unmanifest. This makes that ego, 'I', now become aware (conscious) of problems related to health! The technique, the method of dereliction of the work of taking care properly, no more or no less was the cause of a strong demand by one's own body. To be the immediate supplier (provider) without cutting any item from the requisition slip or demand is not in the habit of the ego, the manager, CEO, of the body! While carbon dioxide is not getting out, toxins and impurities increase and the other one, the fresh one, has to wait outside. That others have to wait outside is also enjoyed by the 'I', ego; now the enjoyer becomes the sufferer, the side is changed, the role and status is reversed and healthiness becomes un-healthiness.

From the movement point of view, more and more push and force is required to activate the other, but how can the extra force and pressure be generated when the upper limit, breaking or bursting point has been reached? It becomes a boarder-line-case. Desire, expectation, ambitions and the planned programmes related to it remain half fulfilled!

The host was to leave the place (SPACE) from within the body; normally the host does not leave and get out, it's the guest who has to get out, to leave. That guest has identified forcefully with the activities and movements of the host, lived like a host, and now the movement procedure shows that the host has to leave, to get out, because it is a copy and not the original! Leaving the body has to be completed skilfully as nothing can be taken (carried) away by the guest. The manifest items remain behind, but is it possible to carry away the unmanifest stock of desire, expectation and ambition? As it occurs, the host is not able to leave the stock, is not able to wait until it manifests, and has to go out, to leave the body 'in the middle' so to speak, and doesn't even know how to be free from this unmanifest stock or whether it is 'carried forward'.

So struggling, managing, pushing to stay while also getting rid of the stock at the end of that time period was observed by the other as hopeless! Wait and watch the struggle 'to be or not to be'. The giver gives and the receiver is not there, while the taker has no strength to take, and for receiving there is no readiness or preparedness because of the on-going struggle inside, that "Who are you which is going to push me out of my body"?

When body intelligence has decided to close down the show and close the theatre, what can the actor do? The actor was the guest artist. As the street lamp needs a post or pole, as a flame needs cotton thread and wax together for a candle (or a cotton wick and oil to burn together in a pot), in the same way, that holy breath or astral light-body (a composition) is provided to carry out the work. A living body becomes a dead body, The functional aspect is the stopping of that ENERGY. Death is declared of that holy breath, astral light, who lived inside the body with a specific name and form.

Then, who becomes the ghost? That host who carried away the stock of desire along with the plan and programme as an imprint or impression was the guest. That is why 'g' indicates the previous title of host as GHOST, who is not free from the desires on one side and, on the other side, becomes free from the body. Now, without the living body, like the house owner searching for a rented house or accommodation, who is it that can provide it for a paying guest?

ENERGY is searching for a living place to carry on the plan and programme and that place as a space should be covered, encircled: the space within and not outside, not an open space without the cover of a body, is useful to that ENERGY. Now this is free and not free ENERGY because of both past impressions and no cover (living body) as a place (space) to live.

SPACE is a PLACE where the instrument is kept and it has occupied the SPACE and PLACE as a body. It can be either very small or very big as size and numbers are not important for SPACE where there is no problem of accommodation. ENERGY is inside the OPEN SPACE and ENERGY is inside the CLOSED SPACE and ENERGY is inside the 'more closed space' which is closed by forms of ENERGY. And that becomes the shape of the space according to the form, name or term, even the number, which is given to it. Each individual is digitalized and now known by a bio-matrix with certain digits: a group of digits for the country, then specific area, then place or person from bigger and broader, general and common to a very specific and particular, two extreme points covered by the bridge of digits. On one side, there are many specific and particular groups of digits, on the other side, they are all connected with one country code, and different countries with their country code in one list, an international collection (list).

There can be a two-way connection of many and one. Many are connected with each other and although they are at a distance from each other, they remain connected and in contact through communication, transportation and travelling. Many are one becoming and belonging to each other, they are not remaining separated and, as they are together in this way, they have to be separate from this so-called togetherness and oneness. On one side they know why they have to be together and not to be separate, so they make an effort to achieve it as they know that being together is important; however, they don't know how important it is to be separate from the togetherness (oneness)! To know on the basis of information, and taking for granted that the source of the information is genuine and valid, there is no need to check and test. Trust and faith, and believing that the provider (informer of the information) will not cheat, means there is an expectation to be honest and honesty from the other side!

What about one's own side? Because of that own side there is expectation from the other side, now both are expecting honesty from each other, and they are honest relatively! This 'honest relatively' is accepted by both sides, and so there is no need to mention honesty because it is included in that relativity: it is and it is not honest!

This type of honesty and honest information is knowingly accepted because it is coming from honest, so it becomes honest information. Honesty from both the sides is taken for granted! So, no doubt, in acceptance of that information and with confidence, it becomes ready to pass on or be used. Honest information can be moved on further in two ways: as it is it is passed onto the other or it is used for a specific purpose. The utilization has given the result, and the result of the result is joy or sadness, happiness or unhappiness.

Who is wrong? Is it the doer? No, the doer is right, best and perfect. Then what is wrong? The Information? No, it is honest, and the source is honest, so how can it be wrong? The two are not wrong, which means this side is not wrong, it's the other side that's wrong! What is or which one is the other side?

Other than the two, the third one is on the other side; this one does not belong to the two, when the two are not wrong this one can be wrong, and how it can be wrong is possible to know, to find out, to investigate and to prove with evidence! This has given rise to argument, explanation, justification and classification to prove it is and it is not wrong! Relatively, both are right and both are wrong. ENERGY is ONE in both of them, so ONE has two sides which are opposite and this opposite is in the other, not in 'me'! While 'I' and you or you and 'I' (me) exist, two are existing, we and they become one with the opposition inside, as 'I' and you or you and 'I' (me)!

Either they know ENERGY is ONE, and even after that, they try to show, to prove wrong and right, or that they don't know ENERGY is ONE, and because of that they try to show, to prove wrong and right! How can it be proved that they don't know ENERGY is ONE, that ULTIMATELY it is ENERGY, or to consider that they know very well that ENERGY IS ONE and ULTIMATE and UTLIMATELY IT IS ENERGY?

Why do they have to prove this? What will be achieved? How can ONE ENERGY prove that its own side is better than the other side? So, one has two sides: which side is better? How can 'one' decide or find out? Is it because of the two sides that there is one side, or is it because of one side that there are two sides?

From one's point of view, these are the two sides: with which side to connect, is it either/or both the sides equally? From the sides point of view, the two are different and opposite, connected and one; oneness is established with two complementary opposites. So, that one belongs to which side? Is it more, less or equally? Are you ENERGY or SPACE? How can you say? To prove this one has to do more? How can SPACE do more?

Energy can do more, it's possible, so Energy can prove 'I' am the one who is here and there, inside this and that and although 'I' am 'ONE', 'I' am also many. SPACE is SPACE, a non-moving principle. So, Energy has to carry space to give form and shape to SPACE. Energy gets the form and the shape first and then SPACE gets that form and shape inside and it becomes those together as if one, not two! It is the need and requirement of Space in a different way, at different levels, in different forms of Energy, so it becomes a transaction between the two forms of Energy. This means that two needs one space! One has to give up the right and claim for Space!

Who can do that? Who will do that? How can Energy change its nature? To acquire, possess, to have, to snatch, to take away, etc., is easier, then why stop? It's better to take up the challenge and prove, and then the winner can have the Space. Both agree to prove, to win and enjoy that space as a place!

Have you seen that SPACE is similarly trying to have SPACE? Two SPACES and ONE ENERGY? How can space be a winner or looser? It is ENERGY, its movements and its forms, that challenge and risk for the achievement. SPACE remains there and there, ENERGY can't remain there and there: ENERGY came, it remains and it moves further in SPACE! Constantly moving and changing, energy is impermanent. The winner and looser is Energy, the stronger and weaker is Energy.

It is ONE, ultimately ONE, and even after that it tries to prove: 'I' am the ONE and only! Energy challenges Energy and takes a risk to prove itself so that Energy can accept, recognize and be ready to appreciate 'me', 'my', and 'mine' Energy the ego! Individuals are many. A higher and super ego is one ego! EGO is ONE ultimately and its forms are many!

Why do two forms have to prove themselves for one space? When the two know that space will remain, they will move from there! Ask the Energy form, "you don't know this?" The immediate answer is "yes, I know"! Do you know what you don't know? Which one is bigger and larger, known or unknown? Instead of giving the answer, it replies, "yes I know"!

Ignorance is opposite to this, and gnosis means 'to know'. According to knowledge, an action and performance was carried out, and the result has shown a lack of knowledge while, on the other side, it was a knowledge-based action and performance and now it is not because of the result. So, it is knowledge and it is not knowledge, that is the lack or absence of knowledge, or ignorance.

That is on one side while on the other side is the knowledge, "I know". This 'I', the ego, puts a limit on knowledge and the gnosis (the whole) becomes partial, a part. So, from the action and performance point of view "I know", so 'I' decide to do and have done, which has given the result, has shown and proved that the known part was insufficient in getting a better result. A lacking, an absence of knowledge, was also there, which was not considered and acknowledged by that 'I', the ego. Therefore, the expression "I know" gives more emphasis and stress to the known part, rather than the not known part, or the to be known part. This expression, "I know", is very common and works as a blanket or cover to the other side, which no other can discover. The best use of an avoiding mechanism is to divert the focus of attention from one side to the other side, swinging in such a way that shows one side all the time and moves further, without showing the other side!

That's why there is the need of many blankets, or covers, just as if it is too cold, or there is too much use of intellectual property, its logic and reasoning, to justify, to clarify, to explain, etc., etc. In order to cover ignorance, the best covers of all are anger and crying, to accept it as "I know"; that way, 'I' was not knowing enough! And what's more, 'I' was not trying to know before taking the decision and action, because it was considered and taken for granted that "I am the best, the perfect, the right".

How can there be a mistake in the action or performance? There is no doubt, even no doubt on doubt by that doubtful one, because the doubt was in the other's decision and action, and so there's no need to have a doubt by the best one, the perfect and right one that is 'I', the ego, the source of the doubt! The result has started shaking confidence, it is difficult to accept and correct, repetition of the result has removed the cover of the ego, 'I', in a painful way: Energy gets exposed in Space! Without cover, shelter and protection insecure is the preparation for the security from inside, not from outside! What is unknown by Energy is Space/SPACE, and the known is its own side that is Energy/ENERGY. Gnosis has agnosis, agnostic, and agnosticism, with gnosiology. The compass of the knower as an individual is smaller in knowing all because of its limitation, and to focus knowledge from one side, or to cover up both sides, to be in-between, then also it is difficult to cover up both sides because to cover up both sides from far, far away from the centre, the 'I', the ego, has to be higher and higher, to be away from the ground, the centre!

How far should that one be away from the ground, the centre? First, the map position. Here, the 'I', ego, was bigger in the surrounding area, and that area was smaller; later on, bigger becomes smaller and the surrounding area becomes bigger and bigger! The "I know" was the bigger in relation, now it has changed and bigger becomes the smaller because of the change in relation, its relativity! As and when that 'I', ego, has expressed "I know", the doors of further learning are closed! On one side it tries to move further, and on the other side closes the door, which allows it to move further by its own expression and action! A big bang by the door closing creates hurt and injury because of the closed door, which does not permit (allow) it to move further. The ego, 'I', gets hurt and injured because of that "I know", which itself is ignorance and is the cause of pain and suffering, because it has closed the door on knowing further!

What is according to the one individual is not the same according to the other individual because of their different positions and standpoints. Although the object to know is one and the same (and also common to all), even after that, their knowledge is not the same, it is different from each other, and to prove "I know" better than you, each one is busy collecting and creating evidence for their knowledge giving the possibilities to compare, to evaluate, to judge, that ENERGY and its actions and performance in SPACE! SPACE is taken for granted, and ENERGY becomes the object of knowledge by the knower, ENERGY; the process to know, the link between the two, is also by ENERGY – the trio in SPACE! Further, that which remains unknown, agnosis, is also an ENERGY!

What you are not, how can it be known? Energy can know about Energy; what is not Energy, how can Energy know about it? In which way can Energy know? Is it through being Energy to becoming not Energy?

ENERGY becomes SPACE – to write this sentence is easy! It is grammatically correct, but does it mean that ENERGY really becomes SPACE? The reader is just flowing and considering the possibilities that Energy can play role-playing and become Space. This means that it appears as a space, a quasi-steady state! Developing from the performance and actions of this role, Energy plays many, many roles constantly, one after the other and many at the same time. So from the role point of view, each one is different and from the appearance point of view, Energy as a principle is the same, is ultimately Energy. From the background point of view, each appearance has its own contrasting background, and the other background is the contrast of the contrast, which is SPACE, a common background for each role played by Energy!

The seen is different and is related to the past, seeing is the present connection, and yet to be seeing and seen is related to the future. The constant flow and middle portion is life, which is connected to the present and different from past and future. The flow is flowing, this is recognized by that one who is not flowing and not the flow, and not even flowing with the flow as a companion, opposite to the flow. From this point, the description and narration of the flow, and the one who flows along with the flow, who describes and narrates the flow, provides one more description, narration. Two seemingly different, approaches to the one object that is the flow – a constant movement of Energy!

How can this two be one? Is it through accepting or rejecting each other?

From the flow point of view, it changes constantly. The two-way possibility is to consider the change in a contrary way to make it more convenient and comfortable, or not to consider other related changes, to be fixed only with one possibility. The flow of Energy becomes the object, which has no objection to the other side: for some this is the illusion and for some others it is not the illusion because the two have two opposite standpoints of one and the same object! From their standpoint, the two are correct (right) as well as opposite to each other. This situation occurs because of the ONE ENERGY FLOW, which can be described as a river, it has two sides that are opposite to each other, and the flow is flowing continuously. The two sides automatically appear because of the flow!

How many does it become? Three! Two sides and one constant flow are three! Also, because the flow is the divider and the divider has made or created a division, created two. The flow is a dividing line, two sides becoming two out of one! ONE was before and because of that ONE and the flow, by flowing over something, on something, it creates two sides and then appears as three, instead of two! Again, there is a third ONE who notices this two or three together. The position or standpoint of this third one, to look at these three or two and to make a statement about them, is also important to notice because the third one is very many, and their statements criss-cross over each other as their position (standpoint) is different from each other! The statement is accepted and appreciated by the fourth one, who becomes the follower to carry forward the message of the statement to the fifth one. A common baseline is from where all are emerging like sprouts, breaking the cover of the seed and moving in two directions just as a sprout and root. The seed is one point, and now becomes the line to connect the upper and lower part as a stem. Constant change, transformation and conversion is going on because of that ENERGY FLOW.

The illusion is created by Energy, the illusion is perceived by Energy, and it is an illusion, expressed in particular ways by Energy. Again, this expression (statement) is ignored and neglected by Energy, while it is appreciated and accepted by Energy also!

The cause of illusion is ignorance. One of the causes of happiness is illusion. In this way, happiness becomes related to illusion and ignorance. This happiness is on one side and, on the other side, there is also HAPPINESS, which is opposite to related happiness! This becomes the cause of curiosity and research for better and better happiness, more and more happiness, and this in turn becomes the base of the inference to start imagining or thinking of that happiness which is free from relativity, which is not related

SPACE is free from relativity; it is not related because it is not ENERGY. SPACE is the ENVELOPE, the COVER, is HAPPINESS: to discover, to find out, to get it again, it becomes the final GOAL, target, or aim to achieve, to have, for that ENERGY. Energy is also an envelope, a cover, and as happiness, it makes, forces and pushes to discover, to find out, to get it again, it becomes the goal, target, aim, to achieve, to have it, for Energy. To move from unhappiness to happiness becomes the goal, target, aim and instead of reaching the other side, Energy reaches to its own peak of happiness, and then turns into, changes into, transforms into, converts into, unhappiness because of its own constant movement.

All different forms, structures, systems and their functions engage to have that particular specific result of happiness! As Energy has two sides, it is possible to be half happy, 50% happy, and not completely, totally 100% happy, because the other half is unhappy, and that is why it is said, 'the glass is half full and half empty'. This means that a pot, a container, a box, a glass, a body, a cover, a space, cannot be filled 100% by ENERGY because full and half is related to the size, and size ULTIMATELY is the bigger, and the content is Energy: the container is Space/SPACE and that's why all the time, in different ways, it remains half full and half empty.

The quantitative approach is related to size, and the terms of expression for it are 'full, half, quarter,' etc. The qualitative approach is different; it does not give more importance to size, measurement and quantity. All the time Energy is the content and the container in two different ways, and also the third one who works with these two, and a fourth one also who observes, sees, or becomes the witness, to this movement, and the fifth one is the common base, to start, to become any one of them!

Darkness is another term for ignorance and illusion. That darkness means absence of light, a normal, natural light that is SUN light. Instead of that, any other light is light, and it is not light because it is not SUN light! Clarity is because of light, and lights have differences in them from their source point of view. Ignorance is called darkness because of the absence of SUN light (illumination), and it is not ignorance and there is no darkness when there is the availability of such light. This 'light' is presence, and when perceived clearly there is no illusion but only clear perception through that light; that's why it is suggested that it's better to keep it off that light to avoid making mistakes and suffering pain! Energy is the source and provider of that light; it makes that object of perception and selection brighter. This means that the object was perceived in that light and the projector has projected onto that object making it become more colourful and lively, natural and attractive. Energy is ready for any type of make-up, because through make-up things can appear much more beautiful and remain attractive for others, which or who are also Energy! Plus is moved and attracted by minus, and minus is also attracted and moved because of plus!

Is it possible to be free from plus and minus?

Who are you? Only plus? Only minus?

Or are you a mixture of plus and minus?

Both are the signs of Energy. Which one is stronger, more dominant and prominent within you? Or in 'me'? Better to check and find out!

Plus is moving to give, to deliver.

Minus is moving to get, to take, to snatch, to take it away.

Both are moving and meeting.

What is the minus giving back after getting from the plus? What is the plus getting back after giving to the minus? This shows how the binding principle of the 'law of action' works as a binding agent between these two (plus and minus), and how it keeps them together.

The movement is the movement. Then who is moving along with it, or is it only movement? Then, is it solely Energy? Then, is it not because of ignorance (illusion) that it has to be illuminated properly through a different light? Then, plus is the past of Energy, and minus is the other past of Energy. Then, what is this movement for: to give and to get, to receive and to give, to take, to snatch, to take away from plus Energy by minus Energy? Why? Or is it an action and performance by Space? If it's not SPACE, then what is SPACE there for?

To support, to provide, to allow, to permit the movement to be changed, to transform and to convert, to become more and more spacious for the movement of Energy is the answer. Energy becomes the obstacle of its own movement, and becomes spacious for its own movement. When it becomes spacious and allows movement, this does not mean that it becomes SPACE although it seems to be, looks like and appears so. This behaviour appears so generous and open, kind and gentle, in order to put (create) that impression in the other Energy, or other part, side of Energy. To consider as a space that spacious appearance, without establishing proper knowledge, it becomes erroneous knowledge.

From the similar and difference point of view,

- Plus is two,
- Minus is two, and
- Zero is also a two and one
- after that zero is also a two!

These two are similar and different. Two gives the choice and option to select one out of two, which is considered as a substitute for the other one; it is also considered as an alternative to the other one! The result makes it clear that the selection was not clear, or that it was unclear, and that illusion was there because the selection was not done properly. The reason for it, the justification or explanation for it, is that distinguishing the difference between the two as one similar appearance was not properly carried out because of partial knowledge. That partial knowledge as "I know", was not able to decide (distinguish) impartially without coming under the influence of the partial knowledge "I know" and so becomes limited knowledge on one side and, on the other side, it becomes the well-known popular term 'ignorance'.

What does "I know" mean? It means that in the beginning and at the end, through the result, 'I' did not know! It means 'I' was ignorant. For this result, clarity and knowledge existed in the past, so it was carried out at that time, but the result didn't happen, it happened in the future, was yet to come, so it was unpredictable because of the probability and possibility for the result, which remains unknown, but not without expectation. However, the result is not related to the expectation of the performer, the doer, 'I', the ego. When it was carried out it was in present time, then that present time became the past, and the future which was yet to come arrived and became the present giving and showing the result and along with it ignorance, idiotness, foolishness, stupidness, or cleverness or wisdom! These characteristics belong to the performer, the doer, the 'I, ego, while the illusion belongs to the object to select for the performance.

From the correction point of view, to remove the illusion, to overcome the illusion, which is a mixture of the two (similar and different), the difficulty of recognition has to be overcome. What makes it difficult to recognize the right one is the lack of patience, too much hurry, not able to wait, partial knowledge of that which is 'known', too much confidence in one's own selection and decision, etc., etc. All these are related (connected) to that performer, doer, 'I', the ego, which is the inner side of that outer side where illusion exists, or where it is there in various forms of objects.

Naturally, it's better to do the correction inside rather than outside, which is bigger than inside and becomes the cause of confusion and illusion. To do the correction inside is easier, while outside doing the correction is more difficult. The projector is inside, ignorance is inside, partial knowledge of "I know" is inside and erroneousness is also inside, constantly!

Knowingly this is done by the doer, even if it is done as a reflex action, which means that habit becomes the controller of the action, and the action is done as if without any decision, without involving or engaging the 'I', ego. This in turn means that what was to be done is decided automatically because the habit is developed and formed to perform automatically and that doer, the 'I', ego becomes the non-doer, or as if it were that "I am not the doer". This stage or state of being is equivalent to that statement, for the ABSOLUTE ONE is the DOER and I am not the Doer, the 'I', ego. This expression shows wisdom, while to make use of the statement and to impress the other's Energy, that Energy changes gear (or transforms) into automatic from the manual operating system and hands over all tasks to the auto system and becomes free to enjoy the freedom!

The habit is the set-up of a specific and particular programme inside to do the work outside, where two appear as one and the same, even though the Energy within is the responsible one, not the Energy outside, which looks like (seems to be) appearing as one! The knower has to know about the object, then selects the object to use because of the possibilities of wrong use, misuse, abuse, or correct and proper use. The knower becomes the doer, the doer becomes the enjoyer and later on the enjoyer becomes the sufferer. Because the habit becomes the doer who does automatically, the results are enjoyed by the enjoyer who was the doer in the past, and now, in the present, appears as if that one is not the doer but has given up.

Energy has given up, surrendered, to Energy, or is it to Space? In which way is it given up, surrendered? To be indifferent after giving up (surrendering), the right action to do now becomes the duty of the other, or the habit to do, to perform, in the same way, continuously. A mistake occurred, it happened, it was not in the planned programme; the habit (a mechanical action, an automatically controlled action) becomes interrupted inside and is reflected as a mistake outside, not the old one but the new one, and out of imagination and thinking to get the idea about it, that action becomes the mistake.

Is it not a creation of the inner Energy to create a new mistake? The result of the mistake is outside. It's not enough to recognize and accept the mistake as a mistake so the correction has to be achieved in order that it's not repeated, for it not to re-occur or happen again and again, yet where was the correction done by Energy? The correction is done, it is a correction and it is not a correction because the form is corrected not the system, or the system is corrected while the structure remains the same (unchanged), so it becomes a partial correction, not a total one! So, it is and it is not a correction and the chances for a new mistake remain open for appearance because it is Energy, it has its own freedom of movement: the mistake is part of that free movement!

From Energy's point of view, it is a mistake and it is not a mistake, because it is a continuity of the action in one way or the other! The flow of Energy was flowing in one way or the other! The ego, 'I', doer, was more concerned and interested in expecting a better result and was disappointed because of the result of the mistake (action)! To be ready or not to be ready to accept the result becomes a dilemma, a question for the enjoyer of the result.

What to do? Can it be to become the doer again, to enjoy again? The interruption of this result in the continuity of enjoyment makes it obvious that the result is not the same, not even similar, so now the enjoyment is different.

What to do? Can it be to identify with that different result or not to identify? Or can it be to become the doer again to bring change to that different result through doing in a different way than the previous way of doing?

How was it done? Who was the doer at that time? The habit was at that time the doer and became the enjoyer, allowing the habits to become controller of the actions and movement as it became auto-control, auto-movement, auto-response, etc. This shows a change in the role of one Energy into the other energetic role with the same Energy! At the same time, the activity of the previous role was carried out by the automatic systems of Energy. The memory storehouse for each different programme of the automatic system, for its function, is immediately available. Somehow the memory carries impressions of the neglect and disregard, the avoidance and lack of care, and that also reaches the automatic system as a blank recording where no programme of action or activity is recorded. This means that forgetfulness becomes spontaneous as a part of the developed habit of a particular action done by the doer, 'I', ego, at that time (which is now past with reference to today's time). The enjoyer was the doer who now becomes the sufferer of a forgetfulness cultivated in the past but which now gives flowers and fruits! To achieve one, it was necessary to neglect and ignore the other and the achievement has given happiness.

Then what happens to that action of the other side? How does it give the flowers and fruit to the doer of the action? The happiness of achievement has come and gone because it is part of Energy's function to move constantly. The question is why did the doer become happy? The answer is because of happiness, unhappiness is also available to the same doer without any effort. So, unhappiness becomes effortless, or it is effortless to become unhappy while effort is needed to become happy!

To maintain constant joy and happiness outside with effort to show and demonstrate to others as if there is no sadness outside but which appears, so where is it? It is inside, it exists inside! How long can it remain inside without affecting the outside? How long is it possible to carry the load of sadness within and show (demonstrate) happiness outside without allowing the natural change. Is it possible for Energy?

To cheat is possible; that becomes the illusion for the other's ignorance who is using light but it is not SUN light. The absence of light is darkness and that is ignorance yet it is not the absence of light altogether, although the light is not sunlight. It is not ignorance because the other light was present and darkness was removed; it is as if darkness disappeared for a short while and then appeared along with the appearance of the result, and illusion was proved, idiotness was established, stupidity was manifested, and foolishness becomes the cause of enjoyment!

The cheater is ENERGY, and the teacher has Energy! ABSOLUTE AS A TEACHER, and related as a teacher and cheater! Learning directly from the teacher and indirectly from the cheater, Energy is one and the roles are two; learner has a choice to learn from one role and to avoid, or not to learn, from the other. It's not easy, because the learner is in-between the two phases or stages with ignorance on one side and illusion on the other. The learner has to learn how to distinguish the difference between the two. This means learning to differentiate the difference between the two out of one and then to select one and to know the other one, and to utilize the selected one properly. The learner is also part of Energy. Which one is teacher and cheater outside as well as inside? A trio exists inside!

While the opposite of Energy is SPACE ABSOLUTE, that also exists inside as a background, taking it for granted, so a trio appears on that ground: two on one side and one on the other side, so they are three in total and two as a side! This two as a side, to know by any term, belongs to a terminology. To reduce the number again means to consider the two sides together as one, and it becomes one having oneness and remaining inseparable. This two as a one belongs to ENERGY to ONE, then the background becomes zero, or the opposite, and that is Space, SPACE. Again they become two as opposite to each other, as well as inseparable.

So, they are together as one and become one having a oneness up to a certain limit, or to a certain extent. Again, it becomes possible to look and to conclude that one is appearing firmly, strongly and clearly on the other. This other very, very often comes into use, it is related with the other at the same time as not being related, and exists in the area free from relativity. This other is a background, a space for Energy.

The journey of analysis starts from the point of 'I', the ego, the doer, as an investigator and thinker, etc., up to the end-point on the opposite side of that point. In connection to the starting point, this opposite point appears as one point, a common acceptable point for all different starting points; there are many, many points on one side connected by ONE Point known as ENERGY. It is inside and outside at the same time. Outside it appears as one common point, inside as one particular, specific point. Ultimately it's ONE Energy: ONE ENERGY inside is many, and many particular, specific energies altogether become ONE ENERGY. This is the only side and ENERGY is the base and source of everything. This is not accepted by the other. It's the nature of Energy to be opposite, so in a natural way they (the others) have taken the standpoint that the background SPACE is also to be considered equally important: it is not only Energy, it is SPACE where Energy exists! SPACE is a PLACE for ENERGY to Exist.

Not to agree, to oppose and to find a new point which also exists, is the work of Energy. Once it becomes opposite, it remains opposite: in this way, it becomes the supporter of the opposition, the opposite of Energy that is Space, and starts to propagate from the side of SPACE. Automatically Energy becomes the second. After that, SPACE is established as ONE without a Second! This state of existence is beyond the limit and capability of Energy.

How then can Energy become a Space? If it can, then it can reach up to that state of existence! From the point of view of SPACE with particles, it means SPACE with ENERGY. Beyond that is SPACE without particles, without Energy. SPACE without particles becomes void, nothing, vacuum, absent, and becomes the GROUND of and for the BACKGROUND.

Distance is measured in light years because it is far away from the point on the Earth. That Dark BLACK BACK GROUND and its GROUND as SPACE, ONE without the second, has opportunity to be seen by one's own eyes. In this way, SPACE becomes

Two – with and without, and as
Two – higher and lower, and as
Two – outer and inner, and as
Two – polluted and unpolluted!

Along with these two 'qualities' of SPACE, ENERGY has its own two sides:

negative – positive,
or plus – minus,
or male – female,
two opposite – at the same time.

The varieties of the two are known by different terms and expressions as: two, or dual, or dichotomy, or double, and a mixture of these two makes or creates double duality with the possibility to unite (connect) in a wrong way, either because of illusion or ignorance. That is why clarity and purification are important.

The possibilities of mixtures with different permutations and combinations become immense. ENERGY was free and became bound, connected and united with its own opposite forces, forms, systems, structures and functions. The ONE was free, and is now searching for freedom without being bound, for freedom without responsibility. That ONE was alone and single, then that one becomes double and is always together having a mix of impressions, which become the guiding principle and force for its movement, together and separate.

The graduation and degradation of Energy and its movement from the SUN to the Earth is constantly giving and receiving. The giver is the SUN and the receiver is the Earth and the other planets with their moons also. Earth is a living body, and a living body is an Earth also! Earth is a receiver, while the living body on the Earth also becomes a receiver from the giver, the SUN. The giver SUN is giving in such a way that it appears as if taking away to give back in a different form. So, it becomes a change, a transformation and conversion, and that process is known as Nature, and the environment is governed by the SUN as a governor.

Looking to this method of recycling, the living body (living being) has changed its status of being from receiver to taker, and is able to take away; it prefers to take rather than to receive to avoid obligation. Not satisfied and happy with this, the living being wants to have more and more and it prefers to snatch, to grab, to have as a quick possession and to develop ownership of it. Ultimately ENERGY as a ONE has to move in the same way, without any change. How is this possible?

Change is another name (term) for Energy! From the SUN to the Earth and living being there is a descending flow of Energy from the higher level to the lower level, from the centre to the periphery, from in to out. The ONE who gives all the time is known by specific, particular terms, and the other one, who takes, snatches and grabs is also known by specific and particular terms. This has created and developed the fear, to monitor, to control, to regulate the other related and connected Energy. The living being as an Energy plus Space together have a choice to move in two directions, either higher or lower. The direction is leading towards the destination of two opposites known by a popular term, and recognized and accepted by the other with different terms of their terminology.

A living being is considered as existing on the base line, on the zero line; below the base line the area is minus, while above the zero line (base line) the area is plus. The Energy of the living being moves freely in any direction, and as a result of that movement the area is decided and declared, and accordingly it gets the further result. Descending impressions are stronger, and to counter those impressions and to ascend as a result of counter impressions (and to have, to create and put on those impressions) that living being has to be or live in a particular, specific way without any specific relation or communication with the other Energy. This is known as a discipline, to be able to have, to achieve, what is decided! Each movement or action has its own base line, middle line and central line, and along with it, its result also has a possibility to be either above the zero line or below the zero line. Where the result has to be is decided by the action, activities and movement.

How to do? What to do? When, where, and why to do? This is decided by Energy, the doer, the 'I', the ego! According to the decision, the action, activities, and performance at that time appear as if they are in the middle (centre) and not away from the zero line. The preferable and expected movement is above and not below the zero line; not to be in the minus is the goal, aim and target of the decision makers.

How is this possible for Energy? How can it be known and decided that this is the plus and this is the minus? To descend, to go down, to fall, is easier and not more difficult; after that it requires more effort to remain in a neutral position without being in either one or the other side. To move on the middle line, or middle path, to be in the centre forever and not be back on the periphery, is the most difficult task for Energy. To be there just for the time being for enjoyment, to fulfil responsibilities, or to complete and finish any work, to be there up to that time and after that not to remain there, is the goal, target, or aim of ENERGY. So, in this way, it is a goal, target and aim to be there and also not to be there; that's why there is change, and change becomes another name or term to express ENERGY!

As it is a descending Energy from the SUN, it has to be ascending also. There are two types of ascending: one is ascending and the other is not ascending but looks as if it is ascending: it is and it is not ascending because it has to descend after a certain limit or distance, or it is not going to meet the centre point.

The SUN IS THE CENTRAL POINT for the Energy of a living being (living body) as an Earth, and Earth as a living body. What is the result of the meeting with the SUN? Energy knows, so it avoids the meeting. In the beginning, at the starting time, it looks like Energy is moving in the right direction to meet, to unite, to join, to combine and to become one with the SUN. Later on, after a certain distance is over, then it is possible to discover that the right direction at the beginning (the start) becomes wrong at the end! By successfully avoiding the meeting it was relieved that it survived and was happy to have one more chance or opportunity to try. So why not fail rather than pass and move further?

What is it finally, ignorance or illusion or both from two different points of view?

Because there is relation and connection to the Energy, both exist because of that particular, specific, ENERGY. The way to describe this and make it clear with the help of the other, becomes a choice or acceptance, because the GIVER SUN gives constantly, while the constant receiver has changed the role and state of being. Absence of light is darkness and is comparable with ignorance; that darkness is removed through or with the light, which is knowledge. This means it is not that DARKNESS, DARK BLACK and UNCHANGABLE, it is a darkness that is changeable with or through the presence and absence of light, the knowledge.

So, it is knowledge and it is not knowledge because it is not SUN LIGHT, and the knowledge belongs to IT! Looking to the other light, which is not sunlight, it is suggested that it is better to turn off that light because its source is not the SUN! Then, be ready to face the darkness and move from the changeable darkness to the unchangeable darkness, which is SPACE, the DARK BLACK BACK GROUND, ONE WITHOUT A SECOND! Learn to move in the darkness and to reach the object without considering it as an obstacle; it helps to take a turn, to move in the other direction, until the starting point is reached, the point of origin. Up to this time, Energy has to move and move and to keep moving, but it expects to be steady like SPACE!

Movement, when it is not recognized, is considered steady, but it is the slowest movement known as the quasi-steady state. Similarly, the giver is giving to get back more than that which is given, and for this, there are many different calculations that the giver is doing.

The giver is two. How can two have in return more than the given? Both are takers, they know how to take more, because the two giver/taker exchanges do the transaction, and Energy has swallowed the piece of Energy to become bigger Energy. It's also necessary to swallow, to eat, to consume, the smaller pieces. Energy has invented many different skills and methods to swallow and to eat, to consume and to avoid, to prevent and not to become the object to be swallowed or to be eaten, not to be consumed on the other side.

Is a one-way business possible? Although they do it knowingly and they know what happens to the other, they expect that it will not happen and that they will remain safe, and will not be the object to be swallowed, to be eaten, to be consumed.

Is it ignorance?
Or is it illusion?
Or is it both?
Or is it something else?
What is it?

Energy can think and try to be one-way, but for how long? It is a constant struggle not to become the object to be swallowed, eaten and consumed, one needs to be constantly awake and aware, to avoid and to prevent it from happening, and for that it becomes more and more clever on one side. On the other side, the cleverness, which belongs to the intellect, is one of the 'outlets' for Energy to move in and out, and it becomes more and more familiar with this movement, which means that automatically more has less on the other side, that is the emotional side.

How to be in the emotional area, how to avoid and prevent it? Here, it becomes difficult for Energy because of its own well-planned deprivation, which has created and developed a starvation inside for a pure emotional approach and exchange! It is a mixed and polluted approach; 'pure' is the label, the tag, and with the help of that light looking to that not pure as pure, and to that which is not permanent as permanent, and to not happiness as happiness, and taking that which is not a centre of the activity, taking it for granted as a centre, is a contrary way.

That Energy has planned 'to be' because it is opposite to SPACE! There is nothing wrong in being opposite, contrary is the normal logic and reasoning 'to be'. In this creation, why not become the creator and have one's own creation, become the owner, the master and authority of it?

With this, Energy has started to change its role and appearance, its state of being, for the specific, particular achievement. It is not one and common for One Energy. Why does Energy have to prove its superiority and to show evidence of it? The answer is because it is ONE and different, with two opposite sides which are in and out at the same time, as well as being the divider which divided and created, made the division: that divider has to be the cause to unite, to join, to combine. Energy's appearance divides and its disappearance unites, combines and joins.

Recognition of the absence indicates knowledge about the presence. Acceptance of it helps to appreciate that absence. The absence of a divider, of division or duality means uniformity, oneness, even-ness out of uneven-ness. That is the process of giving up, on one level, and forgiveness on the other level, which helps to forget and overcome, to get rid of and to get relief. Through acceptance, patience and tolerance, it is possible to achieve that state of even-ness; just do the opposite, the contrary, and it becomes uneven-ness. Moving is Energy, uneven-ness is because of Energy, it is a cause and effect both at the same time, two sides of one coin.

THAT DARK BLACK SPACE is the SWALLOWER to swallow the swallower, Energy!

The way it is swallowed, that way it comes out further as a production, then it becomes the production of creation of that swallowed Energy in another way.

A big time difference, the distance from here to there, is measured in light years. That light belongs to the SUN. FIRE is one, flames are many; ground is one and peaks are many.

SPACE IS ONE without a second; SPACE IS ONE, with a second. SPACE is ULTIMATE as it is considered as being ENERGY as well, which is also an Ultimate and Ultimately Energy.

There are two ways to check, to analyse, a dual approach. What for? To prove and to convey what? SPACE and ENERGY are together, it is accepted by all without a question or doubt. Then together they are, learning and getting educated about how they are together from that one who became one together. But who is learning, who is teacher: SPACE? ENERGY?

The role of SPACE is the Back Ground, while the role of Energy is also a background while it is also in or on the front! In all the movement, action, activities and performances, even in the effect and result, these two are together, both are inseparable. Hunter, prey and hunting is the Energy; eater, food and eating is the Energy; learning, learner and tutor is the Energy.

Then, what is Space doing? Nothing! It is just Being with Energy. The role is played by Energy, to achieve that object, which is Energy. The technique, method, skill and efficiency to achieve that object is also a part and function of Energy. From manifest to unmanifest, up to that level,

Energy and its cyclic movement moves in two different ways, clockwise and/or anticlockwise, it spirals in an upward and/or downward movement, which gives and creates the shape of a mountain or hill, broad base and peak. In one case it's movement, while in the other it's steady, not moving! Have you seen, observed a mountain or a hill which has a peak downward, or a peak pointing down and its base up? This is called imagination: from one to the other shape and form, structure, system and function, from one to the other in the opposite, contrary way.

That's why, what cannot be imagined cannot be thought of; what cannot be thought cannot be decided, that which has not been decided, that won't be done or it is not done, which means that the result is not there of that wrong and/or right. Imagination has the same wrong and/or right result, a group of three. One set of three, which started from thinking not from the imagination, now becomes six in total, and their combination shows the results, the variations. Considering the result as an effect, then the cause is different, and the effect can become a cause to create, to give a further effect as a result.

Imagination and thinking are inside the result of action, which is manifest outside. While the unmanifest imagination and thinking has a connection (relation) with the manifest effect and result, that can be the cause of the manifestation of imagination and thinking inside!

Energy is the cause behind thinking and imagination, and Energy is manifest and unmanifest in these two different states of being that Energy.

The same term 'manifestation' is also used in relation to SPACE to communicate what is common and the same to both Energy and SPACE; the second and related term of manifest is 'unmanifest'. This second term, 'unmanifest', indicates change, transformation, conversion and destruction; this is applicable to ENERGY and is not applicable to SPACE!

From the use of these two popular and common terms, 'manifest' and 'unmanifest', now they can be co-related, combined and united with the other two principles of existence, that is SPACE and ENERGY, from the result point of view. Those who are playing, enjoying, handling and being with the two terms in connection and relation to, in combination with, uniting with Energy are entering into the whirlpool of the energetic movement of Energy! They are attracted and caught by Energy because it has manifested Energy's form, function, structure, system and result as well as its being unmanifest; also, however, both manifest and unmanifest are the state of Energy, yet for SPACE, when it is used, then 'manifest' remains a common term for SPACE and ENERGY. To make it clear for the second term for ENERGY, it is expressed by (communicated by) the terms 'destruction', 'change', 'transformation' and 'conversion', instead of using the term 'unmanifest' for ENERGY.

Then, in relation to SPACE, it is necessary to make this clear because SPACE IS, so it is used and expressed by the term 'manifestation'; but how can it be unmanifest? SPACE is not destructible, it's not possible to destroy the form, shape, structure, etc., because of ENERGY. Energy belongs to Energy.

SPACE around us and around the Earth as a living body is manifest SPACE, a background, while that Black Back Ground, which is a Back GROUND of that Ground as manifest SPACE, becomes Unmanifest in relation to (connection to) manifest SPACE. Because IT IS MANIFEST SPACE therefore, THAT SPACE is considered as UNMANIFEST SPACE, which is the ABSOLUTELY DARK BLACK BACK GROUND! That's why, it becomes necessary to avoid the use of the same term 'UNMANIFEST' for ENERGY; instead of using this, the terms 'destruction', 'destroy', 'transform', 'change', 'convert', etc., can be used for ENERGY to make it clear in relation (connection) to the term 'manifest', which is common for both ENERGY and SPACE! However, the other term of 'manifest', is not common for both Energy and Space. ENERGY and SPACE is the distance, that point which is far away from one's own standpoint or reference point. Up to a certain distance it's possible to perceive and say it's a manifestation; it is also possible to perceive the destruction, change, transformation and conversion. Then a question arises: can the opposite term of 'manifestation' be 'unmanifest'? It is easily considered and taken for granted that the term 'unmanifest' is related (connected) with the future, to that which has to happen but has not yet happened!

From the time point of view, 'unmanifest' becomes a related term because the future time period is related and connected with the PAST and PRESENT. The three phases of time are inter-related (connected) with each other, although it is ONE TIME. Time is a measuring unit of ENERGY; both the terms 'manifest' and 'unmanifest' indicate a cyclic movement, either clockwise or anticlockwise in the movement of THAT ENERGY.

The nature of SPACE is not the same as that of ENERGY, both are opposite: SPACE is considered to be INDESTRUCTABLE, or is it possible to prove, with evidence, that is not INDESTRUCTABLE? However, it is possible to prove with evidence that DESTRUCTABLE is the nature of ENERGY'S form, shape, structure and function, and that it is possible to change, transform and covert also. Therefore, the term 'destructible' is possible to apply to Energy, while it is not possible to use it for SPACE because it is indestructible although it is manifest. Opposite of this is unmanifest SPACE, which is not yet perceived and not yet manifest. It is constantly far away, and constantly going to remain as unmanifest, as unchangeable, non-transformable, and as an unconvertible state. The nature of SPACE is a DARK BLACK BACK GROUND!

Is it possible for a single living being to change, or is it possible for the Earth as a living being to change, to transform, to convert, that DARK BLACK BACK GROUND?

It is even difficult for the SUN to make it bright and to remove the DARKNESS because it is ABSOLUTE DARKNESS, which is absolutely DARK! In that BACK GROUND, the SUN looks like a bright SPOT, a FIREBALL, and the light of it tries to illuminate each and every object, either tiny little particles or the bigger ones such as the Earth!

The appearance of the two in the Back Ground, which is common SPACE, makes a difference: SUN is a SUN and Earth is an Earth; giver is the giver and receiver is the receiver. The giver is the SUN and the receiver is the Earth. The moon belongs to whom? Although the moon belongs to the Earth, the moon is a receiver also!

SPACE is the Back Ground and it is not the Back Ground as it is not the same SPACE. SPACE can be seen as a Front Ground the same as the Back Ground. SPACE is around the object, and the object is surrounded by SPACE. This is known as SPACE is outside, and the object exists within SPACE! The way the object is surrounded by SPACE is the same as when SPACE is surrounded by the object because within the object SPACE exists.

From the existence point of view, SPACE and ENERGY (the object) are both existing in each other! Both are in-between and both are outside. The 'I', ego, me, my and mine is the starting point. This is a small (little tiny) point existing on the Earth. The other side of this starting point and its existence is the SUN, which is also a STARTING POINT.

Looking to and considering these two starting points in connection (relation) with each other they become one starting point again on one side, and the other side of this STARTING POINT SUN – what is it? It is SPACE!

The END POINT is the SUN from the starting point of 'I', me, my, and mine and the ego, and the Earth also! The beginning has an end and the end has a beginning. The END POINT is from one side, and the beginning point, the starting point, is on the other side towards ENDLESS SPACE, the INFINITE.

Who can reach THAT ENDLESS POINT? It is the other side of the starting point which exists, and the existence of the two starting points which are connected to each other are dependent on the existence of SPACE, which is INDISTRUCTIBLE. As it is ENDLESS SPACE, so it can be an ENDLESS BEGINNING, STARTING. That's why there is the TERM 'ZERO', and the figure is applied to IT! In it, it is NOTHING, and that NOTHING is EVERYTHING because in it, NOTHING EXISTS.

The journey is going on, but where will it END? Will it be at the point of NOTHING or at the point of EVERYTHING; will it be to know that NOTHING IS EVERYTHING and that EVERYTHING IS NOTHING?

Those who consider ENERGY as ULTIMATE, for them the STARTING and ENDING POINT is ENERGY, while for others who consider SPACE as ULTIMATE, for them the STARTING and ENDING POINT is SPACE. Those who have a mixed approach, they have the chance to jump from one point to other starting and ending points.

It is possible to prove with evidence that the cause of creation, the starting and ending points, is ENERGY. ENERGY is considered as a FATHER and MOTHER, good and evil, also. The proof and evidence shows existence, because IT IS it exists, so it is possible to prove creation through utilizing the existence of IT, which is ENERGY. Once it is proved with evidence, doubt and questions are removed.

This has established Faith, Belief and Trust in ENERGY. Later on, as ENERGY is a constantly moving principle, this Faith, Belief and Trust also remains in a constantly moving (changing) state from one to another form, structure, system, function and result. Although ENERGY is ONE, of which there is no doubt, in order to start to reach this END POINT, many, many starting points come into existence, known as 'paths', 'the way' to reach to this END POINT.

To agree, to accept and to appreciate this finding is it optional or compulsory? The finding is: ENERGY is the ULTIMATE and it is the starting and ending point for all.

The answer to the question of 'Creation' is given like this: ENERGY is considered as creation as well as the CREATOR. It is the cause as well as the effect. Those who know that the OPPOSITE exists, they also know that the OPPOSITE OF ENERGY is SPACE, and not ENERGY! The opposite of the relativity of ENERGY is the ABSOLUTENESS OF SPACE. On the other side, relativity has an opposite and an opposition in it, while SPACE has no opposition and the opposite is SPACE! SPACE is ONE and the same, either inside or outside; the difference is because of ENERGY and not because of SPACE!

ENERGY can mix and merge with ENERGY, while it can remain separate or together with SPACE! This is a choice, an option, in which way to be together or separate. The togetherness or separateness is not going to affect SPACE. SPACE remains unaffected while, on the other side ENERGY is affected by its different forms, systems, structures and functions. That's why the result becomes the effect and that affected part becomes the cause and, further, the effect turns into (or becomes) a cause for a further effect continuously.

What happens to SPACE? SPACE remains unaffected, unconcerned, the base, constantly; change appears, manifests and remains on that base on a temporary basis. From the unmanifest it manifests, appearing temporarily and disappearing. The cause for each appearance is different, and the same cause from the other side appears as effects.

That's why there is the question: How can SPACE mix with SPACE, dissolve with in Space, merge with Space? Or is it possible for Energy to mix, dissolve, or merge in SPACE? Or Is it possible with ENERGY?

What is easy and possible from the ENERGY point of view, that is to be with or without mixing, dissolving or merging with another form, system, structure and function of the Energy, is not easy from the SPACE point of view!

From the unaffected, unconcerned SPACE point of view, the changing of appearance of ENERGY is transitory and temporary, and also a cause of attraction and temptation; those who know this try to be on the side of SPACE and try to become like SPACE through becoming and developing the unaffected and unconcerned part within. The characteristics, qualities, aspects, features, type and nature of ENERGY and SPACE are within as well as outside for study.

Who will study ENERGY and SPACE? ENERGY or SPACE or a mixture of the two, that is 'I', me, my, mine and ego? Why does ENERGY have to study and know more about ENERGY? Why does SPACE have to study to know more about SPACE? Both know what they are, and what is the use to know what you are not, or what they are not? What is the purpose? To be like that, to appear like that quasi state or appearance, who can do it, ENERGY or SPACE? ENERGY needs to do that, while SPACE has to accept it! ENERGY can change, modify, alter, omit, add to, or multiply, or divide etc., and all that time SPACE can be the observer, witness or the 'Seer'.

That 'I', me, my, mine ego – as a mixture of these two, ENERGY and SPACE – came into existence as a third entity; the combination of that two has made ONE and now ONE has two inside and becomes the cause of the other two, so that they can be one. Then a question: to whom does this one made by the two – that is 'I', me, my and mine, and ego – belong? Is it to ENERGY or to SPACE or to both equally or more or less? The way that two are together as 'I', me, my, mine, and ego, as a manifestation in-between the two that is ENERGY and SPACE, being in-between, there is a choice on which side to be or not to be!

Freedom is provided to move and to unite, to join and to connect, while the result shows and informs about the wrong and right union, joint or connection, and the movement was perfect, that's why a question: why did this happen? Being in-between and having two extreme sides, appears (looks like) a plus and a minus and what appears is not the same and matching to its inner substance, it is opposite, different, so it is not real.

Then what is 'Real'? The opposite of the opposite appearance is opposite, and opposite of the opposite means opposite to that which appears. Because appearance is appearance, this gives two possible ways to be with those two opposite sides.

Although duality is considered as one, when it is more elaborately looked into it becomes double duality, becoming more complicated from the simple dual approach. This is easy to understand but difficult to distinguish and to live by accordingly because to be in-between, to remain without moving towards any side and not to be in contact, not to unite, not to join, not to combine, is difficult. Also, another difficulty is distinguishing the difference between the two that is appearance and its opposite. This means that what it is and what it is not are both together, so it is necessary to distinguish, to know how and which way to be together: on one side together and on the other side separate and far away so that other side also appears as a periphery, or outer circle. As the union (connection) takes place, it takes charge and control over further movement. This appears as if it is a controller of the further movements and its results.

Then a question: what happened to that 'I', me, my and mine, the ego, and doer? Did it try to be out of control, or did it just allow and permit the controller to control and, remaining inside, tried to have a further, new contact. This indicates dissatisfaction and the tendency to search for better than what it has or possesses! This shows the process of together and separate in a cyclic form, and the change of the controller and control.

Is it not a game? For what is it played? For enjoyment, fun and pleasure? Who is getting this, ENERGY or SPACE? Who is giving and providing it, ENERGY or SPACE? How? In which way? Who is the Enjoyer? The doer? Then, who is the doer, is it ENERGY or SPACE?

ENERGY is the doer! The ego and the 'I', me, my, and mine belongs to the mixture of the two, ENERGY and SPACE. The doer role is part or the side of the ego, the 'I' me, my and mine and is because of ENERGY; while not to be the doer and enjoyer but to be the observer, witness, and seer is the role, side and part of SPACE which manifests in the Ego, the 'I', me, my and mine! And that manifestation is known and perceived as a manifestation of a SPACE, or otherwise of an ENERGY!

Does the ego, the 'I', me, my, and mine, belong to ENERGY or SPACE or both? If both, in what proportion are they: more or less or equal? What makes the difference? Is it ENERGY or its manifestation, or SPACE or its manifestation? The process or work of distinguishing and separating is done by whom, is it by the third entity the ego, the 'I', me, my and mine, or by the two ENERGY and SPACE together, or is it any one of them?

First, the mistake is distinguishing.

Second, the error in analysing the mistake.

Third, the correction is done according to the analysis and again the mistake happens, and it happens because of the error and 'to err is human'.

The human being, living being, the individual, is a mixture, or only an ENERGY, or only a SPACE? Is it not a manifestation of them both (ENERGY and SPACE) together in the form of a human being that also has a structure and a system, function and result?

From this manifestation of the two together as one living being, life begins until death occurs as a separation of that two, togetherness becomes the past. Birth is a manifestation of that conception which was manifested inside, from the unmanifest, and occupied the inner space as a place until the time of birth, the appearance outside at the outer space.

Here the intellect is not the designer, the inner intelligence is the designer! The ego, the 'I', the doer, is not the designer of that conception, but the doing process has involved the doer, and the credit goes to the doer, while the role of the doer was 50% which looks like, appears as 100% for that conception as creation!

The theory of evolution points out that the cause of it is ENERGY. It is proved with evidence, step by step, how systematically the formation of the human being and other living beings has been achieved up until today from the time of conception: the meeting, mixing and becoming one out of two, and remaining two inside that one, and from outside to appear as one having two inside! Two are two, there are many ways to know, many different terms used for it, to communicate, that one has two inside!

One is made by two or has two inside, and to appear as one on the other side of THAT ONE, the 'little difference' is with or without having two inside! Two are the sides of a one in the middle, and this middle one has a choice (option) to unite, to join, to combine, with either that one with the two or with THAT ONE without the two. Although the choice (option) is there for selection, it requires a skill to distinguish or to be ready to learn from the mistakes and experience.

So there is a choice and option to correct and connect again, to become one or to remain one, this is also a choice, option! How and which way is it possible to become one or to remain one?

Although it looks simple from one side, it is complicated and complex from the other side. ENERGY is on one side, SPACE is on the other side, and the ETHER is in the middle! That is why the ether is considered as SPACE; also it is filled inside SPACE and becomes the ENERGY field, a place for ENERGY. Two together as ONE, and the term 'ETHER' becomes a common term for both the sides ENERGY and SPACE! Because the ETHER is the state of in-between in the middle of ENERGY and SPACE, this is why it's easy to identify that oneness and to know and understand SPACE with the help of the term ETHER. ETHER replaces the term 'SPACE' while developing conceptual understanding. A very refined form of ENERGY is ETHER because it is not SPACE and is different to SPACE. Having a difference within, ENERGY is known popularly by this term 'ETHER' and it is taken for granted that it is equal to SPACE! Any objection?

The object/OBJECT becomes the object of objection! How can SPACE become either an object or a subject? It is certain that ENERGY can become an object and subject! ETHER is also an OBJECT and SUBJECT, in and out! IT IS

GIVEN AND IT IS RECEIVED BY SPACE TO THE ENERGY FORM!

The first receiver is the ENERGY form and the first giver is SPACE. It looks as if ETHER is the giver and receiver and also a quasi-steady state. The receiver becomes the giver, and creation becomes the creator, to move and to change and to become like that is the basic nature and function of ENERGY and ETHER! Both the terms are apparently different, showing mastery over the adjustment and compromise with the other, while 'SPACE' is also a term similar and considered equal to ETHER, the difference is not considered and, finally, the background remains a ground and background because of the similarity, and the adjustment on the ground is done by the ETHER, ENERGY.

Now, two terms, two formations, and later on further formations in a continuation, an endless, infinite formation! This has motion as well as resistance; without this, minus this, is SPACE, pure SPACE! This is a motionless, resistance-less state. In this state 'less' is the suffix; opposite to this state of pure SPACE, that state has the suffix 'more' to indicate that the limit is crossed: this is the state of ENERGY, ETHER.

SPACE is considered as a distance between two points. Is it possible to have only one point, one without the second point? That point is the ONLY POINT, in it are all the points, which are collectively called and known as the Universe! Nothing is outside of the Universe!

While being in the womb of the mother, is it possible for an embryo to know all the details about the mother? Even if it is possible for this, then the next question is: after knowing in detail about the mother, is it possible to know in detail about the father without getting any help from the Mother? How is it possible? What has to be done to know that? When it is not easy and possible to know about the father, does it mean that the father is not there, not existing, or that it is enough to know only about the mother? Anyhow, the embryo is in direct contact with its own mother. Or is it in contact with its own father? Contact is with the mother directly, and with the father indirectly!

The WOMB is a UNIVERSE!

The MOTHER is a UNIVERSE!

The CREATOR is a UNIVERSE!

Then, who are we? And, where are we?

Out of the UNIVERSE or inside the UNIVERSE?

When it is inside the UNIVERSE, then the UNIVERSE can be a WOMB as well as a MOTHER and also a CREATOR; from different viewpoints, three, and even more terms are possible to apply to the UNIVERSE!

Just as a bird tries to measure the sky and a fish tries to measure the ocean, what the animal can't do the human being, living being, the individual, the ego, tries to do because the bird and fish don't have a cognitive brain function, while this is an advantage for the human to prove superiority in the animal kingdom! The crooked and cunning, the wicked and shrewd, the miser and the greedy, the egotistic and ambitious, all are together with attachment and lust to prove "I am better than you!" and "I am superior to you!"

Together these two, 'I' and 'you', become 'we' and once it is possessed then they say it is 'ours'. Then comes the choice of whether to divide the possession equally, or more, or less? Is there readiness and eagerness to share or to exchange? Isn't it a transaction, a business under the term of or in the name of 'sharing'; isn't this the nature of ENERGY? Why does this common ENERGY behave in this way? Why does it have to be different, becoming the cause of the difference? Is it not the quality which is the cause and not the polarity, as plus and minus, positive and negative?

From the qualitative point of view,
From the quantitative point of view, and
from the polarity ('+ - o') point of view,
the function of the ENERGY and its result and effect
will be common or different from each point of view?

The crooked and cunning, the wicked and shrewd, miser and greedy, egoistic and ambitious, lusty and desirous, attached, etc., are more related to the quality or to the quantity or to polarity? Just think properly, don't be in a hurry for a conclusion, because of the possibilities of mixture and in which proportion?

That's why it is pure ENERGY and it is not pure ENERGY; the mixture has no proper proportion to be pure ENERGY! So, pure ENERGY is considered a higher class and what is not pure is considered a lower class', or as a higher ENERGY and a lower ENERGY! High and low also indicate the area along with the class.

There is a two-way approach and understanding of ENERGY: first, from a QUANTITY point of view, the physicists have studied in detail, second, from a QUALITY point of view, the philosophers have studied in detail!

The two different approaches to ONE ENERGY, from the quantity and quality points of view, each one has their own terminology for communication and expression, as well as schools to educate and propagate the value of it. The individual is an individual having freedom to move on any one of the two paths, to explore what the other individual has not yet done! Up to today this activity is continually going on and the two are remaining as two, although the two belong to the ONE ENERGY: in separate ways both are remaining and also maintaining their contact (relation) with THAT ONE ENERGY.

In a different way, even today this difference is not allowing the two to become one! It is difficult to separate quality from quantity and quantity from quality because it means that the two exist in one and belong to ONE ENERGY. The existence of the two in one has to be distinguished by the individual first, and then each one has to be connected separately with ONE ENERGY in a different way, which means that the destination is the same: the pathways to reach it and the starting points are different, while the destination, the end point is the same, ONE ENERGY. The first thing to accept is that the two are in one object to perceive and that the perception is selective. What is not selected remains as it is, is neglected because two different individuals (with different backgrounds) have carried out the selection on the basis of selective and neglective perception.

Now, two individuals are on one side, while on the other side there is ONE common object but it is different because of the two which are together in that one!

From the ENERGY point of view, ENERGY is inside both sides, the individual and the object. Then why are there two? Individuals have a difficulty and problem in accepting each other and becoming one from the ONE COMMON ENERGY point of view, and to neglect and ignore the difference, which is the cause of the different. Instead of ignoring and neglecting what has to be, that is not neglected and ignored, and what has not to be neglected and ignored, that is neglected and ignored, which means that it becomes difficult for the two to remain without crossing each other, cutting each other's plans and development!

How can they become complementary to each other? What has ONE ENERGY to achieve from these two?

ENERGY is ONE, so there is no question of achieving and adding or increasing the achievement. However, while the ENERGY within makes attempts and efforts to prove, to increase, to show, to demonstrate, to be different and separate, ENERGY appears and seems to be not one and more than one. The purpose becomes the cause of transaction and exchange of business at different levels and places between the two ENERGIES, although it is ONE! Selective perception, specialization and narrow vision help to develop separation from the other flows of ENERGY!

From the source and origin point of view, although the term 'Energy' remains common and one, it becomes two not one, it appears as one, is considered as one, because two are inside the one; here, two are the ENERGY form, having two different sources or origins. One is solar Energy, which comes from the SUN constantly and is known as a constant giver or distributor. The other one is a constant receiver, the Earth. It has its own ENERGY. ENERGY within, fire within, flame within and because of this EARTH as a living body, and a living body as an Earth, is considered and accepted.

The meeting of the two Energies at a different level with a different purpose creates a mixture where two become one, appear as one, are accepted and established as one; and that one, having doubt, no confidence and no trust, fears to loose its own state of existence that it has acquired, that it has possessed, and which is held by the ego, the 'I', with full power and strength, so that no other form of ENERGY can take it away! It is well prepared for a fight and struggle, to keep and not to give or loose it. ONE ENERGY, two forms, each one trying to be one, ready to give up, while the other one is ready to acquire and possess. Two opposite patterns of behaviour. How can this be recognized or distinguished? Who will do it? ENERGY? Why, what for? It will not be a selective perception, biased and prejudiced conclusion. This means that ENERGY becomes the evaluator and the evaluation of that object is done by Energy, which is ENERGY on the other side. The report of the evaluation is evaluated by ENERGY.

Why does ONE ENERGY have to do all this process? Is it not necessary and important to give names, code numbers and terms to express and communicate, to make it clear what is meant by ENERGY? Everyone knows this, but not how to use it in a proper way, and for each one a proper way is different; although they are opposite to each other, ways are proper!

Is it possible for SPACE to use ENERGY or is ENERGY using ENERGY? The USER is ENERGY and the USER has energy to use, the USER is using energy, what for? Although ENERGY is ONE, it is and it is not the same because the USER/ENERGY is different from the object to be used. From one point of view, the two are different and opposite, not the same, just as one who eats the cake and the cake itself, one who drives the car and the car itself, one who sits on the chair and the chair itself. A long list is possible: two are two and go together to remain as two, and go together to become one with the help of the two!

All the signs on the calculator are for ENERGY because it has a form, function, system, structure and results and effects. The calculator is needed for fast calculation, by that one who is not the calculator! The one who is not the calculator is the USER of the calculator, the two have Energy for their function, to obtain (get) the result. In this way, it is and it is not the ENERGY. Then what is it?

The existence of the third one, the Seer, Observer, the Witness, does not belong to these two sets of ENERGY; also SPACE within belongs to the third one, the Seer, Observer and the Witness.

Where is the position of the 'I', the ego? ENERGY belongs to the 'I', the ego; and to SPACE, the 'I', the ego, belongs. The process of assimilation and segregation, separation or the metabolism with anabolism and catabolism is going on continuously at various levels, for different purposes. What is the Result?

Now, the separator is ENERGY, separation is done by Energy, and the process of becoming separate is the result and means, one becomes the two again!

From the quantity point of view, quality point of view, and source and origin point of view, there is simple duality and multiple duality! Simple is easy, while the complex is multiple duality, and because of the complexity of multiple duality, simple problems have difficult solutions.

Who is the Creator? The creation is the creator to create this multiplicity in duality, through creating its own creation, own world, and to develop, to become the owner of it, because it is my creation, it's mine, it is me who has created this! I am the owner, possessor and property holder. What belongs to me is not yours; however, I am ready to share with yours! Are you ready to share with me what belongs to you?

ENERGY is communicating and expecting with ENERGY. How does it appear? The common term is one, and the given term, the names to code, to communicate, to express, are different from each other, so that it is possible to distinguish the difference between the two, and possible to identify and be recognized by the third one that is also an ENERGY? ENERGY is the cause of duality. The progression in duality and with duality makes double duality, then furthermore, it turns into multiple duality, which is basically a DUALITY that is a minimum figure or number. When the second becomes the first one, then the FIRST ONE becomes ZERO and the place of the FIRST ONE is occupied by the SECOND ONE which appears as a first one! It is even ready to appear and become a Zero against ZERO.

That's why ETHER is considered as SPACE! It is and it is not Space! ETHER is ENERGY and ETHER is not ENERGY! A change of standpoint (viewpoint) makes the difference.

On the one hand there is ETHER, ENERGY and ENERGY'S form, structure, function, system, and results and effects; on the other hand there is SPACE within, SPACE outside and SPACE BEYOND, which is a DARK BLACK BACK GROUND, as an ENVELOPE FOR AND OF the UNIVERSE. The existence of SPACE is taken for granted, while ENERGY, in the form of Ether, becoming ETHER, appears as Space because of the oneness and togetherness. That's why 'two', 'Double', 'Dual', and 'Second', etc., terms came into use to clear up various objects.

The living being', individual, is second, first, or zero or the third person? Who changes the role and becomes the owner, is it the second, first, zero or third? To know duality and to be free from duality are two different ways of life!

In the same way, to know the ABSOLUTE ONE at the intellectual level and to live the life accordingly or not is a choice and option. Because the teachers of History, Geography, Chemistry, Physics, Maths etc., etc., are not living the life of their selected subject, why does the teacher of Spirituality, Yoga, Vedanta, etc., etc., have to live their life according to their selected subject? Are the teachers and preachers allowed to be free or is it compulsory for them? Who decides? ENERGY? OR SPACE? ENERGY can decide, while SPACE cannot decide, it has to be allowed and permitted! As SPACE can't stop, ENERGY exhausts and develops the fear to stop, to die, to lose its existence! Is it not a funny situation that the immortal has a fear of death? Who is going to die?

In the process of realization, first they say the SUN is moving, then they say the Earth is moving, now they say the Galaxy is moving! Then, who is steady? Where is the steadiness? How did this idea or thought come, from where did it come? Because of the impression of the STEADY STATE, the quasi-steady state came into use, to communicate, to express that particular state as a quasi-steady state!

Is SPACE testable? Is ENERGY testable? Who is doing the testing, SPACE or ENERGY'S form, structure, function, system, etc., etc?

Evidence of testing is the result, the effect. Today, faith, belief, and trust are based on testing and a testable object, which can be proved with evidence, as the existence of ENERGY OR SPACE? Through the testing and proving, providing evidence for verification, it is possible to transplant faith, belief, and trust from one side to the other side, and as a result, there is beautiful order in chaotic conditions, situations and circumstances, which becomes a puzzle and problem to solve. Each solution provides many problems and puzzles: isn't this a 'nice' trap of multiple duality?

Simple duality has an easy way to solve and not to repeat and recycle, while in the case of multiple duality, the solution and problem, or problem and solution, are together: how can one be without the other? It is not an ABSOLUTE ONE, it is a multiple one; that's why it is possible to be together with this one and separate from that one!

Each living being, individual, is a single one, alone, mono, uno: how many are they? One in one way, and many in another way! Much more and many is because of plus by plus: either increasing slowly, or multiplying and increasing with speed, not slowly! Speed in the movement to increase, and to be faster than the other is the nature of ENERGY, or it is the nature of SPACE?

SPACE increases and decreases and becomes the cause of change in pressure, which again becomes the cause to change that pressure, to increase and decrease the movement, the flow of Energy, from one side to the other, from one direction to the other direction. Change in pressure, is known as high and low pressure. This high and low, hyper and hypo, up and down, and so forth, again becomes the cause of the various changes which indicate no stability and no steadiness. Furthermore, this change loses control over the movement and becomes out of control, from balance to change and movement becoming imbalanced.

As this imbalance becomes the base, the equilibrium changes and turns into dis-equilibrium. As this happens it gives a further push to bring change into harmony, so it becomes disharmony: in the movement of each one, the harmonious-ness now is not there, doesn't remain. Sure, it is an impression, a memory, but the impact remains and the expression becomes "I was healthy, now I am sick and ill", the ease has gone and disease has established – within; the 'Peace' has gone and disturbance becomes established within: then what is outside? Silence, pin-drop silence, absence of sound, outside, not inside! What has to be inside, that is established outside; what has to be outside, that has the chance to establish inside: chaos inside, while order is outside. As a result, beauty and beautification is outside, so automatically it follows that ugliness and distorted unity and clarity is inside.

Is it because of SPACE? Or ENERGY? Energy is the cause and effect, the problem and solution, the question and answer, the plus and minus, positive and negative, high and low, etc., etc. The different pairs are set against each other at different levels giving different results because it is not ONE ABSOLUTE RESULT. That's why the different, different terms have to be used, to differentiate the difference between the two in one! This is also done by, and has to be done by, Energy and not by SPACE! The process of transformation ends with transcending, fear restricts and controls and doesn't allow loss of existence of the 'I', ego and the doer, the

ENERGY within to transcend, to convert and to become SPACE! A gap between the two is the distance between the two, the more the freedom then the more the distance in the gap and SPACE between the two: a little hairline crack is enough to increase the Space and gap, to break the unity between the two, the relation of the two! Two are the points, the extreme end of the point, a standpoint, a viewpoint, and opposite to each other.

Between the two points, or between the two, what exists? ONE SPACE! COMMON SPACE! Two together become one with togetherness. What happens to that SPACE? While there is that oneness through togetherness of the two, SPACE remains separate and distinct. Later on, two again become two from togetherness and oneness, and SPACE again exists between the two and reappears from outside of that oneness and togetherness. Although it is outside from the oneness and togetherness point of view, that SPACE is also in-between, outside as well as in-between the two.

The second point is far away and it exists and existence of it gives the possibility to that SPACE, which comes outside as a result of oneness and togetherness, to become the SPACE in-between the two points, point related and ABSOLUTE. The related one is made by two which have established oneness (togetherness) and become one out of the two; so the SPACE in-between the two has skipped outside, and that one becomes a compact one, a compressed one, a combined one, joined, united and one, looks like ONE! Is it?

The difference between this related one and the ABSOLUTE ONE is possible to distinguish by developing patience, acceptance and tolerance. Because the cause to become one changes, then another cause comes next to the previous one, that is the cause of a separation, because change is the nature of ENERGY and the cause is not the ABSOLUTE, it's a related cause: it is changing and along with it its result and effect are also changing. This means that SPACE comes back (re-appears) between the two. That's why one can just wait and watch that unity, joint, combination, oneness, togetherness. Wait and watch means to take distance and space and not to be involved, not to interfere. It's a chance (an opportunity) to become Space, to develop the characteristics of Space, to become the third one, then to be one of them, the 'two' and craving, to have a desire to become one, to be together, to belong to the other one, or the other one to belong to 'me', etc., etc. All this becomes an interruption and distraction from that role of the Third One.

This is considered as a fall, to be back, to come down, to try again and again; that's why there is trial and error so as not to repeat the same mistake, and the error in analysis of the mistake becomes the cause of the repetition, of the mistake. Not to have mistakes and errors means perfection and obsession for perfection, which will not allow action and is restricting while creating fear of making mistakes on one side and, on the other side, creating desire and expectation for the best result between the two phases, the 'I', the ego, with a question mark. To do or not to do? What to do?

Who created this confused state of being? Who developed and achieved it? Was it ENERGY or SPACE? The doer is ENERGY, not Space! The pressure (either high or low, positive or negative) is the cause of movement, the expansion and contraction, the increase and decrease of pressure on one side and, on the other side, the movement in any direction (up and down, in and out) and by this both sides affect each other, again from one side. On the other side, the constant temperature (heat) from the SUN through its rays becomes the cause of an increase in temperature; while on the other side, the constant rotation of the EARTH on its own axis is a constant receiver, which becomes the constant provider of the minus heat area that is cold to the heat of the SUN. This occurs constantly from dark night to bright day, and again it appears from bright day to dark night. The movement is important, it is because of fire within the Earth and fire outside, the SUN! The constant giver and provider of heat is the fire and this is also the cause of movement.

The movement within and the movement outside, and the movement within the movement; this is in the same way as a body is moving because of the movement within. The outer appearance of the movement is the cover, the body of the inner movement, and the inner movement is connected and related with ENERGY, a constant moving principle!

The inner movement is related (connected) with life and death, also death does not stop the movement: death is the stopping of the function of the reflex action. However, the movement starts after the 'stop' and death is declared; that movement is related (connected) with death and not with life. Death is the opposite term to life, it is the end of a life, a 'full stop' to that continuity, activity and functional movement of and by the two. From birth life begins and up to the end (death) it remains: it does not mean that the end of a life is the beginning of death! There is no beginning and end! While there is a beginning and there is an end of a life on one side, on the other side, there is no birth and no death, therefore no life. There is no beginning and no end to that Absolute Principle!

How is birth and death possible for ENERGY and SPACE? The Principle never dies while we survive! Even after that it remains! That's why 'birth and death' is a related term, not an Absolute Term, and it's not applicable to ENERGY and SPACE directly! Indirectly it is related and connected.

So, when there is no birth, there is no death and there is no life, then how is it? What is it? Without all this process, who are you? And with all this process, who are you? How can one identify the identity without having any identification mark or sign? How can it be recognized?

So it is difficult to accept! That's why it has no appreciation!! This is from one side and, on the other side, questions arise: why not recognize it, why is there no acceptance, and why no appreciation? Then the thinking starts, the prognosis and speculation, and then the conclusion and judgement, and a decision for the other side from this side! It's a swinging of the 'I', the ego, between the two, either in a clear way, or in a confused way! This process is going on continuously on one side and, on the other side, a continuous collection of the result of the process accumulates. On one side, 'I', the ego, is busy as a processor and, on the other side, is busy as a collector (receiver): manual on one side, automatic on the other. There are many roles to play and change takes place automatically – the flow of water's movement carries the swimmers either by swimming or floating. One has a choice to decide and act, the other has given up the choice and right to decide and act while being in the flow of the movement, which is because of ENERGY.

Is it not surrender to that principle of movement, the ENERGY, the Divine ENERGY, the MOTHER? Is it not being an adult and becoming a child with the manifestation of that innocent nature of the child creating full affection and love towards that MOTHER? Is it possible for that adult to do so, or does that one just become worshipper of the MOTHER?

All actions are done under the able and proper guidance of the intellect, which means that the inner one who calls for action does so without knowing when to do what! The doer, the worshipper, follows all the guidance that can be found, listens to all instructions, being happy in the beginning and unhappy at the end because of the change! This means that the calculations, speculations and prognosis, the conclusion, judgement, decision and action, although seeming to be right, become wrong.

Why does this happen? In analysis, in checking and re-checking, the error remains; however, correction is done up to a satisfactory mark and then there is readiness for a new mistake and the old result. Until this situation is rectified and corrected, the process goes on automatically. Doing is on one side, happening is on the other side; manual is on one side, automatic is on the other side; cause is on one side, effect and result is on the other side. To be on one side and to move to the other side, as well as to pass through the phase, state, place, spot, the point of the centre, in-between, in the middle, without becoming established there, results in passing through, going through, and to be back, all the way back. Back is the back of the back! So, to move further, to go ahead, is to return back!

Where? Came from where? ENERGY and its movement came from SPACE, and has to go back to SPACE, it is the PLACE for ENERGY, that's why it tries to be in SPACE, either within/inside, or outside.

Now, to be within (inside) either SPACE or in itself means being ENERGY. Here, in this case, ENERGY tries to be outside because the existence of inner SPACE is either not recognized or accepted. So, being in SPACE within, ENERGY tries to be outside, to come outside, to go outside, because the existence of inner SPACE either is not recognized or not accepted. Again, being in SPACE within, ENERGY tries to go outside, come outside, because of the strong base of non-acceptance and refusal to recognize. So, there is no appreciation and, on this basis, ENERGY becomes rebellious and tries to break the rules, the walls of conditionings, morals and manners, etc., to be free and to be out of that. This shows that ENERGY is the block, rule, condition, and wall, etc., on one side and, on the other side, ENERGY as non-acceptance, is not ready to recognize and starts struggling, fighting, quarrelling and declares war against ENERGY!

The opponent, enemy, the rival, is it ENERGY of ENERGY or of SPACE? How is it possible? SPACE provides the place to be, but who decides in which way to be there? Is it ENERGY or SPACE? Clean and clear is SPACE. Or is it dusty and dirty? Is this because of ENERGY? It is because of ENERGY, which can be either clean and clear or dusty and dirty, because SPACE and ENERGY at one point come together, have oneness and cannot be separated from that togetherness. That's why the term for this oneness (togetherness) is 'ether' and it is considered in two ways: clean and clear or dusty and dirty. Now, what it is being had (enjoyed, used, etc.), that can be provided, and this means that what is provided from the side of ether can either be clean and clear or dusty and dirty.

To whom is it provided? Who is the receiver, and who is the giver? Is it ENERGY or SPACE or a mixture of both? The answer is that the MIXTURE is the GIVER AND PROVIDER, and the mixture is the receiver; on both sides is the 'I' (EGO) and the 'i' (ego) as an original and a photocopy: the two are similar and difference exists. This mixture is multiplied in size and number: the ONE reflects in that multiplicity and multiple duality becomes the challenge for the individual. This is because from the outside (the outer point of view) duality is illusion, while from the inner (inside point of view) it is ignorance (incomplete knowledge) – in the middle, between the two points, the 'I', the ego, enjoys wielding power and developing fear to lose and so increases the grip on holding, using strength, force and pressure.

The pressure required to survive and carry on the functions and activities, from the survival point of view, is the foundation; from this base, demand increases and achievements are gained through pressurising the pressure to adjust, to co-operate, to adopt, to support and to fulfil the increased demand and achievements. Thus there is the need and requirement of strength and force for the enjoyment of power in any field, in any activity. This pressure becomes the cause of the 'hair-line crack' and break-up of the limit, the capacity and the ability to be with that much pressure which has built up from the normal range. This in turn becomes difficult to bear and the strength to tolerate the pressure becomes less and less on one side and, on the other side, irritability and reduced tolerance, anger and a change in behavioural pattern becomes easy to observe, to notice, while for that individual it is normal behaviour! No change in it!!

The increase in pressure increases the tension and the wall becomes tense, hardness increases and elasticity decreases, rigidity manifests, rigid it becomes, ready to break! The technique to decrease pressure helps to release tension and the tense walls regain their elasticity thereby allowing (permitting) stretching to occur within the limit again and again. This is possible to control and manage through proper movement; both expansion and contraction are needed. On one side, the individual gives importance to development, progress and expansion and, on the other side, contraction becomes less important, with no special effort made to pull back, to get it back, having no control over it, which means there is more expansion on one side and less contraction on the other.

There is a limit to both sides. Within the limit, within the provided margin of the plus and minus areas, movement should be for healthy survival. Instead of that, both more and less converts this into unhealthy survival and later on it becomes difficult to pull back, to get it back, because of the constant force and pressure which moves from in to out, inside to outside, from the centre to the periphery. This constant flow in one direction with effort becomes the cause of fear on the other side: what will happen to that establishment with the reduction of force and pressure towards expansion? This fear of the unknown and of the future becomes the cause of worries and anxiety.

The answer and the solution to the problem of who can give is the one who created it! The creator of fear is the ego. "I have fear", is the expression, fear is the creation, and later on,

creation becomes the creator,
effect becomes the cause,
symptoms become the cause, and
happening becomes the doer!

All this is because the coin has two sides and is kept not in a vertical position but in a horizontal position, one side down and the other side up. It is not important which one has to be up and which one has to be down, but who decides? It happens and how is it kept? Which side is up? Why is it that this one has to be up?

The answers are ready. This shows the two sides: one who asks and answers, and the other is the coin. On one side two are there, one who asks the question and one who answers; on the other side, there is one object, the coin, and questions and answers are related (connected) to that object.

Who prepared the coin? To whom does it belong?

A few more questions easily arise, which means it becomes an unending process, consuming the time and energy of the individual. The individual takes the opportunity to run away, to avoid, to skip, and with the help of the various questions, moves from one point or topic to another until it becomes comfortable, bearable and convenient. The solution appears as consumption of the work (just like alcohol to an alcoholic) and the individual becomes a workaholic to overcome certain, specific problems, through engaging and keeping busy with tight work schedules. This shows that there is no time, no space, to do any other activity because all the Space is occupied by the mind to overcome the problem; there is no time for the body and fatigue, exhaustion, tiredness and weakness starts. The gross physical ENERGY needs recharging for better functioning and results, while the workaholic has no time for it.

Push and pull, force and pressure, strength and power, etc., are all used by the 'I', the ego, for two goals: one apparent and visible; the other one, hidden and known by the ego, the 'I'. The picture appears as: the driver prefers to drive, while the indicator shows that fuel is going to run out and soon the tank will be empty! In the case of reality, one on the street and the other on the street of the Life: what does the driver have to do in the two types of situation?

One is visible, known and possible to imagine, to think of the result and consequences; while in the case of the Life related street, how can the driver decide and select or choose the 'street' for refilling, recharging, a place to stop? That is a Space to stop? Although the driver can have a wish, the pilot can have a wish and desire, the doer can also have a wish and desire to be on the path (street), to remain constantly and continuously. Is it possible?

The first chance is to the driver, pilot, doer, controller, etc., and the next is to the vehicle. Who decides to stop and not to move further, is it the same ENERGY or are they two, not one? The need of a garage, clinic, dispensary and counselling: why is it needed and required when One (the individual) expresses "I know how to do and what to do". Then why has that independent become a dependent to those systems?

Why can't the one who is alone manage, arrange and solve the problem without being together?

Why is it that freedom on a temporary basis changes (converts) into binding? What is the reason behind it?

Whose play is this and who is the player? Is it because of illusion or ignorance?

Where does fear exist, is it inside or outside? Where does grief and sadness exist, is it inside or outside? Where does happiness and joy exist, is it inside or outside?

Is illusion because of ignorance? Although they are two, in one way the two are one outside and, in another way, inside. To know one, the other needs to be known! Ignorance does not allow the individual to distinguish, while illusion creates obstacles in the process of distinguishing; similar they are but not the same, so different they are as well as similar. The same has to be found out which is inside as a part and outside as a part. Combination of the inside and outside parts in a correct and right (proper) way becomes wrong and not proper as the result comes of that combination, joining, union. To have a divorce, two are not going to marry! On one side, by avoiding marriage, the long process of divorce is avoided; on the other side, the formation of the family is stopped; and on the other side, formation of the group starts because family and group are similar and because there is more than one individual. The difference is the binding material and relation in a specific, particular way, so the group remains as a group, while the family can be a family at the same time as being a group.

The individual seeking a sense of safety and security starts searching for what a family can provide that the group cannot provide, and for what the group can provide that is difficult to achieve from the family! Cleverly avoiding the binding (the marriage) and the long process of divorce, being independent, the individual starts searching the group for safety and protection and to be secure. The search for a group which can accommodate independence on one side while, on the other side, the search for a group to depend on, to have that togetherness, oneness, goes on. The group is a creation of one individual, a single one! After the formation of the group, that one merges inside the group and the group as a creation becomes the creator of further creation! It belongs to whom? Is it to that single, one, individual, or to a group as a one, one single group having its own force and mobility? A group has its own ego and own 'body'. That body can accommodate all that is possible, as many individuals as possible and, depending on the purpose and motives of the group, its activity starts to have (to achieve) the decided fixed result or hidden goal, also!

Which type of ENERGY is working and functioning in it? The group shows (demonstrates) strength and power, while its quality manifests through activity! The group is like a magnet, having a magnetic force to attract and also distract! It has its own limitations. It's a body, a cover, which is made by many, one by one: although it appears as one, it has many ones in it. 'We', 'our' and 'us' is on one side, while 'you' and 'they' are the terms for the other side!

The single 'I', alone, is on both sides. Ego is one of the group, which is made by many egos, one by one. This means that the ego can be made by many egos – the group ego and individual ego are different; the first one is made by many as a collective ego, which is stronger and more powerful than the ego of a single individual. Here in this group ego is a mixing, merging and surrendering of one into the other for a specific reason or particular purpose. Security is taken for granted after joining the group through the required process. The collection of the ego takes place through togetherness and oneness of the single individual one to and with the other, and among them one ego of the individual is working as a manifest ego of the group. The manifestation from the un-manifestation becomes the cause of further manifestation. In the case of the group ego, the group leader is the manifestation of the manifestation: is it or is it not a case of a manifest ego having its own ego?

How can two egos exist in one single individual? Dual ego becomes the cause of conflict and confrontation, confusion and chaos, anger and hate, etc. The presence and appearance of the manifest ego of the group is maintained; later on, the absence and disappearance of that ego leaves impressions behind while the group exists until a new leader is either selected, elected, appointed or deputed to lead the group.

The seed gives a sprout which moves upwards, grows up, and then the root goes downward to hold onto the ground, to get food and water to survive. The seed on one side and the seed on the other side, one is outside and the other one is inside. One leader is outside, while the other one is inside. To lead is the nature of ENERGY, the group is a form of ENERGY; the single individual represents a small amount of THE ENERGY with quality also. The group is a big amount of ENERGY, quantity along with its quality. Body, head and tail is all ENERGY or SPACE?

SPACE is SPACE, it gets the shape of body, head and tail along with ENERGY. SPACE, which gets the shape, is known as ETHER. And ETHER is considered and taken for granted as SPACE. The question is, why are the two different terms coined? Two terms, 'SPACE' and 'ETHER', used to communicate one, to express one, what is meant by that? Or this?

ENERGY and ETHER are easy to prove with evidence; even on the basis of this evidence and proof, it is difficult to perceive SPACE, which is not ENERGY and ETHER. Because of the oneness and togetherness, it becomes difficult to perceive SPACE, which is not ENERGY and ETHER.

WHO can perceive whom? Eyes can't see their own eyes; only in a mirror is it possible as a reflection! Then what is seen, is it the eyes or the plain glass which reflects? It is difficult to differentiate while seeing one's own reflection in the mirror! What is reflected is an object, the reflector is also an object, both are ENERGY in two different ways. How is it that SPACE can be the object to reflect and the reflector as the ENERGY?

Particles are the reflectors reflecting the SUN'S RAYS and spreading light around, creating brightness and also providing colour with a spectrum. The bright colours and light are spread by many, many particles on one side, while the source of light, the SUN, is on the other side, and the area between the two is SPACE. Spread by the light (reflection), brightness shows the presence of light and darkness indicates its absence. Brightness and presence of light is further related (connected) with the day which starts with sunrise, then mid-day, then sunset and night begins with the starting of darkness and absence of light, midnight, and then the end of night and beginning of day. Two joints, two times, two opposite directions, two expressing the rising and setting of the ONE SUN! This happens because of the rotation (movement) of the EARTH but the individual perceives it in a different way, in an opposite way! Apparently it is correct (right) so it came into expression, and it became a popular and established fact accepted by all. Like this, countless established (and incorrect) facts are accepted by many individuals. Basically the Earth is round, having a curve; however, on this basis the historical square, flat, angle and angular notions have been developed and established.

ENERGY is a flow of movement in two different ways; the starting point for both is the same as it has freedom of movement and can change its way and nature of movement ad infinitum. It is ENERGY, not SPACE! SPACE can't move like ENERGY. ENERGY 'carries' SPACE, so it appears as if SPACE is moving, but actually the two are moving or either one of them is moving, and that is enough to change the scenario, the picture, the environment.

Because of this it looks as if SPACE is moving and that the point of the observer is not moving. So, one is a fixed unmoving point, while the other is not fixed and is a moving point: the gap between the two is SPACE that can be measured as a distance between the two points. Freedom is the gap between the two where SPACE exists. Friction, conflict, fight and quarrel indicate that Space as a place between the two is not a peaceful place, or that there is no peace in-between, so it is a disturbed Space or a SPACE full of disturbance, which in turn means it is a disturbed state of ENERGY. Instead of freedom it appears as bound and develops the need and desire to be free from the binding.

How is SPACE bound, and how will SPACE be free from the binding? It is through the movement of ENERGY as it opens and closes that there is both freedom and binding. Positive and negative, plus and minus belong to the same ENERGY and are the hooks or connections which are connected and separated from each other.

From the ENERGY point of view there is freedom and binding and also from the SPACE point of view there is freedom and binding. They appear to be different and have a difference in them, while both have a common (similar) term of expression and communication. In this way, different and similar becomes the choice, the option, for individuals to develop their own intellect or wisdom!

The individual is single, one, alone, and 'only' is the term used, but this is not properly applicable to the single individual; only one is allowed, the question is what about the other? So, the individual is not only, single and alone as there are many individuals who are also single, one and alone! The two terms are 'only' and 'also'. To avoid debate, argument, quarrel and conflict it's better to use the term 'also' instead of 'only' for the related one and, for the ABSOLUTE ONE, it's better to use 'ONLY ONE'.

To have peace without disturbance, the wise and intellectual and the not wise or otherwise have a choice or option to select, to decide, to act and as a result they can have peace without disturbance. To know similarity and difference is on one side, and to act and do accordingly is on the other side. The result and effect comes after doing, after action, as a happening; the result, effect and happening gives satisfaction, peace and happiness.

To know only develops insecurity and disturbance and the desire to know more and more develops into that state of "I know". Later on it comes out in expression and communication as "I know, I know", which means indirectly to say, "now change the topic or keep quiet"! With this attitude there is no consideration of that new thing, information or knowledge given to 'me'. Instead of recognizing it as new, accepting it as new and appreciating it as new, the expression "I know" puts cold water on the burning fire or desire to have appreciation and recognition from the other! The one who expressed it does not get hurt; the one who gets hurt can't express it! Ego is on both sides: "I have expressed", "I got hurt", the individual, single, one, alone each tries to teach a lesson to the other. Both have a choice and according to the guidance within each one is deciding and acting.

To know duality and to come out of duality are two different things. To know duality is very simple and easy at the intellectual level. The dual 'trap' is ignorance on one side, illusion on the other, and in-between the two the 'I', ego of each individual enjoys the different roles and positions, and each ego becomes more than one with superimposition or layers one upon the other. How many layers the 'I', the ego, has goes on and on! That is why identity crisis occurs because of identification with the different identities! The group ego is an example from the 'post and position' point of view. The layers, one upon the other, cover the centre, the ego, the nucleus, the cause of pain and the suffering. The layers work as a shield and protect the ego; knowledge becomes the cause of disturbance: how much to cover and how much to expose, to hide or not hide the fear becomes controller of action and behaviour. This is all highly connected with the ego and the 'I am-ness'

The layers are working and appearing as covers, as blankets. The seed has these layers and a shoot comes out of it, later on a root also comes out of the seed. It's a two-way journey, upward towards the light and open-ness known as the sky, and downward, away from the light, moving for food and water, to hold the ground and support growth, progress and development, which gives flowers and fruit. The seed was one; it becomes the tree with flowers and fruit having seeds within.

ENERGY in different forms with different names and shapes known as per the appearance becomes popular and well-known. ONE becomes many, and many have the ONE within. Life begins and death has to be! Combine, unite, join and then separate; to combine, unite and join it becomes cycle and re-cycle.

There is fear of losing existence because the enjoyer is enjoying existence. Being ENERGY is not enough, becoming is more important. The effort, attempt and journey is towards that decided destination to become. Being ENERGY, a constant moving principle, the individual starts learning how to move, to walk, run, and jump because the teacher (as ENERGY) is ready to teach all necessary lessons to the learner, who is ENERGY! ENERGY becomes the investigator to investigate the source and cause of one's own existence and of the Universe. Being the cause and source, ENERGY as ULTIMATE becomes the investigator and comes to the conclusion that ENERGY is ULTIMATELY ONE!

Knowing from the result, with evidence and proof, it is proved that ENERGY is the ULTIMATE CAUSE, the CAUSE of the CAUSE. The knowledge of this result and ULTIMATE CAUSE becomes the ground and the cause of further research and investigation, to find out that ONE ENERGY. This is undertaken by each single individual ONE separately, in their own way, in a different way, and even after accepting the previous result, a new investigation to find out that OLD and ANCIENT ENERGY is made in their own way, to get satisfaction and later on appreciation and the prize! The prize giver is ENERGY, and the receiver of the prize is also ENERGY; through ENERGETIC CURRENT both are connected and related, they are two? Or are they one?

Although it is ONE ENERGY, in reality it is not one but two and SPACE is the gap between the two, the distance between the two!

While these two exist, SPACE exists, either between the two or covering the two as one! Combined, joined or united, two are together with togetherness and oneness, then separation on one side, cycle and recycle, together and separate, while on the other side, together with SPACE. How can ENERGY be separate?

How is it possible to expect to be alone when ENERGY and SPACE are always together? The craving to be alone, considering "I am alone" and lonely, not belonging to anyone and no one belonging to me, makes the loneliness stronger and stronger until finally aloneness is resolved in togetherness. Fear of insecurity develops within the one who is alone and who prefers to be free and independent. In the search for security, which is made by two, shelter and protection develop. Who can provide this type of security? The cause and origin of movement and disturbance is the insecurity. Who creates it? Who develops it? Is it ENERGY or is it SPACE?

To live alone, to enjoy life and fear death: insecurity develops within that alone individual!

Is being alone an illusion?

Or is being alone ignorance?

Or is being alone the decision to do what is not possible?

Or is being alone cheating, avoiding, escaping, running away, not accepting and refusing togetherness?

Or why be alone, and for what purpose?

Or is being alone an acceptance of togetherness while at the same time being free and independent in togetherness?

In togetherness, oneness is the ground and because of this there is the existence of life and life related activities on this ground or in this ground or from and through etc., etc., the ground: who exists?

Are there two?

Or ONE ONLY?

Or ONE in two ways?

According to the standpoint, viewpoint, reference point, the expression and communication by the individual for satisfaction, peace and happiness uses different terms, connotations and material to make it more and more clear. However, because of limitations it becomes difficult to express (communicate) the TOTAL and COMPLETE picture even partially, or incompletely, or in a limited way.

On one side, true and honest effort is made to explain THAT by all in their own way and it becomes the common point; while, on the other side, THAT common point becomes the uncommon point because of limitations: each one has their own points to express and communicate and are ready to give understanding rather than to get (to have) the understanding!

Is it not a funny thing that fear of destruction becomes the cause of peace? Is it not so that greediness and ambition to become the controller and owner have developed fear and destruction as a tool and mechanism to exert control to become the owner?

ENERGY has chosen and selected the path to become the controller and owner through creating and developing fear of destruction, considering it as the easy method. So, each one becomes busily engaged in showing and demonstrating their power and strength of destruction in order that it can generate (create) fear and then comes readiness to adjust, compromise and exchange. Profit and loss, gain and loss, winning and defeat, are the result. Revenge and punishment, anger and hate develop along with the result. To destroy and to finish becomes the aim, the goal, the target and the creative Energy becomes useful to create destructive items: this is the use of one's own creativity.

Is it use, misuse, abuse, wrong use, or proper use?

Fear of destruction and fear of loss indicates construction and to have without construction the destruction is not possible. Without having in the first place it's not possible to lose. Creativity is needed for both sides, and between the two phases (ends) is the middle phase, which is to maintain and that also needs creativity. This means that the utilization of creativity takes place in many different ways, for various purposes. From the duality point of view, it is destruction and it is not destruction because it is just transforming from one form into another and a change of the formation becomes destruction. Instead of fear having to destroy, fear becomes the cause of destruction.

It is not destruction because it is not ABSOLUTE DESTRUCTION; that is not possible either for ENERGY or SPACE. Or is it possible?

Fear becomes the cause of friendship, apparently it is and it is not at the other level! Conditions are created, and conditional it becomes, so then the need to be unconditional! To be free and not to be bound and have conditions, commitment and responsibility, this is also one type of condition and limitation created by the 'I', the ego, just as not doing is also doing at that level. The world of linguistics or the linguistic world and the material world, this dual world becomes the means, the tools, the path, the way, for the ego, the 'I', to utilize both of them or one of them and, as a result of that, the wheel of ENERGY moves and keeps moving because 'where there is a will there is a way' and where there is a wheel there is a path!

The PATH and the PLACE are SPACE: what remains ultimately is the place, SPACE, not the 'I', the ego!

To know about SPACE, and to become like SPACE, and to be SPACE for the other, is the choice and option.

And, to know about ENERGY, and to become ENERGETIC, and to be an ENERGY for the other, is the choice and option.

Fear comes to enable which condition? Because control is not there and control is there, the controller knows the benefit of control, and that's why it is not ready to lose control, to give up control.

The two different movements: with and without control; and certain specific, particular, movements through which, although they are without control, it is possible to develop control through proper and judicious training. That developed habit, later on, becomes the controller and the CONTROLLER loses control over the movement at any level.

The CONTROLLER is the ego; from the doer it becomes the not-doer through allowing permeation of the habit to control the faculty of decision. This means actions become automatic, so it appears that actions happens automatically! It is true and it is not true because happening without doing is not possible. And doing gives the feeling and sensation, and experience, while the feeling by mistake is connected with thinking. How can thinking give (create) feeling? Who is the creator?

First there is projection on the inner screen, then perception of the projection, then cognition from the perception. As a result, there is the manifestation of "I know", then rejection or acceptance. On the basis of this, further development happens: one is negative and the other positive.

First, the decision to project is made on which basis? The source is memory (impressions), which belong to the past and not the future. Projection has its own 'colour'; the projector has to decide about the projection, then there is perception and cognition as per the projection.

From the qualitative point of view, the quality of the projection is on one side while, on the other side, what is projected has its own quality. ENERGY is the projector, is the projection of Energy and is the perception and cognition of Energy. The ENERGY to become the receiver is to get, to have, then to start giving through becoming a giver, a 'projector', and a game of self-cheating starts. The ego, the 'I', the unit of ENERGY, is separate like an atom or particle; each unit of Energy as 'I', the ego, starts and begins the exchange, later on it becomes a transaction, and later still it becomes a trading.

Why does SPACE have to enter into this business? How can SPACE be a projector and where does the projection project, onto which screen, is it the screen of SPACE? Who can perceive and recognize this, is it SPACE or ENERGY?

SPACE as a place becomes the storehouse of memory, preserved in that ETHER as a SPACE and from there it can come up to the manifestation level where it is possible to see and perceive.

Thinking works as projection and feeling develops out of it, giving the possibility to perceive and develop cognition. The knower doesn't know what is the base of thinking and starts expressing, communicating, deciding and acting according to the feeling which is generated and created by the thinking. Who is the thinker, is it ENERGY or SPACE? The result gives the answer through pain, suffering, unhappiness or joy and happiness.

Thinking is a movement, and the movement is of ENERGY. So, thinker and thinking become ENERGY because SPACE is not the thinker and thinking, also not the feeling! SPACE can be nothing but SPACE! SPACE just is. Only after understanding this is it possible to be the evaluator and to do the evaluation. This is done by ENERGY, not by SPACE! That's why the question: to be or not to be SPACE or ENERGY? Who decides? Is it SPACE or ENERGY?

Who are you? Do you know? How do you know whether you are ENERGY or SPACE or both as ETHER? Do you think or feel that all individuals are one and the same or are they different? All are SPACE, ENERGY, and a mixture of both: three possibilities. Who is who? And what about the other?

The need, necessity and requirement to know each in its own way: is it possible to keep all separate and distinguish them through their own quality, characteristics and aspects, to coin the terms and later on, using numbers (digits) to differentiate becomes the fashion of the time? The world of linguistics and information has covered up the world of the material. The individual has to deal with these two worlds: although the world is one, it becomes two, dual, double and each one of the two has again furthered their own creation. Double or dual, the simple dual becomes double dual, complex dual, multiple dual and multiple duality on one side while, on the other side, is oneness and One, and ONE, and ZERO!

The driver can't drive the car as the vehicle is in ZERO, neutral gear! Forward gear is plus and many while reverse gear is minus and one without an option! Why? All drivers accept this condition of gear system arrangement: zero to start and back to zero after finishing. Is this also possible for the driver to do in day-to-day life?

Vehicle and driver on the street or motorway never mix and merge to become one; without becoming this they flow and flow like a river made by drops of rain merging with each other! They have separate identity, mechanical movement and varied appearance to create difference. Is it not this that is the function and nature of ENERGY, the ego?

River becomes one with many raindrops in it.

Light becomes one brightness with many colours in it.

Universe becomes the one including many in it.

River is flowing, drops of rain are running together.

Traffic is moving, each vehicle keeping a space, a distance, in-between.

Light is one in a day as daylight, it appears as many lights as daylight disappears!

Universe is one, like a womb or egg. Who can count how many are in it? Who can measure the size and dimension of it?

SPACE is the covering layer; ENERGY is also covering the layers, one upon the other. SPACE covers the Universe; one ENERGY covers the SPACE in it. There is ONE SPACE with many forms of Energy. The individual is a mini universe; the Universe is one having many, many mini universes within.

To know the ONE and SPACE within or outside is the choice and option for all. How can one know this?

Is cognition the first, or does perception have to be first? Is movement from outside to inside better or is inside to outside better; from mind to body to manifestation outside or from outside to body to mind? It's a two-way process (pathway): conception within and manifestation outside. What is within is not outside of that 'I', the centre.

There are two bases of cognition, SPACE and ENERGY, two ways to perceive SPACE and ENERGY, two types of manifestation from two different bases of cognition.

Superimposition, layers upon layers, filters after filters, security check after security check, to defend and protect the ego, the duplicate creator! A photocopy machine of the Universe!

Cognition and perception without proper action means that activity cannot provide any fruit or result.

Acceptance is after re-cognition, recognize and then appreciate. Fear of the unknown is because there is no recognition, so no acceptance and no appreciation indicates a lack of confidence, no trust within, then doubt and suspicion appear. This demonstrates faith and belief in ENERGY which has shown its characteristics to shake, to move and to change.

How to welcome the unknown, the stranger; how to receive the GUEST known as death without notice and appointment! The fear of death is because it is not known when it will be. How can death be recognized? Without recognition it is not possible to accept it, to welcome it. How is it possible to appreciate that which is unwelcome and not accepted and so recognize death?

Death as a separation is to be perceived; perception of that gives cognition that it is a togetherness and oneness that has to separate, and that is death. This type of separation as a break up, divorce and death has to be recognized, then it is easy to accept and appreciate because SPACE and ENERGY, the two together as well as separate, always exist! And the individual has a fear of death! Is it not funny?

The individual is the enjoyer of life as well as the sufferer of it. Becoming a sufferer, the individual makes a start to putting the question and asking: why is there suffering? The question, "why is there enjoyment?" is not asked! To enjoy becomes one; suffering is the end of that oneness and togetherness. Death is a declaration that they are separate! They are not together and one; however, they were one! Is it a recycling of ENERGY or a recycling of SPACE?

The knower knows. Who is the knower, is it SPACE, or ENERGY, or a mixture? While the mixture is there, separation has to occur again and again, with or without pain!

How to avoid pain and to accept separation? While the seed exists, the sprout will be available for growth and the root will be available for holding in a two-way development.

How can sprouting be stopped? While there is darkness, absence of light, ignorance will be there and illusion can work effectively.

How to be ready and prepared to receive the light, which can remove the darkness, the ignorance? While movement exists, trust and confidence gives support to the strength and power to move.

How to develop trust and confidence? While freedom and openness exist, knowledge to distinguish the difference between the two from one is available so that selection of one will not be the cause of pain and suffering.

How to develop the knowledge to distinguish, to discriminate and to differentiate the difference between the two from one? While sleep means not awake, there is no awareness and no alertness, it is where night is to sleep and day is to awake. What happens? Day becomes longer and prolongs work to achieve more; sleep at night becomes shorter to recharge energy the natural way. Energy burnout is greater because of more work and less sleep. This forceful waking and pressure of work shows that sleep is not enough and that waking is forced.

How to set this cause of disturbance right and to stop that unnecessary burnout? What to do?

Questions are there because intellectuals are able to work out the right and proper answer. Receiving ready-made answers doesn't give satisfaction because there is no effort expended to discover the answer, which then develops obligation, doesn't it?

The ego is that unit of ENERGY which knows all the tricks that the trade has for what is expected and desired! So, answers to those questions are not provided to the able ego, the 'I', the intellectuals.

What remains once the name, number and form (shape) is removed? It is SPACE and ENERGY, isn't it?

Is this not the ULTIMATE APPEARANCE OF THE TWO AS THAT DARK BLACK BACKGROUND AND THE BRIGHT SPOT, THE SUN, the constant giver and the constant receiver.

The EARTH, as a living body, exists in the UNIVERSE and the living body as an Earth exists as a mini, mini universe!

The world is inside the WORLD.

THE UNIVERSAL WORLD is infinite, while the mini, mini, tiny little universe world, which belongs to each single individual, is finite. So, for one individual, their own world is not the same as (not like) the other individual's world. They are different from each other; each one is a creator of their own world.

In this way, creation becomes the creator and creates its own creation, developing attachment towards it. As a result, 'I', me, my, and mine become part of the ego that is one. This one is connected and related to the SUN, the SOURCE of life, to ENERGY and also to the Earth, and combines with EARTH ENERGY, which is distinct from SUN ENERGY.

The individual is free to decide, to select, to use, one Energy to achieve and develop the other ENERGY. This is how ENERGY becomes the means and the goal!

ENERGY as a means and ENERGY as a goal! EARTH ENERGY as the means and SUN ENERGY as the goal.

Then it is clear that the living body as an EARTH is just a means provided to the 'I', the ego, but it develops attachment to it! That ways and means are provided does not mean they belong to the individual and that the individual is the owner and controller of those means, the manipulator of those means or the buyer and seller of those means!

'Means' are considered as a commodity, they become the consumer and consumption is developed because ENERGY can't stop, can't say no. ENERGY is not able to say ENOUGH'S ENOUGH.

But here, in this writing process,
Enough has to arrive,
A stop has to happen, and
No further writing
Can satisfactorily take place.
This is considered an END,
On the big place as a SPACE.

This end is from my side. Now start from your side! Either accept the presentation of SPACE and ENERGY or reject, refuse and oppose it. The choice (option) is yours.

You are free to destroy either the presentation of SPACE and ENERGY or SPACE and ENERGY itself. YOU ARE FREE to do whatever is possible where you are and who you are to destroy. Destroy what, SPACE, ENERGY? Try it or give up! See what you can do. Otherwise say it's enough and sing the same song of ENOUGH is Enough! Now it's ENOUGH SPACE and ENERGY for all of us. Let it work on its own, in its own way, in its natural way, to provide all of us the Light of Happiness.

THANK YOU
To SPACE and ENERGY
Within and Beyond!
THANK YOU
To Both of You
As one! ONE!!
Salutation to ONE and one!

O – X – X – X – O

Epilogue

You have reached the end. Is it the end? If it's not the end, where else is there to go, what else needs to be known?

Printed in the United Kingdom by
Lightning Source UK Ltd., Milton Keynes
138101UK00001B/63/P

9 780956 211200